Treasury of Newfoundland Stories

JACK FITZGERALD'S

Volume II

Amazing & Strange

Canada Council Conseil des Arts
for the Arts du Canada

Canada

Newfoundland
Labrador

We gratefully acknowledge the financial support of the Canada Council for the Arts,
the Government of Canada through the Canada Book Fund (CBF),
and the Government of Newfoundland and Labrador through the Department
of Tourism, Culture and Recreation for our publishing program.

Cover Design by Maurice Fitzgerald
Layout by Paul Pettipas
Printed on acid-free paper

Published by
CREATIVE PUBLISHERS
an imprint of CREATIVE BOOK PUBLISHING
a Transcontinental Inc. associated company
P.O. Box 8660, Stn. A
St. John's, Newfoundland and Labrador A1B 3T7

Library and Archives Canada Cataloguing in Publication

Fitzgerald, Jack, 1943-, author
    Jack Fitzgerald's treasury of Newfoundland stories / Jack Fitzgerald.

Includes bibliographical references.
Contents: v. 2 Amazing and strange
ISBN 978-1-77103-095-3 (v. 2 : paperback)

    1. Newfoundland and Labrador--History--Anecdotes. 2. Newfoundland
and Labrador--Anecdotes. I. Title. II. Title: Treasury of Newfoundland stories.

FC2161.8.F595 2015   971.8   C2015-904829-X

Treasury of Newfoundland Stories

Volume II

Amazing & Strange

St. John's, Newfoundland and Labrador, 2016

I dedicate this book to my fellow classmates at
Holy Cross School, St. John's

Dedication v
Table of Contents vii
Preface xv

Part 3

Part 4

Part 5

X

Part 12

Part 13

Part 14

Preface

My goal, in the publication of these stories, is to share with as many people as possible stories of people and events that have fascinated me in my research of Newfoundland's colourful history and culture. My sources are many, including among others early newspapers, court records and official reports from the Colony of Newfoundland to authorities elsewhere. Often reports in competing publications may differ somewhat from each other, and I do my best to sift out the facts from conjecture but, since it is impossible to talk to the original writers/reporters, I have to find the common thread in the various sources in order to be as accurate as possible. At times, after a book has been published, additional facts and/or corrections have been brought to my attention, and I have been pleased to update or correct these stories in subsequent publications. I welcome such input from my readers.

Part 1

Wherever you go you'll always find a boy from New-
foundland, He's the pride of every country, good fortune
on him smile, They sail the river Slaney and they cross
the river Nile, Way down in South Africa you'll find them
on the roll, With Peary's expedition they got nearest to
the pole.

-Author unknown

The above verse was taken from an age-old Newfoundland song, which underscores the worldwide presence and influence of Newfoundlanders. It seems an appropriate introduction to the pages that follow, which includes both Newfoundland men and women.

1. Newfoundland Girl Became Part of French Royal Family

Pamela Simms was born in Fogo, Newfoundland, but was raised in a French household along with a child who later became King Louis Philippe of France. Her story is a most intriguing chronicle of Newfoundland's history and, fortunately, has been documented and preserved for future generations.

Pamela's name was actually Nancy Simms. She was named after her mother, Nancy, at the time of her birth in the spring of 1773. Pamela was born out of wedlock, a common practice at that time due to the lack of clergy. This stemmed from anti-settlement regulations imposed in Newfoundland by the British. Her parents were Nancy Simms and English Naval Captain Jeremiah Coughlan.

Coughlan's mission in Newfoundland was to defend the Fogo area from invasion by the French and the Americans. To do this, he built a fort and had it equipped with six cannons. On the side, Coughlan operated an export and import business dealing with fish, oil and clothing. He fell in love with his servant girl, Nancy Simms. This union produced the child Nancy, who to her family was called "Little Nancy" and who in later life, was given the name "Pamela." Coughlan had promised to marry Nancy Simms when the chance arose.

As required by law, Coughlan returned to England in the spring. While he was away, Nancy and her child moved to Dog Bay to spend the winter with her father. The following spring Coughlan returned to Newfoundland and brought Nancy and their child to live at his home in Fogo.

A year and a half later, Coughlan took his family to London with plans to marry. Whether they married or not is not known, and the last known record shows that she resided at Christ Church where she supported herself by doing needle- work.

According to the family history preserved and handed down by Nancy's uncle, Harry Simms, who passed away in 1884 at the age of eighty, her father received a letter from her stating that she was forced to part with Little Nancy in order to leave the country. Another letter, written by Coughlan, was received and claimed that, "The mother and child were being looked after by him indirectly and were being well cared for."

At this point, Little Nancy's life took a fairy tale twist that put her on the road to becoming part of the household of the Royal Family of France. She was just six years old. Madame Felicite de Genlis had been chosen by the Duke of Orleans to care for his children and arrange for their education. He also wanted to bring a young English-speaking child, approximately six years old, to France to become a companion to his children, one of whom was the future King Louis XIV of France.

To accomplish this, the Duke sought the help of a close friend, Mr. Forth, who resided in London. While visiting Christ Church, Mr. Forth met Little Nancy and her mother. He was captivated by her "beauty and childish wit" and successfully persuaded her mother to allow the child to live in the de Genlis household with the children of the Royal family.

Harry Simms recalled:

> The letter that accompanied her, and which is probably still extant said, 'I am sending to Your Highness the prettiest little girl in England.' Madame de Genlis took an immediate liking to the child and changed her first name to Pamela. She looked upon Pamela, and treated her, as she would one of her own children. Eventually, she sought out the child's mother in England and paid her 25 pounds to give up all rights to Little Nancy. Her new identity was Lady Pamela and she was educated at Belle Chase with the prince and princess as companions and friends.

When the French revolution erupted, the Duke sent his family, Lady Pamela and Madame de Genlis to London for safety reasons. However, a portrait of the family, including Lady Pamela, was commissioned by the Duke before they left Paris. The portrait was still on display in the Palace of Versailles up until the 1970s.

A few years later, Pamela met and fell in love with the Irish patriot, Sir Edward Fitzgerald. They met at a theatre where the then celebrated play *Ladoiska* was being staged.

According to Harry Simms, "Fitzgerald gazed raptly at a young lady sitting with a party in a box near his own. As soon as the curtain fell, he had a friend take him to the party in the next box and introduce him to Pamela. Less than a month after their first meeting, Lady Pamela Simms, the girl from Fogo, became the bride of Lord Edward Fitzgerald. The marriage took place at Tourney, France, and M. de Chartres, afterwards King of France, was one of the witnesses of the ceremony." The couple settled down in Kildare, the homeland lodge of Sir Edward.

This happened during the period when the Irish were being mistreated and oppressed by the English and Sir Edward emerged as a leader of the rebellion that grew in opposition to England. As a consequence, Sir Edward was hunted down by the British. To avoid capture, he became a master of disguises and moved from village to village and county to county, always one step ahead of his pursuers.

Fitzgerald was finally captured by three spies and was severely wounded after putting up a valiant battle against the trio. He suffered an agonizing death at his own castle a week later. All he possessed was left to his widow, Lady Pamela Fitzgerald.

Later she met and married Joseph Pitcairn, United States Consul to Germany. That marriage failed and the two were divorced. Lady Pamela then moved to live in France under the name of Fitzgerald. Her efforts to renew the close kinship she had with King Louis Philippe and his family failed. Her dazzling life in European society had come to an end. She retired to a convent in Paris at the age of fifty-five and passed away on November 9, 1831. Fifty years later her descendants had her ashes moved from Mont-Maître to Thames-Ditton, near London where they were entombed in the family vault by her grandson, Sir Edward Campbell, and granddaughter, Lady Selby Smith.[1]

2. Papal Visit to Jerusalem in 1964 Made Possible by a Newfoundlander

When Pope Paul VI made his historic pilgrimage to the Holy Land in 1964 he faced two problems: first, his personal security

[1] The story of Pamela Simms was researched and preserved by her uncle Henry Simms of Fogo and has appeared in several newspapers over the past century.

and secondly, communication was difficult, with people speaking not only different languages but a variety of dialects. The trip was the focus of world attention. When the Pope departed from Rome he received a send-off from Italy's president and the Papal aircraft was escorted by a squadron of the Italian Air Force.

When the Papal plane entered Jordanian airspace, King Hussein sent his air force to escort the plane to Amman Airport. Hussein had strongly supported the Papal pilgrimage and arranged for a team of his military guards to dress as priests and provide security for the Pope while he was in Jordan. In his book, Pope Paul VI, published by Random House, 1966, Alden Hatch describes how the Pope overcame the language problem on the trip.

Describing the Vatican entourage accompanying the Pope, Hatch noted, "To translate his vital conversations with men of many tongues, Pope Paul had a brilliant linguist, Monsignor William Carew." Monsignor Carew, later Archbishop Carew, was born at 155 Queen's Road, St. John's, Newfoundland in 1922.

He was the second Canadian diocesan priest ever to crack the once iron-clad tradition that top departmental jobs in the Vatican went only to Italians. The appointment was reported on in the Toronto *Globe and Mail*, 1961. The newspaper commented, "Since 1953, when he was summoned to the Holy See, Monsignor Carew has not only become a man to watch in Vatican circles, but he is one of the best known Canadian Roman Catholic Churchmen outside his native land." Monsignor Carew was on the staff of the Vatican Secretariat of State.

Among the monsignor's duties at the time was to arrange audiences with the Pope. He had been present when Princess Margaret visited the Pope Pius XII. At the time he was the only member of the British Commonwealth working full-time at the Vatican.

In 1961, he was awarded the honour of Knight Commander of the Order of Isabella; in 1963 he was appointed Knight Commander of the Order of Dahomey and in 1964 was given the High Order of the Kingdom of Jordan. In 1970, he was appointed as archbishop in Spain. Monsignor Carew also served as Apostolic Nuncio to Rwanda and Burundi. In 1976, Pope Paul appointed the talented Newfoundlander to the post of Apostolic Delegate in Jerusalem and the Holy Land.

Another Newfoundlander served Pope Pius XII at the Vatican. Although he did not reach the level of influence achieved by Archbishop Carew, he was the first Newfoundlander to serve at the Vatican. In 1942, the Right Reverend J.F. Kerwin became a member of His Holiness' household. Prior to his appointment, Father Kerwin was parish priest for Port au Port. The Apostolic Delegate to Ottawa in making the announcement on behalf of the Pope said that, "The exalted honour which has been conferred on the new dignitary has been well merited by an arduous life in the service of the Diocese." Father Kerwin held a position among the Pope's domestic prelates. He served parishes in Bay of Islands and Harbour Breton before moving to Port au Port. Kerwin was held in high regard by his parishioners as well the church hierarchy.

Italian-born Cardinal Falconioa, a close associate of several nineteenth century Popes, had a close association with Newfoundland. Before being elevated to cardinal he had served as monsignor at the Roman Catholic Church in Harbour Grace. Falconia was a member of the Vatican's diplomatic service, and was the first Apostolic Delegate to the United States.

3. Newfoundland Hero Captured Chief of Sioux Nation

At the age of twenty-five, Andrew Bulger of St. John's was a captain in the Newfoundland Regiment and one of many Newfoundlanders who fought in the War of 1812 against American forces.

In American history, he is best remembered as the soldier who captured the Chief of the Sioux Nation on the Mississippi River and brought to justice a Sioux Indian who was charged with murder. His superiors described him as, "A man of outstanding courage and endurance."

Bulger's adventure with the American Indians began with an expedition led by Major William McKay and Captain Bulger from Fort Mackinaw on the Great Lakes to the Mississippi River, which penetrated 500 miles into American territory.

Describing the challenging trek, Captain Bulger wrote to Colonel McDougal on December 30, 1814:

> I reached this place on November 30. From the moment of my departure from Green Bay, until my arrival here, I experienced every misery in the power of cold and want to inflict. I suffered more, sir, during this voyage than you can imagine, much more than even I have suffered during the whole course of my life before. The morning we left to descend the Wisconsin River it was filled with floating ice and there was not a meal of victuals in any of the boats.

Bulger successfully led his men in overcoming these severe conditions and launched a successful attack in which he captured the American fort at Prairie du Chien. He renamed it Fort McKay. Months later Bulger had returned to Canada, when the British learned of an American plan to send an expedition to recapture the fort. Bulger was chosen for his toughness and military skills to return as commander of the fort and prepare for its defense.

By the time Bulger arrived, law and order had deteriorated. The Indians were causing problems. There was a shortage of food, and some soldiers were outright insubordinate. Bulger began by quickly whipping the military back into shape. While this was happening, a Sioux Indian killed two British citizens.

The Newfoundland commander retaliated by making a direct confrontation to the Sioux Nation. He took a band of soldiers and captured the Chief of the Sioux, whom he held as hostage. Through persuasion, Bulger convinced the Chief to surrender the murderer. When the Chief came face to face with the murderer, he said to Bulger, "This is the dog that bit you." The man was tried, found guilty and shot by members of the Newfoundland Regiment. The way Bulger handled the situation impressed the British Forces commander who confirmed Bulger's appointment to Commanding Officer of Fort McKay.

4. Newfoundland-Born Hero Became Captain of Presidential Guard

Michael McCarthy and John Neil were Newfoundland-born American citizens who became true American heroes and each received the treasured Congressional Medal of Honour.

McCarthy was born in St. John's on April 19, 1847, and by 1877 he was an American citizen and a sergeant in the 1st U.S. Cavalry. His elevation to the rank of sergeant came after many battles with Native American Indians. The fiercest and most savage of those encounters was the battle against the Nez Perce Indians of Idaho.

The Nez Perce people got along well with the American settlers in their area and they treated each other with mutual hospitality and generosity. However, there were some settlers whose fear and prejudices led to confrontations. Even then, the Indians attempted to avoid trouble and attended strictly to their own affairs.

As the expansion of the west grew with a continual influx of new settlers, Washington dictated policies which negatively impacted the Nez Perce. They were forced to move from one reservation to another. Things seemed to improve after Washington signed a treaty with them, which gave the Nez Perce possession of a place called the Wallowas Valley.

The arrival of a group of white settlers, who ignored Indian treaty rights and began taking away their land, sparked the dispute that led to an all-out war between the Nez Perce and the whites.

Once again, it was the natives who demonstrated goodwill. They tried to settle the dispute peacefully by pointing to their treaty rights. The whites refused to acknowledge this argument and sent a delegation to Washington to advocate on their behalf.

The settlers were persuasive and, after successfully lobbying the elected officials, obtained Washington's support and a military force to back up the decision. Surprisingly, and to the credit of the Nez Perce, Chief Looking Glass held a council with other tribe leaders who voted to accept the white man's law and move to another site which government had offered.

As they were preparing to move, some settlers began to annoy them. One settler deliberately shot and killed a Nez Perce brave. This proved to be the last straw for those among the Nez Perce who were reluctant to give into the white man in the first place. The death of a tribe member sparked open rebellion against the American authorities. Their first move was an act of revenge against the brother of the settler who had killed their fellow tribe member. The settlers now feared a massacre and persuaded Washington to send in the U.S. Cavalry. By this time the Indians were heading for Montana.

Army General G. Howard issued the following orders to Captain E. Perry of the 1st U.S. Cavalry, "Get to the scene quickly, take away from the Indians their loot and chase them back to the reservation." Perry felt that the Nez Perce were not a warring nation and was convinced that a show of force would be enough to bring about their surrender. Consequently, his ninety-member party left Fort Lapwai poorly equipped. They carried only forty rounds of ammunition for their single carbine and twelve bullets for each pistol. A battle was inevitable.

The cavalry was outnumbered eight to one and the Indians were in an unassailable position. Captain Perry saw a strategic point to his right on elevated rocky ground and ordered Sergeant McCarthy to take six men and hold that position at all costs.

The battle that broke out is described in U.S. Congressional records:

> Now the fight began. The Indians broke forth, yelling, screaming, and filling the air with hideous howls and showers of bullets. As soon as this rush was made, it looked as though Hades itself had been turned loose. Eight citizens, settlers, who had been most loud in their denunciation of the Nez Perce and their demands for vengeance, took to their heels and ran away as fast as they could. The soldiers too were not prepared to meet this furious and awe-inspiring onslaught and wavered. Soon most of the men of "F" Troop were hurrying to the rear.
>
> Captain Perry, doubting the advisability of the defence, ordered a general retreat. Captain Trimble felt Perry was making a big mistake. He galloped to the Commanding Officer and pleaded with him to recall the order. He asked, 'What is to become of McCarthy and his men. They are in a strong position. If we reinforce him and hold ground there, we shall check the attack.' Captain Perry was impressed with Trimble's spirit and argument. He reversed his order. Trimble personally led the men back into battle, but there was still confusion in the ranks.

McCarthy noticed the cavalry's change in tactics and hurridly rode from his position to assist his captain in steadying the men. Once the attack was properly organized, he joined his faithful six men at the former post. The new burst of courage and enthusiastic fighting by the cavalry was not enough to withstand the onslaught of the overwhelming Nez Perce force.

Congressional records described the scene:

Once more the troops retreated before the exultant Nez Perce, galloping to some hills which promised protection about a mile away. Their retreat was much faster than the Indians were able to follow. This second retreat left McCarthy and his detail in a serious plight. Completely surrounded by savages, he nobly and heroically held his position against the storming foe.

The struggle was observed by his comrades on the hills, who followed every phase of it with anticipations of awe and terror. Closer and closer the Indians drew their circle around the gallant little band. One could now see them shoot, strike or club the foremost of the redskins. Now it was a hand-to-hand fight. McCarthy and his comrades could no longer be seen. They were swallowed up by the hordes of screaming Indians. The soldiers who were watching from the hill and witnessing the hand-to-hand battle turned away, sickened by the sight. But again, the figure of McCarthy and his little party sprung up in the middle of the tribe. The gallant little band was cutting its way through the hostilities.

Although the odds were against him, Lieutenant W.R. Parnell, inspired by the sight of McCarthy's courage, led a detachment of cavalry to help McCarthy and his men. Two of McCarthy's men, however, died bravely during the brief but savage ride.

The Congressional records continue:

> Reinforced by Parnell's detachment, the little group
> made another stand against the Nez Perce, but in vain.
> The Indian force was so overwhelming that Parnell or-
> dered a retreat. McCarthy seemed to ignore or not to
> hear the retreat order and continued to fight without
> any regard for his own personal safety. He helped a
> wounded comrade who fell off his horse from being
> captured by the savages. He encouraged and tried to
> control the men who had remained with him to fight.
> When his horse was shot out from under him, he quick-
> ly mounted another and slowly guided his men back to
> the rest of his company. During this retreat his horse
> was shot from under him again, and in the chaos that
> followed the courageous sergeant was separated from
> his comrades.

McCarthy didn't panic. He made a dash for a clump of
bushes behind the Indians where he could watch the unfolding battle without being detected. Indians on horseback passed
in front of his hiding place as they chased his comrades who
were running for their lives. McCarthy was filled with anger
and resentment because he could not help his fellow soldiers.
He realized the battle was over and his troops had been humiliated by the Nez Perce.

The records continue:

> The body of a close friend lay nearby, but before he had
> a chance to hide it, a number of squaws came up and
> began mutilating it and removing the dead man's cloth-
> ing. McCarthy realized that his own boots were sticking
> out of the bushes. He quickly slipped out of them and
> withdrew further into the woods. This was enough to

fool the Indian women who believed some soldier must
have left them during a quick retreat.

McCarthy patiently hid out for hours with an empty gun. He
slipped past the Indian women who were busy collecting items
from the battlefield and made his escape by crawling down
the bed of the creek until he reached the timbered mountains
some miles away. From there he wandered over rough territory
which caused agonizing pain to his feet. This Newfoundland-
born soldier hid by day and travelled by night, living on the
scant rations he had with him. Surviving much hardship, he
made it to his camp at Mount Idaho thoroughly exhausted. His
friends enthusiastically welcomed him.

The leaders of the cavalry meticulously documented Mc-
Carthy's behaviour and sent recommendations to Washington
that he should be awarded the Congressional Medal of Honour.

This award led to another great honour: McCarthy was appointed to the position of captain of the Presidential Guard at
the American White House.

5. Newfoundlander Awarded U.S. Congressional Medal of Honour

Like his fellow Newfoundlander, Michael McCarthy, John
Neil was recognized by the president of the United States and
was awarded the coveted Congressional Medal of Honour. His
act of heroism has been depicted in several Hollywood movies
about the American Civil War.

Neil's dangerous adventure was hatched when Union Forces formulated a top secret project to close the final Confederate
port on the eastern seaboard of the United States in order to
bring about a rapid end to the Civil War. Eight men were carefully selected for this mission. Among this elite force was John
Neil, born in St. John's, Newfoundland.

Neil's story is documented in the records of the U.S. Congressional Library, which outlines a major problem in bringing about an end to the conflict. The record reads:

> The splendid energy of the Union Navy in blockading a seacoast of nearly 3,500 miles had such effect that a year after the commencement of the war there were practically only two ports open along the whole hostile coast: Charleston, South Carolina and Wilmington, North Carolina.
>
> They were the channels through which the Confederates, by means of daring and fast blockade runners, communicated with the outer world and obtained all the supplies and provisions they wanted in exchange for their cotton. It was impossible for the Navy to close those two places at the time with the sea forces available and without the co-operation of the army; but the army had its hands full just then in other parts of the theatre of war.

At first the Union Navy tried valiantly to close the ports which were essential to the Confederates and their survival. They succeeded in blocking Charleston, and the Confederates were forced to retreat to Wilmington which became their new base of operations.

On September 22, 1864, Rear Admiral Porter was assigned Commander of the North Atlantic Squadron of the Federal Navy. His main strategy was to close down Wilmington, which was the only port still left open to the Confederates. Without the food supplies and weapons being delivered through Wilmington, the days of the Confederate forces were numbered.

Fort Fisher was located at the mouth of Wilmington Harbour and was heavily defended by seventy-five guns, all mounted behind heavy earthworks. Most ships of the federal forces were wooden which made a direct attack by the squadron dangerous. At this stage, Admiral Porter was frustrated. The solution to his challenge came when General Butler boarded the Admiral's flagship with a daring plan to knock out the guns at Fort Fisher.

Butler's plan called for 150 tons of gunpowder to be placed aboard a vessel, which would be secretly brought as close as possible to the fort and then blown up. The general was confident that the explosion would be powerful enough to level the fort, or at least dismount the guns.

The plan was reviewed and debated among the leaders and strategists who concluded it was feasible providing the whole cargo of 150 tons could be detonated simultaneously. This was enough for Admiral Porter, who immediately telegraphed the Navy Ordnance Department for the powder.

The plan ran into a problem when Porter, in haste, ordered 15,000 tons instead of the 150 tons of powder. Ordnance officials viewed the order with disbelief, but the error was detected and Porter got his powder. Yet that was only after Ordnance sent a telegraph to Porter asking, "Why do you not ask us to send you Niagara and Vesuvias down there. That would satisfy you."

Porter moved ahead with preparations for the mission. He secured the *Louisiana*, an old vessel, to serve as the powder boat to be sacrificed. Once the powder was bagged and stored on the vessel, the admiral turned his attention to recruiting eight volunteers for the mission.

The munitions boat was fitted out for her perilous assignment at Beaufort Carolina. The fuses were meticulously laid using a system of clockwork and candles to assure the required simultaneous explosion.

The Congressional report stated:

With the *Louisiana* now in a state of readiness, Porter sought out volunteers for the mission. The seventy-five guns at the entrance to Wilmington Harbour meant the mission would be in great danger once the vessel came within firing distance of the fort. The admiral succeeded in getting eight men to volunteer for the dangerous task. One of the first to volunteer was quartermaster John Neil, a Newfoundlander. Neil was a crewman of the *Agawam*.

On the night of December 23rd, the plan went into operation. Admiral Porter made one final change just before it got underway. In spite of expert opinion, Porter was skeptical about the clockwork and candle arrangement. He suggested that it would be wise to light some pine knots in the cabin before leaving the boats, so as to make sure of the explosion.

The eight courageous men then set out for the target under the command of Commander Rhind. There was a great deal of tension as the ship sailed into the harbour beneath the enemy guns; they could be blown to kingdom come, if detected. After what seemed like an eternity to Rhind and his men, they finally got the vessel into position beneath their target.

The men acted swiftly in lighting the candles and pine knots. The candles and the clockwork were set to explode the ship in an hour and a half. Having completed the plan, Rhind and his men slipped into the water and began their treacherous swim to a small boat anchored nearby out of sight of the fort.

The explosion did not occur as planned. It took two hours before detonation occurred. As Admiral Porter had feared, the candle work had failed, but the pine knots did the trick. However, they did not cause a simultaneous explosion; consequently, the enterprise failed.

Yet, it was strong enough to cause extensive damage to the fort. The next day, Porter received a first-hand account of what had happened when four Confederate deserters met him on the *Malvern*. Following the courageous work of the eight volunteers, Union Forces followed up with a heavy naval bombardment of Wilmington. The shot and shell crashed into Fort Fisher at the rate of 115 per minute. An hour-and-a-half into the battle the Confederate guns were silenced. The Union Forces had succeeded. Their only casualty was suffered when one of their Parrott guns exploded. Days later, the Confederates surrendered. The strategic Fort Fisher and nearby inlets were then in the hands of the federal forces. President Abraham Lincoln was elated upon receiving the news.

Out of thousands of union troops participating in the Battle for Wilmington, only a handful of men earned the coveted Congressional Medal of Honour. Among them was Newfoundland-born John Neil.

6. Newfoundland Mercenaries in Mexican Revolution

The names of Newfoundlanders can be found in the records of the many wars fought in British history, but one war in which you would not expect to learn of any Newfoundlander's participation is the Mexican Revolution of 1911. In that important part of Mexican history there is not just one, but actually four Newfoundlanders recorded. All four served as mercenaries with Mexican rebel forces.

Their names are included in the records of the famous Battle of Casas Grandes. During this battle, Patrick Sweeney and Jim Baird of St. John's were killed, while Harry Carter and Robert Mugford were wounded.

The revolution was led by General Francisco Madero, who had contested an election against President Portfirio Diez and was defeated. Diez had him arrested and tossed into jail. When

17

Madero was set free he openly rebelled against Diez. The rebel army started with Madero supporters and was strengthened by the hiring of foreign mercenaries. The rebel leader offered the mercenaries $300 a month and promised each of them 5,000 acres of land when he defeated government forces and replaced Diez as president.

The majority of rebel forces were actually mercenaries with experience in fighting wars all over the world. When things got rough at the Battle of Casas Grandes, the inexperienced Mexicans left the battlefield. The others, including the four Newfoundlanders, fought to within forty feet of the federal forces using dynamite and nitroglycerine.

This offensive was halted suddenly when a bullet hit a 100-pound package of dynamite in the saddlebags of the rebel Captain Lloyd. Lloyd was born in Scotland and had lived in Newfoundland before becoming a soldier of fortune. The battle at Casas Grandes lasted for ninety minutes. The two Newfoundland survivors, Carter and Mugford, were carried from the battlefield by their comrades.

After losing this battle, the Madero forces went on to win the war. When Madero was sworn in as president of Mexico, he reneged on his commitment to both Mexicans and mercenaries regarding land grants.

Mugford left Mexico to live in the United States while Carter enlisted in the forces of Pancho Villa. He was with Villa while it was being hounded by General John J. Pershing, an American hero of World War I. When Carter finished his service with Villa, he settled in Mexico City.

According to author and journalist Michael P. Murphy, Carter became fluent in Spanish and married a Mexican woman. They built a home on the outskirts of Mexico City where he was employed by American interests. They had two children together, but regrettably Carter lost his entire family in a fire that destroyed the family home.

Patrick Sweeney lived on a side street of New Gower Street before moving to the U.S. where he joined the U.S. Infantry Regiment and served in the "Wild West." His experience there motivated him to become a mercenary with the Mexican rebel forces of Madero.

7. Newfoundlander Commanded British in American War of Independence

Henry George Clinton was born in St. John's in 1735. When George Washington led his Colonial troops in battle against the British in the great battle for American independence, one of his main adversaries was that same George Clinton. By then, Clinton had become a British general. His father, also called Henry, was Governor of Newfoundland at the time the general was born.

Young Henry was a brilliant young man who enlisted with the British forces while still in his teens. He was an outstanding soldier and his intelligence and courage enabled him to advance rapidly in the military. He distinguished himself during the Seven Years War where he served under the command of Ferdinand of Brunswick. Later, he entered politics and was elected to the British Parliament and knighted by the King of England.

He played a major role during the American War of Independence and initially was second in command of British forces in North America under Sir William Howe. Following the British defeat at Bunker Hill, this Newfoundlander took full command.

In the battle that followed, he matched military skills with George Washington. He had the Americans on the run after capturing New York City which he held for most of the war.

When the tide turned and the American forces won the war, Clinton was appointed Governor of Gibraltar. He had two sons

19

who advanced to the rank of general and his son, also named Henry, fought in the Battle of Waterloo.

Several other Newfoundlanders rose to top ranks in the British military as well as the Clintons. There was General Sir Henry Pynn, born in Bristol's Hope, who served in Wellington's forces. Another was General Sir John Shea who was in command of British forces in India from 1928-1932. Admiral George Bride of the British Navy was a Newfoundlander. He was the author of several books on the art of naval warfare.

8. Newfoundlander Helped Prevent a War

Thomas Scanlon of Water Street, St. John's had no role to play in Newfoundland history. He was simply an employee of the Telegraph office in St. John's. There would be no reason to even mention his name at this time if it had not been for a telegraph message he delivered by horseback on Saturday night, June 12, 1866. Failure to deliver this particular telegraph would have resulted in the United States going to war with Britain.

This event occurred during the American Civil War. At issue was the fact that England had recognized the government of the Southern States, an act which sparked widespread pressure on President Abraham Lincoln to declare war on England.

Thomas Scanlon became an important figure in this episode of history after the Galway liner *Prince Albert* sailed into St. John's Harbour on the night of June 12, 1866, carrying an urgent, crucial message from the prime minister of England for the president of the United States. The secret message to be relayed from St. John's to Washington advised Lincoln that England had changed its American policy and had withdrawn its recognition of the Southern government, choosing instead to remain neutral.

It was important to get this message to Lincoln in time to prevent an American declaration of war. The message was turned over to Tom Scanlon at the Telegraph office in St. John's for relay to Washington. Ordinarily that would have been handled by relays from St. John's to La Manche then along a line of relay stations until it arrived in Washington. However, the telegraph lines to La Manche were down and there was no assurance that the La Manche station was operable. It was indeed a bleak situation.

At this point, Scanlon volunteered to take the message by horseback to the La Manche telegraph station with hopes that it would be in operation. The fate of two great nations and millions of people depended on this message getting through.

Yet, the horseback ride to La Manche had its own challenges and dangers. Scanlon, Newfoundland's Paul Revere, reached a point on his ride where the horse was unable to go any further. He pushed on over rough terrain by foot. This trek was made over bog lands, hills and through streams until he reached a small bay where he caught sight of a ferry. By the time he reached the shoreline, the ferry was on the other side of the bay.

Not ready to admit defeat, the persistent Scanlon caught up with a fisherman nearby and borrowed his gun. He fired the gun repeatedly until he caught the attention of the ferry captain who returned from across the bay to pick him up. Finally, Scanlon arrived at the telegraph station, but yet again he was greeted with frustration; the telegraph system was unmanned and out of order.

Scanlon had not endured hardship to be defeated at this last point of hope. He undertook to repair the system alone, and he succeeded. Finally, he sent off the crucial message and did not move from the station until he received confirmation that the message had been delivered to President Abraham Lincoln. His successful effort succeeded in keeping Lincoln from declaring war on England.

9. The Man They Couldn't Bury!

The religious animosity between Catholics and Protestants in Britain was brought to Newfoundland by its first settlers. A fine example of just how divisive things were is the case of "Bouncing John Moxley." The nickname "Bouncing John" originated only after he had passed away, and was the result of a religious dispute over where he should be buried.

This story has its roots on a street in Carbonear once known as Moxley's Corner, and this is how it got its name:

John Moxley, born a Catholic, was the victim of religious bigotry and became the centre of one of the most bitter religious controversies in Newfoundland's history.

John Moxley married a Protestant lady and the two reared their family in the community of Carbonear. As in all small communities, everyone knew that John had left his faith to marry. However, Moxley never became a Protestant and was described as a "God-fearing man." He read the Protestant Bible and literature regularly but never became a member of any Protestant denomination. He did, however, confide to friends that although he wished to convert he feared doing so because a few of the strong Irish Catholics in Carbonear would kill him.

The bitterness that Moxley wanted to avoid during his lifetime erupted in a major dispute after his death that was not settled until authorities from St. John's intervened. During March 1838, John Moxley died suddenly. While the coroner determined he had died by suicide, suspicion prevailed that he had been murdered. Things began to boil over when his family attempted to give him a proper burial. Neither Catholics nor Protestants wanted him in their respective graveyards.

The family arranged for him to be buried at the Anglican Cemetery but as the minister prepared for the funeral services, some members of his congregation gathered and tried to stop the gravediggers from opening the grave. Because of this interference, the diggers could only dig a few feet. At the conclusion of the Anglican service John Moxley was buried in this shallow grave.

Over the following week, the burial place of John Moxley developed into a major controversy throughout the community. At the centre of the debate was the fact that Moxley was not a practicing member of either the Protestant or the Catholic faith. A small band of Protestants took it upon themselves to correct the problem and in the darkness of night crept into the cemetery, dug up Moxley and unceremoniously deposited his casket on the road outside. This happened several times and on each occasion Moxley was reburied in the Moxley family plot.

When that failed as the solution and Moxley's casket was again dumped onto the road, the clergy from both faiths came up with what they thought to be the solution – bury him in the Catholic graveyard. Although both were satisfied with this choice, church members were not so charitable.

The situation became totally outrageous when a band of men dug up Moxley's casket, which by then was falling apart, took the body out, stripped the cloth lining from the casket and tossed it over a cliff. When a report of these outrages reached the governor in St. John's, a constable was sent to settle the matter. He enlisted the help of the decent people in the community who were outraged by this desecration. This group showed true Christian charity and took control of the matter. The coroner, John Stark, stepped forward and paid for a new casket, and the group buried John Moxley in a hidden wooded place just outside the community.

Moxley had left eight children and an estate valued at $1,200, which was supposed to go the Crown. However, because of the sympathy that developed for the family, the Crown allowed the full amount to go to the widow. Decades after the outrage, Moxley's burial place became known as Moxley's Corner, and Moxley was remembered as "Bouncing John Moxley."

10. Mistress to the King had a Newfoundland Connection

In his play *A Winter's Tale*, Shakespeare included a character named Perdita. In real life, Perdita was the mistress to the Prince Regent of England, later to become King George IV of England.

This Royal mistress was actually Mary Darby Robinson who was born in Bristol, England. Her father was Newfoundland-born Nicholas Darby, who was born during the summer of 1720 to a fisherman's family in St. John's. By 1765, Darby was given the support of Newfoundland Governor, Sir Hugh Palliser to go north to develop the Labrador fishery.

Captain Darby set up headquarters at Cape Charles where he built lodgings, a workshop and a fishing stage. He tried unsuccessfully to overcome the harsh Labrador winters and aggressive encounters with the Inuit. In 1769, British authorities confiscated his goods and equipment and forced him out of business. This action was taken because Darby had employed Frenchmen.

Captain Darby left Newfoundland and became a mercenary with the Russian Army in 1782 at the age of sixty-two. He passed away in a small village on the outskirts of Moscow and was buried in a church cemetery there three years later.

11. First Prisoner Electrocuted in Vermont was a Newfoundlander

Ronald Watson, a Newfoundlander who migrated to Vermont, U.S.A., made news headlines across the United States in 1946 after committing the most gruesome murder the state of Vermont had witnessed in more than forty years. After his execution, a Canadian magazine, *Greater Detective Cases*, ran a feature story with the front page headline, "The Riddle of the Slain Cabbie."

Watson had worked with his father as fisherman in Newfoundland. He first moved to St. John's and worked longshore and fishing to make a living. When friends told him of the American-Newfoundland Farm Agreement, he enrolled. The agreement provided Newfoundlanders with transportation and shelter to move to New England to work on the farms. One of his few belongings was a fishing knife, which he took with him.

One night he had been drinking and socializing at a bar several miles from the farm where he worked, and Henry Teelon was the unfortunate taxi driver who picked up Watson that night. Teelon tried to engage in conversation but Watson was nervous and reluctant. Teelon did not return home that night. Early the next morning the police found his corpse hung over a barbed wire fence and covered in blood.

The police officer noted that there were three gaping holes in the back of Watson's coat as well as two visible knife wounds in the victim's neck. Teelon had been badly beaten and butchered. His forehead over his left eye had been completely crushed.

The investigation lasted several weeks. Vermont police followed up on numerous leads and finally tracked Watson down after finding his name in the victims "call book." "Watson" was the last name written in the book. The Newfoundlander was arrested at the home of his fiancée, Joyce Green. He quickly confessed to the killing. Watson told police he wanted to buy an engagement ring for Joyce and robbed the cabbie to get the money. Henry Teelon had been murdered for his day's take which totalled one hundred and six dollars.

Watson explained that he viciously attacked Teelon because he could not get up enough nerve to take the money. He wanted to be sure Teelon was dead first, so he stabbed him repeatedly.

The murder weapon was his fisherman's knife, which he had brought with him from St. John's.

The trial was a short one and the decision quick. It took place in the Supreme Court of Vermont and captured headlines all over the United States. Ronald Watson was found guilty of murder and was sentenced to be electrocuted. He became the first person to be executed in Vermont since 1906.

12. Newfoundlander First to Volunteer in U.S. for World War I

Dr. William B. Giles, a Newfoundlander, was a noted medical doctor in the United States and Argentina. He was born in St. John's, the son of Captain Edward J. Giles, a former master of the Red Cross liner *Silvia*. Giles held impressive medical credentials. He was a graduate of Harvard Medical Postgraduate School, Tufts Medical College and the New York Poly-Clinic Postgraduate School. This St. John's native was one of the first volunteers sent by the United States Army during World War I to France. He served there as surgeon in a French military hospital. When the U.S. joined the Allies, Dr. Giles was attached to the U.S. Navy hospital ship *Comfort*.

During the first years of World War II, Dr. Giles was renowned in Argentina. The following item appeared in *The Standard*, an English daily newspaper in Buenos Aires dated April 1, 1940:

Possibly unique in the annals of Argentine medicine is the announcement that Dr. William B. Giles, only American trained physician in the country, has completed all the examinations and legal requirements for re-validating his title and has now installed consulting rooms.

Dr. Giles went to Argentina on an American observation tour and decided to stay there. In order to practice his profession, he had to comply with the medical laws of that nation and re-validate his credentials. During his career in Argentina, he was recognized as one of the country's finest doctors. Giles, before going to Argentina, taught at Bellevue Medical, New York and was attached to the Children's Hospital, New York and the West Side Hospital.

13. Boston Street Connected to Newfoundland Family

Moran Square in South Boston has an interesting Newfoundland connection. Like many Newfoundlanders in the 1920s, Mr. and Mrs. Moran left their St. John's home and moved to the U.S., settling in South Boston at 119 Marine Road. Their son, Leonard, was born there in 1932 and subsequently joined the U.S. Army, serving in the Korean War.

Sergeant Moran, twenty-two, made newspaper headlines across the United States in 1954 for performing a daring act of courage, which resulted in the life of a young marine recruit being saved.

The incident took place on January 7, 1954, at Fort Dix, New Jersey, where Moran, a veteran of the Korean War, was instructing recruits in the handling of grenades. One of them accidentally dropped a grenade and Moran swept into action. He jumped into the trench on top of the recruit, thus shielding him from the explosion that followed. He took the brunt of the explosion.

A valiant effort was made to save his life. He was rushed to the Army hospital but the best efforts of doctors failed to save him. The recruit, Private John D. O'Callaghan of New York City, received minor flesh wounds. Captain Harry Lapham, public information officer at Fort Dix, said the recruit was attempting to toss the grenade, when it hit the parapet and rolled back into the trench.

O'Callaghan told reporters he had actually tossed two grenades. He explained, "When I was tossing the second, I fell to the ground as instructed, but I apparently threw it too low and it hit the parapet. Next thing I knew, Sergeant Moran was on top of me covering my body. About the same time, I heard an explosion." Major General C.P. Ryan at Fort Dix documented the recommendation for the Congressional Medal of Honour to be posthumously awarded to Moran.

This was not Moran's first courageous act. In the Korean War, Moran saved the life of Private John F. Norton during enemy gunfire. At that time, while bullets were whirling around the two men, Moran pushed Norton to the ground and shielded him.

To honour Sergeant Moran's memory, the South Boston Council named a square in Boston, Moran Square, after him. The president of the United States posthumously awarded Sergeant Moran the Congressional Medal of Honour.

14. President Hoover's Adviser was a Newfoundlander

During his term as president of the United States, Herbert Hoover's right-hand man in Europe was a Newfoundlander named William Goode, who later became Sir William. In a book on Newfoundland, written by Premier J.R. Smallwood and published in 1931, Smallwood wrote:

> The name may not convey much to American readers, but in certain parts of Europe, Sir William Goode's personality loomed for a while in large proportions. He was born in Newfoundland, the son of the Reverend T.A. Goode. He served for a while as purser in the British Merchant Marine, then for a while, in 1894, in the 4th U.S. Cavalry. When he left the cavalry, he became night city editor of the *New York Recorder*, and in 1895, he was made city editor of the *New York Mercury*. Later, he was employed by the Associated Press and represented them on Admiral Sampson's flagship throughout the Spanish-American War. After the war, he was sent to England for six years. Eventually, having left the Associated Press, he became news editor and then managing editor of the *Daily Mail*.
>
> He was unofficial adviser to the Hungarian government. During the war, he was liaison officer of the Ministry of Food with the U.S. and Canadian food administrations.

He was organizer of the National Committee for Relief in Belgium and in that connection became the right-hand man in Europe to Hoover. He was president of, and British representative on, the Austrian section of the Reparation Commission. [2]

15. Newfoundlander Rode with Roosevelt's Rough Riders

Before becoming president of the United States, Theodore Roosevelt led a military group known as the Rough Riders. The Rough Riders fought in the Spanish-American War, and a member of the Riders was William Maher of St. John's, Newfoundland.

Maher moved to the United States to become a cowboy on the Western prairies. He became an expert horseman and gained valuable experience as a pony express rider.

While working as a pony express rider, he earned a medal for his courage in fighting off bandits who tried to steal the mail. Maher had little trouble joining Roosevelt's Rough Riders, as he was with Roosevelt in Cuba and fought with him in the historic Battle of San Juan Hill.

16 Newfoundlander a Chilean Military Hero

Early in the twentieth century, the Chilean government made a continent-wide search to locate a Newfoundland man named John Fallon. They initiated a newspaper advertising campaign asking that John Fallon, or anybody knowing his whereabouts to contact the Government of Chile. The advertisement was brought to the attention of Fallon at his hometown, Harbour Grace, Newfoundland.

---

[2] Smallwood, J.R. *The New Newfoundland*. The MacMillan Company, New York, 1931.

The reason behind the search was that Chile wanted to honour a man whom they considered a national hero. Fallon had gained notoriety in Chile during a military battle while serving with the Chilean Army. John Fallon was born in Harbour Grace in 1860, the eldest son of Head Constable Luke Fallon. For a brief period he apprenticed with William Grubert, shoemaker. However, he had a burning desire to see the world and experience adventure. Fallon moved to the United States where he enlisted in the 15th Infantry Regiment of the U.S. Army.

After serving a term with the army, Fallon learned of a war going on in the South American republic and left the United States to enlist in the Chilean Army. During one of the many battles he fought there, he took daring action which inspired his fellow soldiers and earned him a place in Chilean military history.

During the battle, and with his army in retreat, Fallon refused to fall back and continued to put up a spirited fight. He was determined that his unit should hold their ground and fight. While under heavy fire from the enemy, he seized and carried the Chilean flag to the top of a hill and firmly planted it for all to see. John Fallon's determined fighting attracted the attention of the retreating troops and they began to turn back and fight. After being hit by an enemy bullet, Fallon held one arm around the flagpole and encouraged his comrades to fight.

When the war ended, he was awarded a medal for bravery. Soon after, he returned to Newfoundland and settled in Harbour Grace. As the years passed, Fallon became a folk hero in Chile and the government again sought him out for one more honour. When Fallon learned of Chile's advertising effort, he responded and was pleased to learn that he had been awarded a lifelong pension from Chile. John Fallon passed away on December 21, 1922. He left four sons: Luke, David, John and Christopher, and one daughter, Mary. A fifth son, Stephen, was killed at Beaumont Hamel.

17. Newfoundland Hero of Spanish-American War

John Cooper was born in Trinity and later moved to the United States. While living in New York, he joined the 15th New York Infantry Regiment. On May 1, 1898, Cooper was a member of the expeditionary force going to Cuba to fight in the Spanish-American War. This turned out to be one of the shortest wars in world history. It began on April 21st and ended on August 12th, three and a half months later. The conflict was fought mainly in Cuba and the Philippines.

By the time Cooper arrived, the Spanish Army was controlling two strongpoints. These were the village of El Caney and San Juan Hill, both in Cuba. Cooper was in the middle of both battles and was at the front of the troops making the major assault at Fort Santiago where fierce fighting caused many casualties on both sides.

A soldier near Cooper who was carrying the Stars and Stripes was shot and killed. As the soldier fell, Cooper seized the flag before it hit the ground. Cooper encouraged his fellow soldiers to push forward amidst the heavy gunfire; inspired by this Newfoundlander's example, the men fought zealously and the Americans succeeded in winning the Battle at Santiago and the Spanish-American War.

John Cooper was hailed as an American hero and awarded a medal for bravery by the United States government. He was given six week's leave, which he used to visit his family in Trinity.

18. Plymouth Rock's Squantum Learned English in Newfoundland

Newfoundland history has recorded an intriguing, captivating, connection between the early settlers of Newfoundland and the first settlers in New England. It is the story of a Native American Indian, which historian David W. Prowse described this way:

The romantic adventures of the Indian Squantum, his infamous capture by Hunt and his subsequent slavery in Spain, his visit to Cupids, and his later services as friend and ally of the Pilgrim Fathers reads more like a scene in a cheap novel than the true story of a poor Redskin. Squantum was taken captive by Thomas Hunt, one of John Smith's captains in the expedition to New England of 1614 [This was the same Captain John Smith whose relationship with Pocahontas is well recognized in American history.]

Squantum was among sixteen Indians taken captive by Hunt and sold as slaves in Malaga. Squantum was highly intelligent and quickly earned the trust of his captors who allowed him more freedom of movement than was accorded to other slaves. After four years in captivity, he met the captain of a ship which was part of John Guy's colony at Cupids and on a trading visit at Malaga.

Squantum gained the captain's trust and arrangements were made to smuggle him aboard the ship which was destined for London and then Cupids, Newfoundland.

It is not known just how long Squantum resided in Cupids, but we do know that while there he met a couple of figures who played a part in the settlement of New England. These were Captain John Mason, a scholar and an officer in the Royal Navy, and Captain Thomas Dermer, a colonist with Guy. It was Captain Dermer who took Squantum to Plymouth to satisfy the curiosity of several prominent merchants there with interests in colonizing New England, thus allowing Squantum to return to his people.

The first pilgrims who arrived in New England were astonished when approached by a Native Indian who spoke good English. He developed a close relationship with the pilgrim colonists and taught them to plant Indian corn, and to use fish manure to make it grow better.

Prowse recorded:

> Squantum was their guide, philosopher, and friend; clothed in an old soldier's uniform, his heart swelled with importance. He made his fellow countrymen believe that from close association with the white men, he had gained the control of disease and death and that he could bring them out of sickness or bury them at will.
>
> This remarkable Indian spoke three languages, and had embraced four religions; first, his native heathenism; secondly, the genial friars in Malaga made him a good Catholic; Mistress Anne Mason converted him into a sound High Churchman; finally the Brownists captured him. His last request was for Governor Bradford to pray for him that '...he might go to ye Englishman's God in heaven.'
>
> The early part of Governor William Bradford's history is full of Squantum and his services to the Pilgrims.
>
> The death of Squantum in 1622 was followed by a short period when the Indians ceased to trade with the pilgrims. Governor Bradford said that Squantum provided valuable services to the colonists and '...he will be remembered.'[3]

19. From Baker to Restaurant Chain Owner

While Patricia Murphy was growing up in Placentia, Newfoundland, her childhood friends called her Patsy Murphy. When Memorial University was officially opened on October 9, 1961, Patsy was among the special guests on the podium seated next to Eleanor Roosevelt, wife of the late president of the United States, Franklin D. Roosevelt, overlooking the largest

[3] D.W. Prowse. *A History of Newfoundland*. Boulder Publications, St. John's, NL.

parade ever held in Newfoundland. By that time she had accumulated a most impressive background.

Patricia Murphy's parents were Mr. and Mrs. Frank Murphy, general store owners in Placentia. Patricia moved to New York in 1929, at age twenty-three, after receiving a scholarship to study music; upon arriving there, she went to live with her uncle. She adjusted quickly to the big city and felt confident enough to move out on her own. Patricia found a furnished room in Manhattan for $4 per week and supported herself by working several part-time jobs. She began by playing the piano during lunch hours at a restaurant near Columbia University. A second job involved colouring postcards and she was paid $3 per hundred.

However, her rise to fame and fortune in the United States was a very difficult route, as this was during the Great Depression. On her forty-five-minute lunch break, she regularly dropped into a place called The Step In Restaurant. One day when she turned up for lunch there was a gone-out-of business sign on the door. It was this experience that put her on the road towards developing one of the largest chains of fashionable restaurants in the United States, The Candlelight Restaurants.

Patricia saw the closed restaurant as an opportunity to become self-employed and she succeeded in renting the facility for $25 weekly. When it came to choosing a name for the business, she settled on The Candlelight Restaurant.

A cooking talent learned from her mother in Newfoundland was making outstanding scones. She decided to make that her specialty but called them "Popovers."

In 1938, Patricia opened a second Candlelight Restaurant in a building in Manhattan. Businessmen from Wall Street began dropping in and picking up orders of scones to bring home, and her business grew rapidly. She upgraded her restaurants to luxury establishments and continued to expand until she had ten such restaurants, with her main one catering to 1 million customers a year. She added to her holdings a gift store in Florida.

One of her restaurants had an 800-car parking lot with a special limousine-shuttling service to take customers to the main entrance. It included a pond, a bridge and a dazzling assortment of flowers and plants.

In 1930, after being in New York a year, she married a stock broker. The marriage failed and was annulled. At a New Year's Eve party in New York City, she met Navy Captain James E. Kiernan. Soon after, they were married but sadly, Kiernan died of a heart attack on October 6, 1957.

At the time she was invited to attend the opening of the new Memorial University of Newfoundland campus[4] by Premier J.R. Smallwood, she was living on a spectacular estate in Florida with greenhouses, a swimming pool, a marble cabana and forty-eight acres of floral beauty, illuminated at night by thousands of lights. Patricia Murphy had a special interest in horticulture, specializing in orchids. Even that interest turned into a business success. She set up a perfume manufacturing factory which extracted perfume from the orchids and marketed them under the names of Green Orchid, Gold Orchid and Regina Rose.

This Newfoundland-born lady won many awards for her flowers including a commendation from Queen Wilhelmina of the Netherlands. Her most valued recognition was the highly respected papal honour known as Lady of the Equestrian Order of the Holy Sepulchre of Jerusalem.

---

[4] Prior to this opening, Memorial University Collage was located on Parade Street.

Part 2

20. Newfoundlander Invents the "Telidon"

Herbert Gideon Bown was born in Badgers Quay, New-foundland and has likely been forgotten today. Yet he invented something in the early 1970s that was grabbed up by interests in six countries, including the intelligence services in the U.S., and *Time* magazine. It also played a key role in the explosion of personal computers on the scene.

What was this invention Bown developed? The name of the product is as forgotten in Newfoundland today as Bown himself. It was called the "Telidon," which turned the television screen into a giant information centre. News media across Canada predicted that Bown's invention would propel Canada into leadership in the field of electronic information gathering.

By the 1980s the Telidon was being used in the United States, France, Japan, Great Britain, Germany and Australia. The first private organization to use the Telidon was *Time* magazine, which used it to extend its electronic publishing to deliver information to American cable companies. The *Los Angeles Times* followed *Time* Magazine soon after. Bown's brainchild made it possible for information to be stored in giant memory banks and had the ability to be used in home television sets.

Newfoundlander Herbert Bown became an Officer of the Order of Canada in 1985.

21. Newfoundlander Related to El Cid

William Johnston was one of the founders of the established Newfoundland firm Baine Johnston Ltd. He also had an interest in genealogy. While engaged in researching his family tree, Mr. Johnston made an outstanding discovery that was significant enough for him to visit Paris, France in an effort to meet with the wife of Napoleon III.

Johnston was more than surprised to find in historic records that he was not only related to El Cid Campeador, Rodrigo Diaz of Spain, but also the French Empress Eugenie, wife of Napoleon III. Furthermore, among his distant relatives was the Earl of Fingal who served as British Ambassador to the Spanish Court in Madrid. It was the Earl's daughter who married a Spanish Don, a descendant of the historic figure El Cid. This daughter was an ancestress of Empress Eugenie.

While the branch of the family bearing the Earl's name had died out, the family fortune remained unclaimed in London. William Johnston had now uncovered an unsolved family mystery, with a fortune waiting to be claimed. Armed with the information that held the answer to this problem, he set out to include in his work the powerful Empress and her husband Napoleon III. With their support they could all share in the abandoned family fortune.

Unfortunately, his timing was off. Using his business connections, Johnston obtained letters of introduction to the French court. For a full week he was dined and entertained by members of Napoleon's court. Of course, they were all impressed by his claim to be a relative of their Empress.

However, he had one flaw that aroused the suspicion of French officials: he could not speak French. This was a major concern to them because at that time the Emperor had to contend with powerful enemies in his own country.

One Paris newspaper editor was so convinced that the

Newfoundlander was a conspirator that he flatly refused to help him. After the many suspicions got to Napoleon's top aides, they pondered the situation and concluded they would not take any chances. This resulted in Johnston being refused access to the Emperor and his wife. William Johnston returned to his Newfoundland home a very disappointed man but with a terrific story to tell.

22. Newfoundlander Became a Giant in American Broadcasting

Newfoundland-born Frank Knight, after leaving Newfoundland to live in the United States, went on to become one of the top names in American broadcasting, in both radio and television, during the first half of the twentieth century

In 1952, the *New York Times* highlighted his abilities as a national American broadcaster. Knight was born in St. John's and had served in World War I with the Royal Newfoundland Regiment. After the war, he decided to study medicine at McGill University. Following his first year, his interest turned to acting and he moved to New York City where he obtained parts in several Broadway shows including, "House Unguarded."

It was through his work on Broadway that he discovered his powerful speaking voice, which might be more useful in radio broadcasting. In 1926, he began as an announcer with the WABC in New York. His most famous assignment was covering of the arrival of German Graf *Zeppelin* to New York on October 15, 1928, which marked the first commercial flight of an aircraft. The *Zeppelin* travelled from Germany to New York, covering 630 miles in four days. It passed over St. John's, an event witnessed by thousands.

A year later he was working for the CBS Broadcasting Corporation.

Frank Knight became best-known as the announcer for the Columbia Broadcasting System's television program, *Chronoscope*, which was sponsored by the Longine Watch Company. He was also host of *The Longine Symphonette*, a popular weekly classical musical broadcast heard in Canada, United States and Newfoundland.

Historians claim, "Knight had the kind of voice that bordered on the pompous but was very popular." In 1952, Jack Gould, a critic with the *New York Times*, wrote: "Knight's commercials were delivered with an almost cathedral formality. They tend to induce such a feeling of social inadequacy that a viewer might be forgiven if he found himself wondering whether he was really eligible to buy the product."

Frank Knight and his wife Mildred Wall, also of St. John's, died from burns suffered in the fire that destroyed their New York apartment in October 1973. Frank lived long enough to be taken to hospital but died a week later on October 18th. He was seventy-three years old.

23. Labrador Man in "Operation Deep Freeze" Mission

Newfoundland-born Jack Bursey was decorated by the United States government for his role in the secret mission, "Operation Deep Freeze," which was launched at the Pentagon. Bursey was born on the northeast coast in St. Lunaire and was sent to school in the United States by Dr. Wilfred Grenfell, who recognized the boy's brilliance.

After completing his education in 1927, he responded to an advertisement calling for people to participate in an expedition to the Antarctic. Over 50,000 applicants responded, and from among these Jack Bursey was selected. A big factor in that decision was that he had lived his early years in northern Labrador.

The Artic expedition was led by Admiral Byrd to carry out exploration that lasted two years. This valuable experience was a strong influence in him being singled out by the Pentagon.

After becoming an American citizen, Bursey joined the U.S. Navy and moved up the ranks to lieutenant commander. The Pentagon placed him in command of the team responsible for reconnaissance, which was the most important part of Operation Deep Freeze. Under Bursey's leadership, his team blazed a 600-mile trail into the frozen wastes of Marie Byrd Land for the tractor-train that would follow to construct the base. The purpose of constructing the base was for scientists to record simultaneous worldwide phenomena such as weather, magnetism, gravity, etc.

When completed, the base became known as Little America V, Antarctica. Bursey's letter of recommendation for the award noted, "During this period [November 1st to March 1957] your competence, integrity, moral courage, ruggedness and untiring efforts contributed materially to the success of Operation Deep Freeze."

Jack Bursey was most humble about receiving his award. He said:

I was raised as a cod fisherman on the bleak rugged shores of the northeast coast of Newfoundland. I was trained to know the sea and learned how to take care of myself in rough weather or smooth. When the ice broke up we coasted along the shores in our schooner, and as a boy I helped my dad bring her into a snug harbour on many a stormy night. In the winter I drove the team of dogs, our only transportation. I was hardened by the cold and the blizzards that swept in over the coast.

24. Newfoundlander Collaborated with F. Scott Fitzgerald

John Gallishaw is an important name in Hollywood's history. He was a top consultant and writer for Paramount

41

Pictures, Columbia Pictures, Metro-Goldwyn-Meyer and Universal Pictures. He started the Gallishaw School of Creative Writing in Cambridge, Massachusetts, which turned out a host of outstanding television and screen writers. He collaborated with F. Scott Fitzgerald on the screenplay for a couple of his books. Among his Hollywood friends were: Clarke Gable and Cary Grant. Newfoundlanders can be proud of John Gallishaw who was born in St. John's in 1890.

Gallishaw's family eventually moved to the United States where he earned a degree from Harvard University. In 1917, during World War I, while still at Harvard, he volunteered for the Canadian Forces but later sought and obtained a discharge in order to join the Royal Newfoundland Regiment. Gallishaw made the move as a means of moving to the battlefront much quicker.

However, once the military brass saw that this young man had a Harvard degree, he was assigned to the war office in London to keep and manage the Regiment's records. Yet, his thirst for action was so strong that he stowed away on the military transport ship taking the Newfoundland Regiment to Malta and turned himself in at sea. At this time, he asked to be assigned to battle duty.

Gallishaw was granted his wish and he was assigned to 'B' Company, which turned out to be his first and last battlefield experience. While participating in the evacuation of Gallipoli he was wounded, and after a period of hospitalization was shipped back to his home in the United States where he completed his studies at Harvard. Five of the books he wrote became part of the English curriculum in American universities. In 1961, he returned to St. John's as a guest of Premier J.R. Smallwood to attend the official opening of Memorial University.

25. Newfoundland Writer Nominated for Academy Award in 1934

George Hembert Westley, author of *House of Rothschild*, was actually George Hippisley, who was born in Harbour Grace in 1865 and had moved to the United States in 1895. His book was turned into a Hollywood movie starring Robert Young, Loretta Young and George Arliss, which was nominated in the Best Picture category at the Hollywood Academy Awards of 1934.

Other American bestselling books written by Hippisley, under his nom de plume, included: *The Maid and the Miscreant* and *Clementina's Highwayman*. He co-authored with Robert Neilson Stephens: *The Man's Game*, *The Intruder*, *Doctor Presto* and *The Scarlet Pimpernel*.

Hippisley passed away on September 25, 1936.

26. Outrageous Assessment of Newfoundland Life in 1861

George Train was a freelance writer and an adventurer and was practically run out of England for his criticisms of British tradition. Once back in the United States his first comment was, "Thank God I am back among Christians!" In 1861, he riled-up Newfoundlanders for writing the following after just two hours in the city:

The town is laid out upon the plan of the intestine arrangements of a lapwing, a well-known bird sometimes used as an eel trap — one street running through the centre. On entering the harbour, I was reminded of Aden, only more fish and less rock. Then it looked like Hong Kong, with less houses and more oil vats. It is not unlike Auckland, but like the harbour of St. Thomas in the West Indies than anything else. Plenty of water and a fine anchorage. Every house is a fish market. Every carriage is a fish wagon.

The boys look like young codfish that had fattened with the bait. The girls like haddock. Fish forms the topic of conversation. The men have a fishy look, many fishy minds and unto them are born fishy children. The fort on the hill showed evident signs of there being fish in the vicinity. Both sides of the harbour are terraced with dried fish.

Order breakfast, they bring you fish. Dinner, you get it boiled and fried. You sell. They pay in fish. You buy. Fish is the staple, the lingua franca of the colony. The people are hospitable. They entertain you with fish. The hotels are primitive. Imagine lollypops and jujube being sold in the front window of Boston's Tremont or Revere! Warrington's [the Union] Hotel is their best. Toussaint is a Frenchman but his café au lait is not Parisians!

Soon after he arrived back home in Boston, George Train was tossed in jail for disturbing the peace at a public meeting.

27. How Newfoundlanders Spend Time in Heaven

American pilot Cy Cadwell visited Newfoundland in 1927 to join in the search for missing pilots Nungesser and Coli. Although he expressed many insulting comments about Newfoundland and its people, he made up for it to many with the following story:

They are a wonderful people, these Newfoundlanders, and theirs is a wonderful country. Never before have I experienced so much kindly helpfulness from so many people. They are simply kindly folk, and even in the short time that we have been here I have grown to love them. These folks are hospitality plus. They love their country and their homes, and are fonder of Newfoundland than Bostonians are of Boston.

The standard tale here is of the visitor who went to Heaven and found: the Americans, Frenchmen, English, Germans and all the other nationalities, enjoying themselves immensely, wearing halos at a cocky angle, singing and carrying on and simply tickled to death with the place.

Over in one corner were a bunch of miserable-looking people chained down to the golden floor. They were Newfoundlanders who had to be chained down to prevent them from walking back home.

28. The Bareback Seal Rider

Man has ridden on the backs of many wild animals, but what about a man riding bareback on a dog hood seal? Well, it happened and the act earned Paddy Dunn of Cupids, Conception Bay, the distinction of being the only known person in the world to have done so. This adventure at the seal hunt took place in 1878, when Paddy was a sealer on the *Panther*, which was under the command of Captain Abram Bartlett.

One day, Paddy was making his way over the ice with six other men, all led by the master-watch. In time, the men came upon a family of three hoods. Mother and pup took to the water, but the mean looking old dog stayed and faced the sealers defiantly. Before the group could decide on whether or not to kill the hood and tow him back to their ship, Paddy Dunn strolled over barehanded and unarmed toward the dog hood.

In response to Paddy's daring approach, the hood reared up to his full length, bared his teeth and inflated his hood tightly, which gave him a ferocious appearance. Without warning the seal savagely lunged at Paddy, who side-stepped the animal. While his fellow sealers watched in awe, Paddy repeated the manoeuver several times, like a matador fighting a bull. On each pass the seal missed its target by inches.

To the witnesses' astonishment, Paddy suddenly side-stepped the seal and then jumped onto his back. The fight became more ferocious as the angry seal snapped fiercely, twisting and turning in an effort to sink his teeth into the rider and tear him to pieces. Each time the seal twisted his head sideways, Paddy would strike it with a blow to the side of the head, which would cause the seal to turn his head and then he would strike him on the other side.

The battle went on for fifteen minutes and Paddy kept his cool throughout the confrontation, hanging on to his position on the hood seal's back. Finally, weakened from the battle, the old seal rushed towards the edge of the ice pan and dived into the water. Paddy was able to jump onto the ice just before the seal went over the edge. Witnesses later recalled that if Paddy had gone over the edge of the ice pan the angry old seal would have torn him to pieces.

29. Leon Trotsky Visited St. John's

During World War II, Joe Smallwood's radio program *The Barrelman Show* was the most listened to radio program in all of Newfoundland. The show ran from 1937 to 1943. Although it was only a fifteen-minute program that was broadcast from Monday to Saturday, people eagerly anticipated it.

Those were the days of battery-operated radios, and people in the outports who had them welcomed neighbours who did not. The program began with the ringing of a ship's bell six times. Then, as one Cappahayden resident recalled, "The house went quieter than the Orangeman's Hall on St. Patrick's Day." This temporary silence was broken by the voice of Smallwood who mesmerized his audience with the most attention-grabbing stories he had collected from Newfoundland's past.

An especially remarkable story was one he told during June 1940, which drew an interesting Newfoundland connection with a giant of world history. That man was Leon Bronstein, who became famous as Leon Trotsky, the father of Nicholai Lenin leader of the Bolshevik Revolution in Russia in 1917.

When the revolution broke out, Lenin was in exile in Switzerland and Trotsky was in New York. Lenin and his colleagues returned to Russia by way of Germany and Poland, using a special sealed train provided by the German government. Trotsky was travelling separately and had boarded a steamship bound for Europe. When the ship docked at Halifax, Trotsky was arrested and imprisoned in an internment camp. This stay was short lived.

Trotsky, by invoking his technical American citizenship, was relased and purchased a ticket on the *Christianiford*, which was leaving Halifax for Scandinavia, where he intended to make his way to Russia. Little did he know, but soon after departing Halifax the ship would wreck on the Southern Shore of Newfoundland's coast and he would be forced to spend a week in St. John's before resuming his mission.

Fortunately, not one of the 1,100 passengers on the *Christianiford* drowned. Smallwood told his listeners, "If that man had been drowned in that wreck, there might be no Fascist state in Italy today ... No Nazi state in Germany. No World War."

All the passengers were brought to St. John's by special trains, where they were given accommodations throughout the city. These accommodations included the Seamen's Institute, the Prince's Rink, and a few hotels. Leon Trotsky went to the Cochrane Hotel where he registered as Leon Bronstein.

Smallwood noted, "There is little doubt that without his organizing genius the Red Army would never have been able to withstand the attacks of the White Armies. The Bolshevik Revolution would have been broken, and the whole history of the world since 1917 would be a vastly different story from what it actually has been."

30. Benedict Arnold's Visit to St. John's

In 1786, Benedict Arnold arrived in St. John's, Newfoundland, where he booked passage for England. After the American

War of Independence, Arnold moved to New Brunswick where he established a small business. Once established, he set out, via St. John's, for England to bring his family to their new home in New Brunswick.

It was in St. John's that he met Newfoundland's famous George Cartwright. The two became friends and shared a cabin on the brig *John*, of Teignmouth, England, which carried passengers from St. John's to England.

The name Benedict Arnold became synonymous with the word "traitor" during the American War of Independence. He had joined the American forces after the outbreak of the American Revolution, where he quickly moved up the ranks in the military. As an officer, he led attacks on several British forts and quickly moved up to the rank of general. General Arnold was lauded by Americans when he successfully defeated the British at Bernis Heights.

Yet, Arnold was not content fighting for the American cause. He shocked many by defecting to Britain, where he was made an officer in the British military. In 1780, he led the British in a victorious battle in which he destroyed Richmond, Virginia.

While awaiting the departure of the brig *John*, he and Cartwright shopped along the Lower Path (Water Street) gathering supplies for their own use. These included two sheep, several hens, a good supply of vegetables and other provisions. However, the cross-Atlantic trip was a rough one and during one major storm the sheep were washed overboard along with many of the provisions.

Strict rationing of food was enforced due to the losses. The treachery of Benedict Arnold surfaced during the emergency when, unknown to his new friend Cartwright, he swiped a supply of water from the cabin they jointly shared so he could obtain an increase of water from the crew's rations. Arnold hid the water for his own personal use. It was only after arriving in England that Cartwright found out about Benedict Arnold's betrayal.

31. Newfoundland's Connection to World-Renowned Scientist

William McGregor was an accomplished astronomer, mineralogist, botanist and world traveller. He contributed volumes of information which were valuable to the world's scientific community. He was the first of many to succeed in crossing the island of West Guinea by way of the Stafford Ridge. It was an arduous task requiring great effort, which he overcame by struggling less than one-mile per day. Throughout this expedition, McGregor discovered several species of the famous Bird of Paradise in addition to identifying many unknown specimens of animal and vegetable life.

McGregor is remembered in Newfoundland as Sir William McGregor, the island's governor. In that capacity, he studied the Newfoundland fishery which in previous times had suffered due to lack of information. Sir William's efforts were aimed at providing the British Colonial Office with reliable information to assist in negotiations regarding the welfare of the country. He also served as governor in New Guinea and Lagos, West Africa.

Sir William McGregor was the only Newfoundland governor to be awarded the Albert Medal, the civilian equivalent of the Victoria Cross. He also earned the Gold Medal of the Royal Humane Society of Australia for saving several lives at sea at great personal risk.

32. Newfoundlander Received German Iron Cross in World War II

Cyril Gardner of British Harbour, Newfoundland, was presented with Germany's top military award during World War II by a German officer in the presence of a seventy-member German platoon. This Newfoundlander was serving as a sergeant with British forces and did nothing to help the German cause or to betray his country. Instead, he performed a remarkable humanitarian and courageous act by risking his own life to save the German platoon.

This incident began when a heavy fog moved in over the battlefield during a battle between Gardner's unit and the Germans, which caused combat to come to a complete halt. Gardner, who spoke German, loaded his machine gun and under the cover of darkness and fog made his way into the German camp by speaking German to the sentries.

Once inside the camp, he captured the officers first, then the remaining soldiers. By the time he was finished, he had disarmed the entire troop. The sergeant ordered them to put their hands over their heads and then escorted them towards British lines. When they neared the allied soldiers, an English officer greeted them. He immediately congratulated Gardner for his heroic deed then prepared his gun for firing. The officer explained to Gardner that he intended to shoot all the prisoners on the spot.

The officer's actions stirred fear amongst the prisoners. When they realized the Englishman's intentions, they stepped backwards. At this point, Sergeant Gardner drew his gun, stepped in between the officer and the prisoners and ordering the officer shouted, "Put your gun back, or for the first German that falls I'll shoot you." The officer hesitated and seeing the determination in Gardner's expression put his gun away and retreated.

The German commanding officer, who wore many medals for bravery, stepped forward and saluted Gardner. He removed the German Iron Cross, which he had been awarded by Hitler, from his own uniform and pinned it to Gardner's chest. The German soldiers applauded the action.

Lieutenant Gardner died in battle on April 14, 1917.

33. Inside the House of Bard Johnny Burke

Author Michael Murphy served as a member of the Royal Newfoundland Constabulary in his younger days. His father Jimmy Murphy was as famous in old St. John's as the bard Johnny Burke. The two wrote and published ballads and distributed them on broadsheets throughout St. John's. Murphy and Burke were also best friends and lived in close proximity to each other.

Murphy recalled his visits to Burke's house as a child. Burke lived on Prescott Street with his sister Annie. Murphy gave a rare insight into the life of Burke, the writer of so many Newfoundland songs, the most famous of which is the "Kelligrews Soiree." Murphy wrote that on every visit he was met by Annie, "… accompanied by a veritable host of huge cats, who stood around her like a bodyguards. Annie generally wore a long black dress, fastened tight around her midsection, and wore her hair tied on the back in what was known as a 'bun.'" According to Murphy, "Annie Burke had the gift of gab and loved greeting visitors. She was also a great baker, and there were always lots of pies, cakes and buns."

People from all walks of life in the town were welcome at the home of Johnny Burke; all he required was sobriety and the ability to play a game of cards. Murphy said that although Burke liked an occasional nip of the "creature" he would not tolerate drunks on his premises.

Burke's prized possession was his gramophone and of all his songs, his favorite was "Cod Liver Oil." Murphy said, "Burke laughed just as heartily at the last playing of it as he had laughed at the first. The gramophone was later raffled and was won by my nephews. I don't remember what became of it after that."

There was a time in St. John's history when the 'Ballad Monger' was a local institution. Perhaps the last of the Ballad Mongers was Johnny Jones of Pleasant Street, whose popular works were sold well into the 1960s. His best work was "The Liquor Book Song."

The songwriting credit for both "Cod Liver Oil" and "The Liquor Book Song" were wrongly claimed decades after the passing of both writers by another person.

Johnny had a theatre on Bell Island just before World War I, which was popular among the islanders. Murphy recalled, "James Esplin, otherwise known as 'Fox Maule', a native of Ontario, played the piano at the theatre and sang the illustrated songs so very popular at the time. The song that really caught on with the miners was, "Harrigan That's Me!"

34. Sir James Pearl, Founder of Mount Pearl

Sir James Pearl, a British naval hero has a plaque honouring his memory in front of the court house in Yarmouth, Nova Scotia. He was born in 1790, the youngest son of David Pearl and Eunice Allen. His maternal grandfather was Major Jeremiah Allen who served with British forces in the French and Indian wars under General Wolfe.

The plaque reads, "In Memory of Captain Sir James Pearl, R.N., K.H. Naval Hero - Empire Statesman served at Trafalgar, the Basques Roads, Welcheren and other famous Engagements. A leader in the Procuring of Parliamentary Government in Newfoundland. Knighted 1836, Born at Kelley's Cove, this country, 1790. Died at Mount Pearl, St. John's, Newfoundland, 1840. Erected by the Yarmouth County Historical Society 1959."

He is best remembered in Newfoundland as the founder of Mount Pearl, which was originally named "Mount Cochrane" after Newfoundland's governor at that time.

Sir James Pearl was an outstanding hero of the British Navy before settling in Newfoundland. He joined the British Navy at the age of eleven and by fifteen was a midshipman. He quickly rose to officer's rank on the ninety-eight-gun British warship, *Neptune*.

Pearl fought valiantly in the Battle of Trafalgar at the age of fifteen, which earned him a promotion to the rank of lieutenant. He was one of the volunteer officers who led the battle which destroyed the French fleet at the Basques Roads. During this battle, Pearl was seriously wounded and was actually blown right off his ship the *Mediator*.

Sir James distinguished himself in many naval battles during his career. During the Burmese War he commanded 500 boats and thirty transport ships, and once rescued 200 Chinese sailors after their ship broke up and sank.

The founder of Mount Pearl received a host of honours in recognition of his bravery and military achievements. The British Patriotic Fund presented him with a sword, the King of the Netherlands presented him with a gold medal, and British merchants at Canton presented him with a plaque in honour of his rescue of the Chinese sailor, which they felt had exalted the British character among the Chinese. Upon his retirement in 1827, he had reached the level of commander. He arrived in Newfoundland in 1829 with a grant from the British government of 1,000 acres of land. He presented the order to Governor Cochrane and selected 1,000 acres in the area now known as Mount Pearl.

However, when he tried to survey the land, the governor was petitioned by the local residents with applications for Crown land in the same area. The governor settled the matter by allowing Pearl to claim 500 acres instead of the full 1,000 in his grant. Sir James agreed and claimed the balance of his grant in another area. He named his estate Mount Cochrane in honour of the governor and used his own money to build a public road through his property.

Sir James Pearl was also among the fathers of Responsible Government in Newfoundland. In 1839, he took petitions to London requesting Responsible Government and presented them personally to King William.

Pearl passed away on January 13, 1840, and was buried in the old Established Protestant Cemetery near the court house on Duckworth Street.[1] Soon after his death, his wife moved to England where she passed away. Tombstones not claimed seemed to have been stored and later placed along the western perimeter of the churchyard. The exact location of the grave of Sir James Pearl is not certain. Newspaper clippings and photographs of the old graveyard taken in the 1880s show that the entire area had been dug up and graves removed. These were relocated to other cemeteries in the city.

Mike Murphy, in his book *Pathways Through Yesterday*, said that Sir James Pearl deserves far more recognition for his role in bringing Responsible Government to Newfoundland than historians have credited him with.

35. How U.S. President Helped a Newfoundland Woman

The story behind how one president of the United States helped a female Newfoundland farmer is a remarkable story of an extraordinary woman. That woman was Ann Hulan who, in the early nineteenth century, was known around Newfoundland's coastal communities as the "Queen of St. George's."

Ann Hulan was a spirited and courageous leader who founded one of the first and largest farms on Newfoundland's west coast. When William Epps Cormack made his historic walk across Newfoundland in 1822, he stayed as a guest on Hulan's farm.

Along with managing her farm, Ann also owned a small cargo ship called the *Industry*. She was no ordinary merchant-type boss. Ann frequently worked alongside her men when unloading a cargo, paid fair wages and treated them with respect. She

---

[1] In the 1880s, graves and tombstones were removed from the cemetery and relocated to other cemeteries.

was known and respected as a fiercely independent woman.

In August 1812, the *Industry* under Captain Clement Renouf became involved in an international incident and drew the attention of President James Monroe. Many American ships had been captured by the British Navy and brought to St. John's. This practice brought American privateers to Newfoundland waters to get revenge by capturing some ships of their own.

As the vessel neared St. Mary's Bay, it was intercepted by a Yankee privateer, the *Benjamin Franklin*, commanded by Captain Josiah Ingersoll. A prize crew from the privateers took over Hulan's ship and sailed it to New York. Because the *Industry* was a small cargo vessel and not part of any military action, American authorities were not certain as to what to do with it.

A court of enquiry was established with Nathanial Davis as chairman. Ann Hulan represented herself before the enquiry and spoke simply and bluntly when making her case. The enquiry members were impressed by her presentation. Davis wrote President Monroe recommending the *Industry* be looked upon as an object of charity rather than spoils of war. The president granted release of the vessel, but due to American law, which disallowed captured vessels during wartime from being released, it had to be put up on auction.

To make sure Ann Hulan was treated justly, the president arranged for her to be the only bidder at the auction and she got the *Industry* back for a token $1 Yankee bill.

36. U.S. President had a Newfoundland Secret

The thirteenth president of the United States, Millard Fillimore, had a skeleton in the closet with a Newfoundland connection. His great-great-grandfather John Fillimore once served as a pirate out of Placentia with Captain John Phillips, a notorious pirate in the eighteenth century.

Phillips came to Newfoundland to work and he settled in Placentia, and for a while trained in ship building. Unhappy with the long hours, low wages and slave-like working conditions; Phillips turned to piracy. He recruited a crew from Newfoundland and St. Pierre and in a short time had a fleet of thirty-three ships. Among the pirate-crews was John Fillimore. Phillips sometimes forced prisoners to serve with him and it is likely that Fillimore was among those.

Several of those who had been captured and forced to serve formulated a plot to seize control of the pirate mother ship. Led by Andrew Harding, the men attacked the pirate crew with carpentry tools. The cries for help alarmed Captain Phillips, who rushed to the deck to see what was happening.

Phillips was hit with a caulking hammer and then attacked with an axe. After he was killed, they cut his hand off and placed it on the yard arm of the ship. Then they cut his head off and pickled it. The mutineers locked the others below deck and took them to Boston where they were turned over to authorities. Phillips head was placed on public display in Boston.

The captured men were placed on trial for piracy, a crime which demanded execution on the gallows. Fillimore was acquitted and settled in New England where he lived for the remainder of his life.

37. Russian Prince Worked in St. John's

A man who, after the end of World War II, tried to settle in St. John's, Newfoundland, and find permanent work was a Russian Prince fleeing Europe. The Prince left Paris in 1947 to start a new life in North America. He arrived in St. John's with a six-week visitor pass and used that time to seek work.

After finding accommodations at Thorburn's on Barnes Road, he began looking for work in the city. When he learned that Pope's Furniture Factory on Water Street was looking for a worker he walked from Barnes Road to the factory to apply. Mr. Pope interviewed him but had no idea he was in the presence of royalty. The man identified himself to Pope as Citoyen (Citizen) Orufosoff. Unfortunately, Pope was looking for a skilled mechanic, which the Prince was not. However, he gave the Prince a day's work in the factory because he felt the man was in need.

The *Sunday Herald* learned of the man's identity and interviewed him at his Barnes Road boarding home. During the interview, the Prince told of his family's history. He spoke of his ancestors invading Russia during the era of Ivan the Terrible. The Orufosoff's were, in turn, conquered by Peter the Great. After the Russian revolution, all royalty were forced to flee Russia. The Orufosoff's fled to Paris. After the death of the Prince's father his mother moved to Afghanistan and the young Prince chose to move to America.

He arrived in St. John's with very little money. After his six-week visitor permit expired he moved to St. Pierre. Within a year he moved to the United States. Mr. Pope was surprised when he later learned that the man to whom he showed kindness was actually a Russian Prince.

38. British Peer from Corner Brook

In 1947, Sir George Philip Grant-Suttie, the son of Colonel George Grant-Suttie, was elevated to the role of baronet at the age of thirteen. Sir George was the grandson of Mr. and Mrs. C.E. Carter of St. Georges. Mr. Carter was born in Scotland and became a commander in the Royal Navy during World War II. The boy's mother married Colonel George Grant-Suttie in Corner Brook, Newfoundland in 1937. After the colonel passed away, his widow married Sergeant Paul Underhill of the United States Army.

Sir George succeeded to the baronetcy after the death of Sir George Grant-Suttie Sr., who passed away in 1947 at his castle in North Berwick, Scotland. Before moving to Scotland to claim his large estate, the young baronet spent a vacation with his grandparents in Newfoundland.

39. Newfoundland Nuclear Scientist Helped Develop the Polaris Submarine

Bill Doherty, born in Badger, Newfoundland, was another Newfoundlander who made a major contribution to the world of science. His father Bill Sr. was brought to Newfoundland in 1907 from Maine by Lord Northcliff to head up the installation of river dams for the A.N.D. Company.

Bill treated workers under his management so well that he became immortalized in the famous ballad by John P. Devine, "The Badger Drive":

Billy Doherty, he is the manager,
and He's a good man at his trade,
And when he's around seeking drivers,
he's like a train going downgrade.
But still he's a man that's kind hearted,
on his word you can always depend,
And there's never a man that works with him
but likes to go with him again.

While living in Newfoundland, William was born. The family lived in Badger but moved back to Maine after Bill turned eight. They often returned to vacation in Newfoundland.

Young Bill Doherty grew up in Maine and became a prominent nuclear scientist. He lived in Maine, but worked on the Polaris Missile Submarine Project at the Portsmouth Naval Base. Dr. Doherty donated his father's old pike pole to the

Newfoundland Museum during Come Home Year in 1966. Before leaving Newfoundland he told reporters, "The advancement in roads, industry and general appearance has been fantastic and Newfoundland seems to have much in store for her." He certainly enjoyed his visit that year, before leaving he caught a seven-pound salmon and a 490-pound tuna in Conception Bay.

Part 3

40. Supernatural Activity near St. John's

The community of Flatrock, just a few miles northeast of St. John's, was the site of dramatic supernatural activity during the fall of 1954. This was not your everyday, spooky ghost story. It was so bizarre that it divided the community, drew the involvement of the R.C.M.P and the St. John's Fire Department, and made the front pages of *The Evening Telegram*. In the end, a priest or exorcist was called in to confront the occurrence.

It all began when eerie, frightening and unexplained things began happening in the home of Mike Parsons of Flatrock. As these events became news across the province, people were convinced a poltergeist, a noisy and mischievous spirit, was at work. The haunting involved a mysterious flame that would burst out spontaneously in various parts of the house. Parsons told reporters he had hoped that some research group would investigate the supernatural happenings. His wife, Josephine, became so upset that she became ill and a priest was called in to bless the home.

The bizarre story began with the sudden appearance of a flame in November, 1954. Mrs. Parsons told reporters, "We were in the kitchen and smelled smoke. In the wood box we found a dictionary burning. There were boughs and dry sticks there, but they were not burning. We were puzzled, but let it go at that."

A few days later, the poltergeist was at work again. On this occasion, Mrs. Parsons and her daughter were in the kitchen, while Mr. Parsons was in the barn milking cows. Mrs. Parsons said, "We smelled smoke and started looking around for fire but couldn't find any. I called out to Dad and Uncle Jim and they came rushing in to look around." The source of the smell was a sack of sugar located in the corner of the kitchen, which spontaneously burst into flames, giving off a terrible odor. A baffled Mr. Parsons told *The Evening Telegram*, "Here's the mysterious thing about it. I touched the sugar sack – just touched it with my hand, and the fire went out."

When reporters went to investigate the reports of strange happenings in Flatrock, they were taken on a tour of the house. They were taken to an upstairs room and shown a bureau with a groove burned into it. The damage resulted when a box of Holy literature resting on it suddenly burst into flames.

In another incident, a doll belonging to a grandchild of the Parsons was resting on the kitchen floor when it suddenly became consumed by fire, which seemingly burst from within the doll. On a separate occasion, a bedroom with no wires or chimney near it had mysteriously burned in several corners after the sudden eruption of flame. The flame died out on its own.

The mystery sparked a great deal of speculation among the people of Flatrock. The most skeptical suggested it was deliberate, so the owners could collect the insurance. However, the R.C.M.P ruled out that possibility noting that insurance was not carried on the property. The Parsons had a summer harvest of vegetables stored in the cellar, and the adjoining barn housed five sheep, a cow, a calf, a horse and twelve tons of hay. They certainly had no interest in losing their possessions in a fire.

It has long been claimed that the priest who responded to the Parsons invitation actually performed the rites of exorcism. Meanwhile, the results of the R.C.M.P investigation, which were inconclusive, were sent to the Justice Department. The amazing flames of Flatrock have never been explained. Some still attribute the happenings to be the work of a poltergeist.

41. Trinity Bay's Connection to the American Civil War

Buried beneath the shadowy waters of Elliston, Trinity Bay, is a cargo of guns and ammunition that was destined for the Confederate States of America during the American Civil War. How the cargo ended up in Newfoundland's coastal waters is among the multitude of intriguing stories from Newfoundland's rich heritage.

The *Thomas Gould Croff* was a gun-running vessel operating between Ireland and Charleston, which was a strong base for the rebel forces. This vessel set out from Valentia, Ireland, for its American destination. At the time, the rebels were desperately in need of the cargo being delivered.

The smugglers had to run the gauntlet of the northern blockade of southern ports along the Atlantic coast. The ship's captain chartered a route through the Straits of Belle Isle to avoid being captured by the Yankees, and also to shorten the course.

Unfortunately, the captain was unfamiliar with northern Newfoundland waters and about sixty miles east of Cape Bonavista, his ship encountered heavy ice and was forced to turn south. The *Thomas Gould Croff* was pounded, bumped and battered by the ice to the point he had to issue the order to abandon ship.

Not long after the captain and crew escaped the doomed vessel, it slowly disappeared beneath the ice taking with it it's vitally important and valuable cargo. It took days for the survivors to make it into Elliston, and by the time they arrived most of them were frostbitten. A few developed gangrene. Only the captain and two crewmen survived the ordeal, the others perished.

63

42. The Logy Bay Spa Mystery

During the period when Admiral Sir Henry Prescott was governor of Newfoundland, from 1834 to 1841, a spa-well was discovered in Logy Bay. This sparked much enthusiasm, and an expectation that it would become a valuable attraction for Newfoundland. In time, the matter was forgotten and continues to this day to be a mystery. During World War II, P.K. Devine appealed to the medical men among the visiting troops for help to reveal the discovery to the world. Devine wrote, "If I can succeed in arousing their curiosity, the problem as to the merits or demerits of the mineral water at Logy Bay may be settled definitely for all time."

The original discovery of the spring water was made by Dr. Kielley, a prominent physician in St. John's in the 1830s and 1840s, who carried out regular calls in the villages near the city and drank regularly from the spring. Kielley obtained the support of Governor Prescott, who agreed to send a sample of the water from the Logy Bay spa-well to his good friend, the celebrated British analyst Sir William Herepath in Bristol, England.

Herepath determined there were nine chemical ingredients in the water: .0450 bicarbonate of iron and .9548 decimals of a grain. The solid contents of a pint of the well-water at 69 degrees Fahrenheit (20 degrees Celsius) were 1,000.016. Devine observed, "It would take a chemist and analyst to properly appraise these figures and compare them with the spa records of other countries, especially in the recorded fact that the solid contents of the Imperial pint amounted to 8.75 grains."

Herepath's reply to Governor Prescott made it clear that the Logy Bay well was a genuine spa, or as he called it, "A chalybeate spring. It is a chalybeate to rather a greater extent than the waters of the King's Bath, in Bath, England. I believe that the waters could be used to advantage if arrangements could be made for the accommodation of invalids near the spring."

Devine hoped that the medical men among the visiting troops would visit and test the Logy Bay spa and make, "... its merits and its curative properties known to the outside world. We may then have tourists coming here in the thousands to drink the waters, which are found by experience to be so useful in dyspepsia, chronic rheumatism and diseases of the skin, etc. The water in Logy Bay is as cold in the summer as in the winter, but I am told that the place has been neglected for many years, and needs a good cleaning up."

Devine's comments were made in the 1940s, when the Logy Bay spa was well-known to many. Since then, its location and memory have long been forgotten.[1]

43. Did the Arsonist call Fred Molloy after starting K of C Fire?

On December 14, 1942, a St. John's resident told an interesting story to the police regarding the night of the Knights of Columbus (K of C) fire on Harvey Road. His name was Fred Molloy, he resided at 4 Bradbury Place and he was a credible witness. Molloy was an accountant with the Newfoundland Railway. The story he told fuelled the German saboteur theory, and to this day it is firmly believed by many.

Actually, there was nothing at all unusual about claims that enemy agents were behind the arson at the Knights of Columbus hostel, after all, World War II was in its third year and the K of C, a hostel for the military, would have been a likely target.

Within a week after the fire, a rumour that German agents had set it had taken root and was being fuelled by a claim that a mysterious telephone call had originated from the K of C hall just after the fire broke out, from a man "speaking broken English."

[1]Mike Harrington, Editor of *The Evening Telegram* on March 14, 1967 sent a copy of P.K. Devine's article to the Newfoundland Historical Society.

This theory prevailed despite the fact that Sir Brian Dunfield, chairman of the enquiry into the fire, concluded it had been the work of a pyromaniac. One of the sources for the German saboteur theory is based on the story that Fred Molloy gave to police two days after the fire.

Molloy experienced something on the night of the tragedy that piqued his curiosity. He took time to investigate the puzzle before going to police. By 3:44 p.m. on December 14, 1942, Molloy had gathered some alarming evidence and was in the process of giving a written statement to Constable Rudolph Nash. The incident that sparked his interest occurred between 11:00 p.m. and 11:30 p.m. on December 12th. The K of C fire broke out at 11:10 p.m. that night.

Molloy said in his police statement:

I was in the kitchen. My wife was present also. My telephone rang. I answered it; a party on the line asked if the telephone number was 3113 or 3311 or some number similar to these. I informed the party making the enquiries that they had the wrong number. My telephone number is 3312W. The party asking for the number was speaking in broken English. I am quite sure on that. It was also a man's voice. In the background I could hear voices. I thought it was laughter at the time and shuffling. I thought it to be dancing.

Molloy's statement was given two days after the fire by which time most of the general population who had never visited the facility firmly believed that the *Uncle Tim's Barn Dance* was an actual dance. The fact is there was no dance at the K of Hall that night.

This is a truth known by any of the witnesses inside the building. The public misconception of this reality resulted from the name used to advertise the weekly Saturday night live radio broadcast from the building of the *Uncle Tim's Barn Dance Show*. Three hundred and fifty collapsible chairs had been set up in the auditorium to accommodate spectators for this on-stage performance. The enquiry determined that there was no dancing going on anywhere else in the building.

Mr. Molloy believed the man on the phone had been drinking and instead of hanging up the phone, he laid it down to prevent any re-calling, which might awake his children. The caller remained on the line and continued talking. What he was saying made sense to Molloy only the next morning after learning of the fire.

Molloy recalled that "over and over again" the caller had repeated, "The house is afire." Molloy told police, "I thought he was trying to get me off the line, in order that he could get his message through, and make the right connection; My telephone number was different from the one he was calling." Originally, Molloy was not sure whether the caller asked, "If this was 3113 or 3311."

In those days a party line system was being used. Telephone numbers in homes using this system had a letter from the alphabet at the end of a four digit number. Molloy's number was 3312W. Private lines used four digit numbers without a letter at the end.

Because of the role this incident had on the birth of the German agent theory, it should be noted that Molloy's on the spot interpretation of the call changed next day when he learned of the tragedy. A part of his statement, ignored on the few occasions this was written about, included, "At the time I thought this man to be under the influence of liquor but since, and on hearing of the K of C disaster, it made me think different, and at the time the man may be excited or nervous."

One has to consider just how much Molloy's impression and memory of the call was being influenced by the rapidly unfolding story. Molloy told police:

> At first when I answered the telephone in my home I could hear this shuffling or dancing in the background plain, then it was after this man kept repeating the shout of "fire!" In fact it died away when the man shouted this over the telephone. When he was repeating this, everything was quiet. After a while the telephone went dead. In my opinion he did not hang up the receiver, if he did I would hear the receiver click at the other end.

Although Molloy originally had been uncertain about the telephone number the caller had mentioned, he informed police that he felt certain the number was 3113. That confirmation came about after his investigation of possible variations of the number and checking the ownership of each telephone number. The number 3113 caught his interest above all others.

He was startled to discover that the number 3113 belonged to the Bavarian Brewery Co. Ltd. on Leslie Street where the brewmaster was a German-American, just the sort of information to cause excitement among investigators. However, this information was later thoroughly investigated by police who ruled out the brewmaster after learning that he was out of town the week of the fire. Yet, this was not enough to satisfy public suspicions.

Another variation of the numbers Molloy toyed with included 3111, which was the telephone number of Marshall Studios at the corner of King's Road and Military Road. It was Marshall who took the famous photos of the fire in progress which appeared in local newspapers.

44. Newfoundland's Famous Author: Nina Nelson

Nina Nelson was an internationally famous writer in the early twentieth century. She was also a Newfoundlander. Nina was the daughter of Claude and Florence Noonan of St. John's, Newfoundland, where she was born in 1915. She was the first English-speaking woman in the world to receive approval to write about Egypt's Royal Family and the Royal palaces. Nina Nelson also authored popular travel books on Egypt, Lebanon and Jordan.

45. Remember Ethel Dickenson

Every day thousands of drivers use Cavendish Square in St. John's, Newfoundland, but very few, if any, pay much attention to the fourteen-foot high monument on the island opposite the Sheraton Hotel. This memorial was erected to honour the memory of a St. John's nurse, Ethel Dickenson. During the great Spanish flu epidemic that swept the world and struck St. John's in 1918, Nurse Dickenson fearlessly worked to help the affected, risking her own health in the process. While accompanying a patient from her home to the hospital, Dickenson caught the dreaded flu. Although she was instrumental in saving many lives, she lost her own battle with the illness and succumbed to it in days.

The inscription on the monument reads, "She gave her life while tending patients at the King George V Institute, St. John's." This institute was used as a fever hospital during the epidemic.

46. The S.S. *Newfoundland* and Smallpox

Smallpox threatened the S.S. *Newfoundland* several years before the famous S.S *Newfoundland* disaster, memorialized in Cassie Brown's book, *Death on the Ice*, which took place in 1914.

What happened during the seal hunt of 1911 to the crew of the S.S. *Newfoundland* may have been a harbinger of what was to come. The ship struck a large patch of seals, which was

69

greeted with much enthusiasm and hard work by the sealers. They were so busy that they lost track of the time and paid little attention to the darkness setting in. When it came, they were trapped on the ice for the night.

There were thirty-five sealers in the stranded group and they had one punt with them. Accepting this predicament, the men prepared for a long, cold night. These were experienced men who put their knowledge of survival to work. The punt turned upside down made adequate shelter from the high winds. The sealers ran, in turn, around the ice pans to keep warm. While this was going on, the others turned their gaffs into firewood and added seals to the blaze, which kept it burning all night. These efforts worked well and all survived the ordeal. They contemplated what would have happened if a fierce, unpredictable storm had struck.

The next day, while hunting seals, they successfully fought off a polar bear attack by firing their rifles, which set the animal running in another direction. Then a danger of another kind struck. It was the dreaded smallpox. When the men began reporting sickness, the captain ordered all to come aboard and they headed back to St. John's.

The vessel stopped at Trinity to consult with the local doctor. He recognized the disease and ordered that nobody be allowed to go ashore. The doctor left and the *Newfoundland* continued to St. John's. Smallpox was already appearing in the city and Conception Bay. When the vessel arrived at Shea's Wharf, near Temperance Street, the ship's entire crew was assessed by a team of doctors from the city. Eleven of the men were diagnosed with smallpox and taken to the Lazaretta (smallpox hospital), on top of Signal Hill. A structure to house the remaining sixty-eight was quickly constructed at Connor's Field on Forest Road. This structure was 150-feet long and fifty-feet wide, and was completed in just one day. While this was being done, they had been ferried across the harbour to the Baine Johnston Wharf.

There they were given hot baths in iron tubs. New clothing was provided and they were forced to walk Southside Road to the town because there was no launch available to take them. It was cold and snowing, which made their walk difficult and forced them to frequently stop to rest.

After everyone was cleared from the ship, some of the healthy crewmen were given $2 a day to help the doctor fumigate it. The task took four days to complete. Despite the misfortunes that followed the vessel, it managed to collect 23,000 pelts.

Then a shocking thing was permitted to happen, which had the potential to cause a major epidemic. The merchant was allowed to sell the seal flippers without informing the public that smallpox that had struck the sealing vessel. There is no record showing that the pelts had been fumigated.

47. Squid Jiggin' Hats

There was a time in Newfoundland's history when fishermen routinely wore top silk hats at the squid jiggin' grounds. This tradition was practiced along the Southern Shore and was started by Richard Sullivan of Ferryland. Sullivan's father was a milliner in Dublin. When he passed away, his estate inherited by his son included a large supply of Irish-style silk hats.

When the large crate containing the inherited goods, including the hats, arrived in Ferryland from Dublin it created a major problem for Sullivan. The shipment was so big he had no way of moving it from the wharf. Sullivan solved this problem by opening the crate on the wharf. It contained a variety of drapes and material and a large supply of tall silk hats. In appreciation for the help given to him by fellow fishermen, Sullivan allowed them to take the hats.

The supply was passed among the fishermen of Ferryland and nearby communities. The men began wearing them at the fishery even when jiggin' squid. The sight of fishermen rowing to and from the fishing grounds all wearing Irish silk hats must have amused any strangers sailing past them.

In time, the fishermen adjusted the hats by cutting them down four inches and then sewing the tops. Others cut the brims off and wore only the high crowns. Some cut only the sides off which left only the front and back parts, these became known as the famous "fore and aft hats" of the Southern Shore fishery.

Richard Sullivan's son, Jim, later became a member of the North West Mounted Police and also fought in the Spanish-American War.

48. The Chance Cove Mystery

The people along the Southern Shore of Newfoundland were bewildered when word spread from community to community that the residents of Chance Cove had disappeared overnight. The community had literally become a ghost town.

Following closely on the heels of the report were some unexplained facts claiming that the entire community had packed their bags overnight and left. They left behind their homes, barns, sheds and farms, and gathered only the things that could be moved.

As time passed, no satisfactory explanation of the mystery surfaced. This puzzle led to claims which were the basis for a tale that has survived more than a century. One word offered the answer – "Ghosts!"

People believed that the supernatural had spooked the people of Chance Cove. Those with relatives and friends who were among those who left Chance Cove recalled being told of the nightly terror that stalked the community. It started after dark, with terrifying screams and cries for help. Some observed spirits and ghosts. The onset of these happenings coincided with the anniversary of the sinking of the *Anglo Saxon*.

A more credible explanation involves what happened after the *Anglo Saxon* disaster of 1863. Three hundred and sixty-seven people drowned in the disaster and the people of Chance Cove helped recover of the bodies and aided in their burials. Travellers crossing the Atlantic to start new lives in America often carried gold in a money belt, which was strapped around their waist. Many of the victims were buried with their belts.

People speculated that the Chance Cove community waited three years to open the graves and remove the belts of gold. They planned to leave Newfoundland, and in the months leading up to the third anniversary of the disaster told anyone who would listen about the ghosts of the *Anglo Saxon* who terrified them at night.

According to this version, on the night of the anniversary the people were awakened by eerie noises and loud agonizing screams. The men in the community rushed to the beach, believing there had been another shipwreck, but found no explanation. After returning to their homes, the haunting resumed. This was enough, the residents packed up what they could carry, left the next day and were never heard from again.

In 1897, John White, a St. John's journalist, and a friend spent a night in one of the vacated buildings in Chance Cove. White noted, "It never rained before or since half as hard as it did that night. We never slept a wink." The two left at daybreak vowing never to return. White never explained why.

Some northern Newfoundland fishermen moved into the vacant homes one summer and turned Chance Cove into a base for their fishing activities. They also claimed that frightening and eerie activities took place there at night. They, too, abandoned the community, but not without putting a torch to it. Not a building survived.[2]

[2]Complete story can be found in Jack Fitzgerald's *Amazing Newfoundland Stories*, 1986.

49. The Sinking of the *Anglo Saxon*

According to historian H.M. Mosdell, an English journal described the disaster as follows:

A pitiful tragedy was the loss of the *Anglo Saxon* on April 27, 1863, at Chance Cove when the sea took toll of 307 persons out of the 444 aboard. In those days there was no Atlantic cable but the telegraph lines extended from the American continent to Cape Race.

That headland was a stopping place for the fast ocean liners plying between Liverpool and New York to exchange with a news-boat, maintained at the station, the latest news of the two hemispheres. The American Civil War was then raging and there was keen rivalry among the liners to deliver the dispatches first.

While steaming through a fog at full speed, the *Anglo Saxon* impaled herself on the rocks. She ran straight into a gulch and the furious waves soon beat her into splinters. The coast folk gathered at her distress signals.

A rampart cliff, a sheer 500 feet above the sea level, defied all hope of assistance by ordinary means. The landsmen had to bring spars and ropes from their boats, improvise derricks, and lower one another down into the boiling surf, where, as a body floated by, the rescuer clutched it and he was hoisted up with his burden living or dead.

When the ship struck, the prow was wedged in the rocks where a score or two survivors lashed themselves there. But the rescuers could not reach them, and the castaways had to jump overboard and take their chances of being saved as the waves swept them to and fro.

The fisher-folk continued their humane endeavours until all hope of there being another living soul on the wreck or rocks was abandoned. The fisher-wives cared for the survivors, and the rescuers when the storm abated, recovered as many other bodies as they could and buried them all in a plot on the hilltop.

In 1900, the United States government arranged for the renovating of the burial place, the earth having been washed away by heavy rain.

50. Gower Street Haunting Makes News

A story of the supernatural which made headlines in the St. John's newspapers took place in 1907 on Gower Street, and upset the neighbourhood for weeks afterwards.

The uncanny story began when a Newfoundland couple living in the United States returned to live in St. John's. They rented a house on Gower Street, near the Victoria Street intersection, and paid three months' rent in advance.

They ended up spending only one night in the house. Stories of strange happenings in the house spread rapidly and reached the offices of *The Evening Telegram*. When a *Telegram* reporter met with the horrified couple, he was told that, "...the woman had been startled in the night by a series of blood-curdling screeches. Horrified, she sat up in bed and saw a woman who had been known to her, but had died several years before in the same room."

Adding to the horror, according to the *Telegram* story, "The apparition was dragging another woman, also known to be dead, by the hair of her head. The woman being dragged was screaming." The housewife passed out and was not revived until daybreak. The couple took their personal belongings and left the house immediately, never to return. The newspaper also noted, "...the landlord refused to refund the rent."

The couple moved to a flat on Goodview Street and the neighbours there later recalled that the woman who saw the screaming spirits never got over her experience.

Meanwhile, in a three-storey, Victorian-style house on Gower Street, near the former Newfoundland Hotel, strange happenings were occurring during the late 1970s. After several families had fled the house, neighbours began calling *Open Line* host Ron Pumphrey to report the strange occurrences. The stories included the sounds of a sobbing child coming from the attic late at night; the rattling of chains; the sound of footsteps from the attic; and blood curdling screams.

The stories continued for some weeks and the landlord found it impossible to rent the vacant home.

After things settled down, a priest was called in to bless each room in the home. Soon after, it was sold and, in time, the stories of hauntings there faded from the public mind.

51. American Ship Named to Honour a Newfoundland Hero

An American vessel, the S.S. *Joseph Squires*, launched in July, 1945, at Portland, Maine. It was named in honour of a great hero, but one who was not an American. This hero was Joseph Squires, a native of Salvage, Bonavista Bay, who was posthumously awarded the Merchant Marine Distinguished Service Cross. Joseph Squires made a deliberate decision to make the sacrifice to save others being threatened. His act of heroism cost him his life. His deed was so meritorious that the president of the United States sent his widow, residing in Newfoundland, a letter of condolence.

When Squires moved to the United States, he found work with the Furness Bermuda Line. In 1937, he accepted a better paying job with the Bethlehem Steel Yard in Brooklyn. A few years later, in 1942, Joseph met Minnie Randall of Trinity Bay, Newfoundland, who was also living in Brooklyn.

In that year, the American government was recruiting experienced men for its Merchant Marine Service. Squires enthusiastically volunteered to join the service. He was assigned to the

crew of the *Maiden Creek*.The ship was preparing to go to Bell
Island, Newfoundland, to pick up an iron ore cargo. Squires was
looking forward to the trip to Newfoundland, but it turned out
to be a voyage he would never complete.

The *Maiden Creek* ran into one of the worst storms to strike
the area in years. The heavy seas pounded her so thoroughly
that she began to sink.The ship tossed and rolled so badly that
getting all the life craft into the water was hopeless.

The only way for anyone to be saved was for others to stay
on board to control the swinging beams, while the rafts were
swung free. There would be no chance for any of those volunteers to survive. Joseph Squires, along with another seaman,
volunteered. Both were lost in the tragedy, and they were honoured by the American government.

In the citation for the honour given, the captain said, "Then
it was that Joseph Squires found his much desired chance to
be useful to this country. With a shipmate, he stayed on the
Maiden Creek to get the boats safely away. In doing, so he gave
up his life, for when the boats were clear of the ship, it was
impossible to save Squires and his shipmate."

52. A Newfoundland Sharpshooter

According to Joseph R. Smallwood, while he was host of
the *Barrelman Radio Show*, Martin Jennings of Codroy Valley
was a legend in his time. The former premier's favourite Jennings story involved an incident that happened at the annual
seal hunt.

On the ice that season was a young man named John McKean
who had never been to the ice-fields before. Smallwood said:

As his vessel hove-to beside a pan of seals, McKean
leaped over her side. He was only a few yards from
the vessel when his feet slipped from under him and

he sprawled on his back in the path of an oncoming dog hood. Pandemonium broke out on board, with men shouting and bawling.

It was obvious to the more experienced sealers that the young lad was in terrible danger. Smallwood continued:

'Silence!' Roared the voice of one accustomed to authority, and save for the grinding of the ship's side against the ice, silence reigned. The seal with fangs bared was already upon John McKean when, this man, Martin Jennings raised his musket to his shoulder. The alarmed captain shouted to Jennings, 'Don't shoot! You'll kill the man.'
'No more for me to kill him than the seal,' answered Jennings, as he pressed the trigger. The seal fell dead. It was shot through the eye, and before it was removed from the unconscious, but uninjured man, someone in the crowd pointed out to the rest that the mouth of the seal was a scant three fingers from John McKean's throat.

53. An Inuit Hero

Sir Wilfred Grenfell performed outstanding work in northern Newfoundland through his efforts to bring health care to people, saving many lives in the process. However, not all Newfoundlanders appreciated this great man. There were many among the pre-1949 St. John's establishment, even to this day, who disliked this man because he had exposed Newfoundland's poverty and human suffering throughout America and Europe, through his fund raising efforts to help the people, thus embarrassing them.

While volumes have been written about Grenfell and his life-saving work in northern Newfoundland, this story deals with perhaps one of his most amazing successes, an Inuit child named Elizabeth. Few people have ever faced the physical pain and suffering as was inflicted upon this poor girl. Her survival is an inspiring story of hope and courage deserving of being perpetuated in this province.

Tribulation entered Elizabeth's life when she was just three years' old, living near Rigolet in Labrador. Her mother was pregnant with her second child and about to deliver. Elizabeth's father set out by dogsled to seek medical help from a community thirty-five miles away.

After reaching the community, Elizabeth's father was seeking a midwife or doctor when a terrible winter storm struck, causing him to be stranded there for four days. He was unsuccessful in finding any help and became intensely worried about his wife and child who were home alone in the storm. As soon as the storm ended, he rushed along the snow-covered paths, driving his dog team as best he could to get home. But he arrived too late.

His wife had delivered the child, but she and the newborn had frozen to death. Little Elizabeth was lying semi-conscious on the floor with both legs frostbitten. Her father acted swiftly to save her. He proceeded to amputate both of her legs below the knee, and then made her stand in a barrel of flour to stop the bleeding. It was a crude, but successful surgery. Miraculously, the little girl survived.

As she grew older, with the help of her father, she learned to move around on her knees. Her father made her a pair of leather pads, which made movement easier.

Dr. Wilfred Grenfell took a special interest in the child and took her to the Grenfell Hospital where she remained for several years. During this period, Grenfell operated on the girl and fitted her with artificial legs. She was then taught to walk on her own, and Grenfell saw to it that she had a chance to attend school. However, his work to give her a future was not yet over.

The doctor's next move to help Elizabeth was to bring her to New York, where she was given the best medical care and underwent eighteen operations by world-renowned Scottish specialist, Dr. John McTavish. In the years that followed, Grenfell continued to supply Elizabeth with artificial limbs.

Elizabeth later met and married a French-Canadian trapper named John Mukko and they settled in Rigolet. They had seven children together. However, poverty continued to stalk them and when Elizabeth outgrew her artificial limbs, she went back to using leather pads. On their own they could no longer afford to purchase new prostheses. Yet, the couple managed well, given the circumstances, but bigger and more tragic problems were about to strike the Mukko household.

In 1918, the Spanish flu epidemic struck Rigolet and claimed the lives of her husband and six of her children. Even during this period of grief and sadness, Elizabeth Mukko remained strong, courageous and full of hope. She buried each member of her family and read the funeral services over their grave. She then set out to build a new life for herself and the remaining child.

Elizabeth took her child and went to the Grenfell Hospital in St. Anthony where she studied nursing and midwifery under Dr. Padden. In 1950, Dr. Tony Paddon Jr. made Elizabeth's story of heroism and courage known. Canadian and American soldiers, impressed by the determination of the young mother, raised enough money to send her to St. John's to get a new set of artificial limbs.

Following this, Elizabeth Mukko returned to Labrador where she raised her child and used a dogsled to travel and provide medical services to the isolated sick in the Rigolet area for twenty more years.

54. Newfoundlander Chained and Tossed into Hudson River Escapes

International headlines followed the feat of a man in the 1920s, who manacled himself inside a heavy canvas bag and had himself tossed into the Hudson River. This was not the great Houdini! This man, who amazed people on two continents, was a magician using the name Professor Whiz. However, his real name was Thomas Fitzgibbon and he was from St. John's, Newfoundland. The professor's amazing feat was filmed by Hollywood newsreel companies and covered by major American newspapers.

Fitzgibbon was the son of St. John's merchant, Thomas Fitzgibbon, who operated a wholesale retail grocery store on Water Street, just west of Buchannan Street. He rivalled Houdini for a few years and performed sold out shows wherever he appeared. He was inspired to become a magician after attending a performance of magician-hypnotist Professor Lawrence at the Casino Theatre in downtown St. John's.

Fitzgibbon befriended the professor who taught him to perform magic and hypnotism. He became so skilled at hypnotism that he demonstrated his ability in the front window of his father's store. A customer of the store volunteered to become his subject. After hypnotizing the man, he instructed him to take up a lying position on a board held up by a barrel on each end. Crowds had gathered outside and inside the store to witness the demonstration.

Fitzgibbon then piled sacks of oats on top of him, which the subject could not otherwise handle. From this performance, he went on to develop a following using the name Professor Whiz.

Upon graduating from St. Bonaventure's College in St. John's, Fitzgibbon brought his magician-hypnotist act to New York and carved out a career for himself. The professor became a popular after dinner speaker in New York. He was also a great athlete and represented the Irish-American Club of New York in many long-distance running events.

Newfoundland-born Professor Whiz passed away at Pennsauken, New Jersey on January 14, 1955 at the age of seventy-three.

55. First Fingerprinting

Criminal history was made in St. John's on August 6, 1934, when the first conviction based on fingerprint evidence was recorded in our court system. The case involved the trial of George Williams, who was charged with breaking and entering the home of Mrs. Edwin Murray of St. John's. Fingerprints left on the window used to gain entry to the Murray house were introduced as evidence in the case. Based solely on this fingerprint evidence, Murray was found guilty.

Not only was this the first time in Newfoundland and Canada that fingerprint evidence alone had won a conviction; it was only the third such case in the British Empire.

56. International Killers Gathered in Newfoundland

In 1947, a rare event in Newfoundland criminal history took place in Gander. A plane carrying thirty-five convicted murderers made a stopover in the airport town. The plane was closely guarded by armed guards. The killers were responsible for more murders in the United States than had been committed in Newfoundland during its previous 450-year history. The plane was at Gander Airport most of the day and during that time passengers were not permitted to leave the plane.

Prior to World War II, the United States sent dangerous convicted criminals back to their own countries. However, it was not practical to do this during the war years and the number of prisoners to be transferred increased to thirty-five. Most of these were en route to Italy and Greece and many of them were involved with the American mafia.

57. The St. John's Noon-Day Gun

A canon fired every day on Signal Hill, and sometimes from the other side of the Narrows, announced noon-time to the people of St. John's for almost two hundred years. People set their time pieces by the firing of the gun. This was a practice that was originated by the military in 1776, the same year the American War of Independence broke out.

The practice ended on March 15, 1949. Some thought it had been suspended because Newfoundland had joined Canada. Although this was a widely held belief, the truth was that there were no available percussion caps (used in firing the gun). With the arrival of Confederation two weeks later, Cabot Tower and its facilities came under the control of the Federal Department of Transport. The department failed to resume the practice. Ten years later, in 1959, the provincial government revived the custom.

Old records show that the custom was not always carried out on Signal Hill. In 1842, the custom was moved to Frederick Battery on the south side of the Narrows. *The Newfoundlander* on January 20, 1842, noted, "A gun will be fired at Frederick Battery exactly at noon each day, which, to a certain extent, will supply the want of a public clock, so much needed in this town." British Admiralty charts of the approaches to St. John's Harbour, dated 1811, refer to the noon-day gun fired daily from the Blockhouse on Signal Hill.

During the nineteenth century, the gun on Signal Hill was sometimes used to announce that the St. John's Regatta was going ahead. It was also fired at midnight, December 31st, to announce the New Year.

58. 'Let Pass' Policy

During the seventeenth and part of the eighteenth centuries, ships needed an approved 'Let Pass' document to enter or leave the port of St. John's. Admiral Montague, governor of Newfoundland, authorized the commanding officer at Fort William to enforce the Let Pass policy.

Under threat of being fired upon from canons on Signal Hill, ships required a signed Let Pass document. A warning shot was fired over the bow of the ship that failed to obtain a pass. This practice was enforced from the 1770s until August 9, 1821 when it came to an end.

Part 4

59. Origins of 'Newfie'

Some Newfoundlanders are not offended by the term 'Newfie,' while others feel insulted by its usage. It has been this way for the past seventy years, and it is not likely to change. Two events occurred during the 1940s that made Newfie famous throughout North America and Europe, and memorialized it in Newfoundland.

It seems the term was first used in 1941, when some American soldiers were introduced to a powerful, locally bottled Jamaican rum, which they christened Newfie Screech. However, in 1943, Newfie was used in such a way that it became instantly known on two continents and exploded into controversy.

In February, 1943, Joan Blondell, one of Hollywood's top stars, while hosting "Command Performance" from Carnegie Hall, New York, used the word Newfie and the slang "Stay where you're to 'till I come where you're at" to introduce the song "Newfoundland Express" poking fun at our "Newfie Bullet." It was done in the spirit of fun, but when Blondell returned to Hollywood she was overwhelmed by the angry letters it generated from Newfoundlanders. The show was heard in North America and Europe.

Blondell defended herself in a letter to *The Evening Telegram,* in which she explained:

In my heart I refuse to believe that the true spirit of the Newfoundlanders I had the pleasure to know, is behind such a petty onslaught upon a person whose every thought and effort since the beginning of the war has been to bring a few moments of cheer to those who are giving so much for us.

For the Newfoundlanders who are outraged, may I say this: I was born in Brooklyn. I would be bent and gray and twisted if I shuddered and condemned those responsible for the endless Brooklyn gags. We Brooklynites have heard them and laughed at them since Brooklyn was born.

Surely on radio shows emanating from the States you have heard the comics mimic New York talk. 'Dis is Toity-Toid Abenue and Toity-Toid Street.' Or that southern drawl, 'Howdy y'all, a'hm shore glad to see y'all heah?'

Several prominent Newfoundlanders defended Joan Blondell through letters to *The Evening Telegram*. John G. Higgins, lawyer and Rhodes Scholar, asked in his letter, "Are we losing our sense of humor?"

Lawyer George Ayre provided the most impressive defense of the actress and utilized a little humor of his own in responding to her critics. He wrote, "It is a great pity that our cowardly, anonymous writers did not bless instead of curse; but they did not. I am prepared to do it for them, and in my simple humble way say:

May heaven bless you, Joan Blondell,
Your form and acting both are swell;
Let those who curse you go to —
Joe Batt's Arm.
And there, I bet, they'll do no harm.

Decades later the word Newfie, or 'Newphie' as Blondell spelled it, is still sparking debate.

60. Newfoundland's Strangest Coincidence

Two vessels, storm-tossed in the North Atlantic, whose incidents were years apart but were travelling identical routes, formed the basis for one of the strangest coincidences in all of Newfoundland history.

The strange happening involved Peter MacPherson, founder of the MacPherson business in Port de Grave in 1811. He later married the daughter of Joseph Furneaux and they had three daughters.

The incident took place when Peter was returning to Newfoundland, accompanied by his aunt after vacationing in England. Their ship was approaching the St. John's Harbour; it was so close that Peter could actually see his home in downtown St. John's.

It was at this point that the strange story began. A sudden wind came up and blew the ship out to sea. The winds increased and caused damage to the ship's mast. When the storm subsided, the crew rigged jury masts; but just as they finished the storm resumed even more fiercely than ever and blew the ship clear across the Atlantic to the west coast of Ireland.

Meanwhile, people in St. John's who had witnessed the sudden storm and the disappearance of the ship were convinced it was lost at sea with all hands on board.

While the people in St. John's mourned the tragedy, the passengers and crew were safe in Ireland waiting for the repairs to their damaged vessel to be completed. To pass away the time, Peter MacPherson visited some of the Irish cottages in the village. In one of these he saw a painting of a man who was strangely familiar to him. But he didn't know why.

The picture impressed him so much that he asked his aunt to come and view it. She agreed, and when she saw the portrait she gasped and collapsed. When she regained her composure she said, "Why Peter, that's your father." Peter McPherson was only eight years old when his father died.

When he asked where it came from the portrait's owner replied, "Oh, that washed ashore on the beach packed in a bale of goods. We liked it and hung it up." Peter purchased it, and when the ship was ready for sailing, he took it home to Newfoundland. He learned that originally the portrait was painted in England and packed in a bale of goods for his father to take to Newfoundland. His father's vessel set out and followed the same route that young Peter's vessel had taken years later. That vessel also ran into a storm and sank off the coast of Ireland, with no survivors. Debris from the wreck had washed ashore at the same place Peter's vessel docked in Ireland.

Two vessels, storm-tossed, on the same voyage, years apart, one lost, the other saved; one with the portrait of the father; the other carrying the son – the odds of them coming together were fantastic. Yet, it happened. The MacPherson portrait did not survive; it was destroyed in the fire that swept St. John's in 1846.

61. Cattle Roamed Water Street

In old St. John's it wasn't unusual to be confronted by a herd of cattle going up Water Street and on other main city streets. Cattle discharged from cargo ships were delivered to their owners who escorted them from the wharves to the various farms surrounding St. John's. Sometimes this led to rather unusual situations, as was the case during September, 1911. The following was reported in *The Evening Telegram* that month:

> Shortly after 2 p.m. yesterday as a number of cattle were being brought up off Pitts' premises, a big bullock walked into Bowring's hardware store, and none knew of its presence until the animal put its head over

Mr. Williams shoulder as he was busy at work on some accounts. He was not a little surprised and somewhat scared, and to get the bovine visitor out without damaging the stock was a problem; men, however, secured it and not a cent's worth of damage was done.

62. The Legend of Kelly's Island

There are many legends regarding the buried treasure on Kelly's Island in Conception Bay. Pirates like Peter Easton, Bart Roberts and Captain Kelly himself are believed to have used the island to bury their ill-gotten gain. Perhaps the most famous and notorious of all the pirates to have visited the island and leave behind buried treasure was the notorious Captain Henry Morgan.

Morgan began his life as a pirate with the support and protection of Governor Thomas Modyford of Barbados. It was in 1668 that Modyford asked Morgan to capture some Spanish ships in the Caribbean as part of a plan to find out the details of an expected Spanish attack on the West Indies. Morgan captured six armed ships, 400 men and a valuable cargo that included gold and silver to pay the troops. He also obtained the Spanish attack plans and for his success was promoted to commander-in-chief of all British ships of war in the West Indies. He was given permission by the governor to attack and loot Spanish cities and the two would share the wealth.

His relationship with the governor became strained when against the advice of the governor, he attacked Panama on February 24, 1671, and took 200 prisoners, 175 mules laden with gold and silver and other valuables. Morgan had not been aware that a peace treaty had been signed between Spain and England. Both Morgan and Modyford were ordered back to England to answer for their conduct.

However, the two succeeded in obtaining the King's pardon and were allowed to continue to live in Barbados. Soon after, accusations were made that Morgan was pirating ships for personal gain. When Modyford learned of this, he became angry because Morgan had not shared the spoils with him. He demanded that Morgan give him a fifty percent share of the loot. Captain Morgan refused and the governor withdrew all official duties assigned to the captain and cancelled all letters confirming these responsibilities.

Captain Morgan chose to live a life of piracy and as he sailed from the shores of the Caribbean he told his men, "Our only country now is the deck beneath our feet." During the fall of 1672, Captain Morgan captured several prizes including the *Trade Wind*, which had a valuable cargo of goods and gold. He pursued and captured another vessel which was on its way to Spain with wine, spices, gold bars and silver bars. The hold of Morgan's ship was filled with stolen treasure. However, he was running out of food and would not risk pulling into any port in the West Indies.

Morgan now turned his attention to Newfoundland. The pickings on the Caribbean were now few and Morgan knew there would be many fishing ships on the Grand Banks of Newfoundland.

Over the following six months, he captured twenty-five ships on the Banks and took what food and water he needed. In order to continue his piracy, Morgan now needed a place to unload his cargo of gold, silver and other valuables. By this time, the fishing fleets were returning to England and Captain Morgan felt Newfoundland would be a safe place to hide his treasure.

Captain Morgan sailed into Conception Bay and anchored at Kelly's Island. However, before making any move to unload his cargo, he carefully scrutinized the area to make sure there were no others in the vicinity. About a week passed and neither a boat nor person had been sighted by the captain. He now felt confident enough to start the process of unloading the massive treasure from the pirate ship. According to legend the treasure included $275,000 in gold and silver and some valuable gems and jewelry.

Legend also claims that a dispute erupted between Captain Henry Morgan and his crew over how the loot should be shared. The men wanted their share immediately and felt it was their choice where on the island to bury it. However, Morgan convinced them it would be more advantageous to bury the entire treasure in one spot and to leave one man on the island to protect it. Although the crew reluctantly agreed to Morgan's plan, each hoped he would be the person left to guard the treasure.

On the day of departure from Kelly's Island, Morgan is said to have summoned all his men and asked for a volunteer to stay with the treasure. An African member of the crew rushed forward shouting, "I'm your man!" Morgan withdrew his cutlass and with a quick and powerful thrust chopped the man's head from his shoulders. He then ordered that he be buried on top of the treasure and said, "Be rest assured that no thieving hands other than our own will ever touch the treasure that lies beneath this ground."

A map of the location of the treasure was carved out on a piece of slate and Captain Henry Morgan with his band of pirates set sail out of Conception Bay. For many years after, Morgan continued his life of piracy and built up a band of over 800 pirates. At age fifty-eight, he came down with a strange tropical disease and within six months was dead. According to legend, Morgan had many sites where he had buried treasure including Kelly's Island. However, it also part of the Morgan legend that the buried treasure on Kelly's Island was never recovered.

During the early 1900s, there were reports of several visits to the island by strangers seeking the Morgan treasure and in one instance *The Evening Telegram* reported that some gold coins were found in the bottom of a boat rented by one of the strangers. There were other treasure-hunting visitors to Kelly's Island but none were successful.

The story of Captain Morgan's treasure will remain part of the colourful history of Conception Bay, and also the source of a variety of ghost stories regarding the pirate-spirit who continues to protect the treasure of Kelly's Island.

63. The Origin of 'Foul Weather Jack'

An old Newfoundland saying 'Foul Weather Jack' actually had its origins with a man who served as a vice-admiral of the British Navy during the War of Independence and had served as governor of Newfoundland from 1769 to 1772. The name reflected his bad luck in military encounters.

Lord John Byron led a squadron of warships to relieve British forces who were fighting the Americans in their war for independence. Unfortunately, one of the worst sea storms on record swept over his fleet and caused them to scatter in all directions. This proved to be the undoing of British power over the American colonies. It resulted in weakening the British forces and was a major blow in them losing the war.

A short while later, Byron led his troops in a battle with Count d'Estaing of Granada, but the outcome of that battle was inconclusive. His bad fortune began at the start of his military career in 1740, at the age of eighteen, when he was a mid-shipman in the British Navy. His ship was lost on the coast of Chile, where he and other crew members were taken prisoner by an Indian tribe and forced to work as servants to Indian families. His term as a slave was made easier when an Indian girl became enchanted with him. She brought him extra food and he was treated better than his captive friends. Eventually, Byron and his friends were released and by 1745 Byron was back in England where he wrote a book about his adventures on the coast of Chile.

John Byron was the grandfather of the famous poet Lord George Byron. The poet was so impressed by his grandfather's narrative that he used it as the basis for the shipwreck scene in *Don Juan*. Byron was known among sailors as an ordinary, upfront person who was a little eccentric. They called him 'Foul Weather Jack.'

Lord Byron resumed his naval career and was promoted to the rank of naval commander. He was sent on an exploration expedition to the South Sea where he once again encountered failure. His only discovery was to find out that Captain Cook had been there before him.

In 1769, he was appointed to governor of Newfoundland. While serving in that position, he had his portrait painted by Sir Joshua Reynolds. In the 1970s, this 200-year-old painting fetched $15,000 at an art auction at Sotheby's Art Gallery in London. This painting, and the nickname 'Foul Weather Jack', are all that is left of the legacy of Newfoundland's Governor John Byron. The nickname is synonymous with a person who attracts bad luck.

64. Ships Rooms

Mention the The Rooms in Newfoundland today and everyone knows you are referring to the splendid building on Harvey Road in St. John's that houses Newfoundland's cultural history. How the name originated is not so well-known.

In Newfoundland history ships rooms referred to sections of a harbour set aside for the exclusive use of fishermen to prepare fish for market. No person was allowed to fence-off grounds or build on any land in close proximity to a ships room without the permission of the governor.

St. John's had fourteen ships rooms. Throughout this part of Newfoundland history the cod fishery was of prime importance and construction of permanent housing or barns was not allowed.Temporary structures could be approved by the governor.A survey carried out in 1801 divided St.John's Harbour into fourteen ships rooms.These began near Chain Rock, which was no. 1, and ran adjacent to each other in consecutive numbers until no. 14 in the west end of the city in the Pokeham Path (Pleasant Street) area.

Some of the names they were known by were:The Admiral's Room no.5; no. 6 was Hudson's ships room; no. 11 was Darkusess'; no. 12 was Lady's Room; and no. 13 was Rotten Row, and was later known as Pye Corner.That was in the area below Princess Street.

65. A Dream that Saved Lives

Captain John Gollop had a crazy dream that helped save the lives of all but one of his crew men. It was the kind of story that listeners of Joe Smallwood's *The Barrelman Radio Show* loved to hear, and Joey did not disappoint them.

Gollop's dream resulted in one of the most incredible escapes from death in Newfoundland history. This story took place while Captain Gollop was returning from a fishing trip off the Labrador coast to his home port at Codroy Valley. In addition to Captain Gollop, there were his brothers Henry and Benjamin,Wilson Fiander and fifteen-year-old Willie Owens, the cook.

A fierce storm raged as the vessel approached the Bay of Islands. Panic set in when a huge wave hit the ship, causing it to keel over on her side. Fortunately, the vessel was carrying a shipment of empty barrels, which kept it from sinking. Henry Gollop was unable to hang on and was washed overboard and drowned. The others struggled against the wind and sea and managed to survive by tying themselves onto the ship.

As the wind and waves continued pounding the vessel, the survivors lapsed in and out of consciousness.The men, suffering from cold, hunger and exposure, expected death at any moment. Then a remarkable thing happened.

Captain John awakened from his sleep and announced to the others that he had a dream where he made a boat from the vessel's canvas sails and then used the contraption to get to shore. At first the others were not impressed by the idea, but in desperation cooperated with their captain in turning the dream into a reality.

They had only one knife which they took turns using to cut the canvas. They used the bulwark for the framing and lashed it together with rope. Then they stretched the canvas around the frame. The whole effort was a difficult and slow process because the ship was being tossed continually by the storm.

The contraption sank as soon as it hit the water and the crew's spirits diminished, but not the captain's. Captain Gollop inspired his men to help pull it back on deck and then replaced the frame with a lighter wood. This time the little 13-foot x 4-foot canoe-shaped craft floated. The men waited a few days until the winds calmed and entrusted their survival to Gollop's dream-inspired life-craft. Using oars shaped from the ship's oars, the men struggled until they arrived safely at Chimney Cove.

The little fishing village was deserted but the fishermen who lived there had left a supply of turnips and salt cod heads, which Gollop and crew turned into a hot welcomed meal. After a short rest, they boarded their canvas boat and rowed it to the Bay of Islands where they ran into good fortune. A schooner pulled up alongside the vessel and took the men aboard. They were taken to Corner Brook, and from there finally made it home to the Codroy Valley.

66. How Scotch Heather Came to Newfoundland

How Scotch Heather found its way to growing in Newfoundland is certainly a strange story. Genuine Scotch Heather can be found growing in several parts of Newfoundland. It can be seen on Signal Hill and in the Ferryland area of Newfoundland's Southern Shore.

Heather is not indigenous to Newfoundland and it was actually not brought here with the intention of growing it. A Scotch seaman who was involved in a shipwreck on the Southern Shore during the 1830s managed to save his mattress, which was filled with heather, from the doomed vessel. He carried it on his back to Ferryland. When the load became overbearing, he decided to discard the heather and save the covering. He tossed the heather along the pathway, and nature did the rest. Winds carried and spread the heather for miles and it took root. Today, it is found in abundance in the Ferryland region.

Scotch Heather was introduced to Signal Hill in a similar way. British soldiers often discarded worn-out, heather-filled mattresses throughout the Signal Hill area.

67. Mutiny at the Seal Hunt

A rare case of mutiny on a Newfoundland vessel occurred at the seal hunt in 1922. It involved the *Diana* under the command of Captain John Parsons. The vessel was carrying 8,000 seal pelts when its propeller was damaged by a growler, which is a large piece of floating ice. Unable to move, the *Diana* became trapped in the ice.

The moving tides forced the ice higher and higher until sheets of ice began moving in over the deck. The pressure was so strong that the *Diana* was forced up, out of the water, and remained fixed on its side. Although the captain said there was no need to abandon ship, some seal hunters did. These men gathered their belongings and left the ship. Captain Parsons expected that the necessary repairs could be carried out to keep the vessel afloat.

During the repair work, the engines broke down and the captain used pumps to keep her afloat while employing the sails for movement. When she moved back into the water, word spread that the ship was leaking. At this time, the crew noticed rats leaving the ship and lost confidence in the captain's efforts. This strengthened the discontent on ship.

When the rigging became entangled in ice, Jack Dodd, a crew member, climbed up the yardarm and cut the lines thereby freeing the *Diana*. The threat of mutiny was made when Captain Parsons refused their request to send out an SOS. He gave into the demand and the S.S. *Watchful* responded. Still, owners supported Captain Parsons' position that there was no imminent danger of sinking. This time they threatened to toss the captain overboard if he did not send a second SOS.

Captain Parsons had enough. He pulled a gun and threatened to shoot the first man to approach him. Men came from all over the vessel for the showdown. With forty sealers and crew surrounding him, Captain Parsons rigged up a hose to give the mutineers a shot of steam if they made any effort to overcome him. The mutineers backed off from the showdown and deserted the captain and the ship.

The owners gave up the *Diana* as lost and issued orders to open the seacocks, allowing the vessel to sink. When the crew learned that the owners had given permission to the crew of the rescue ship *Sagona* to take the 8,000 pelts from the *Diana*, they set the vessel ablaze which caused it to sink.

The story of the *Diana* is told in George Allen England's book, *Vikings of the North*.

68. American Magazine Feature on a Newfoundland Despot

In the nineteenth century the little community of Petipas, Little Bay Islands, was dominated by one man who ruled over the people like a tyrant. The atmosphere at Petipas caught the attention of an American journalist named S.J. Benjamin, who was visiting coastal Newfoundland by schooner. It was just the kind of human interest story he was seeking for the series of feature articles he was writing for *Century* magazine. The story seemed so bizarre that he devoted his full series on the subject which he entitled "The Series Petipas Despot."

Benjamin wrote, "A small place like Petipas always has its leading citizen who acts the part of uncrowned chief. In this case it is Mr. Carter. His will is the law." The article shed light on life in a rural Newfoundland community during the nineteenth century.

When the noted American writer visited Carter's General Store, Carter asked him, "Have you seen our police force. Well here it is!" Benjamin was startled when Carter drew out a massive piece of tarred rope about four feet long and brought it hard down across the counter with a resounding blow.

Carter added:

Many times I had to use this when the store's been full of fishermen, sailors, half-breeds, and Indians; all drunk and full of devilry. There was no authority to call upon to keep the peace and I had to lay about this bit of rope to clear the room by hitting left to right.

Benjamin wrote:
Carter is a typical example of the local despot, exactly fitted to rule among the desperate characters with whom he has to deal. Probably such a ruler is better than none in a place as isolated as this and Newfoundland has many of them.

The American journalist was intrigued by the community itself. Unlike the planned and organized streets he was accustomed to. He stated:

Petipas has no streets. It simply consists of an aggrega-
tion of houses perched here and there wherever a foot-
hold could be obtained among the rocky ledges which
comprise the precipitous hill and which the hamlet has
found lodgement. Carter, by force of character, had succeeded in getting the business of the place mostly for
his own hands, and the poor who form by far the largest
number in such a community, look to him for advances
and supplies which result in them being placed shrewd-
ly in his power.

This system of merchant rule, strange to Americans, was
called 'The Truck System.' When Newfoundland surrendered its
independence in 1933, the system was still in use, although it
had been condemned in England 100 years earlier.

69. The Shortest Criminal Trial

The shortest murder trial including, appeal, sentencing and
execution, in Newfoundland's criminal history took place in
just three days during October, 1794. The event also included
a penalty rarely used in Newfoundland. In handing down the
sentence to the two men who had been found guilty of murder,
the judge sentenced both to hang, with the added indignity of
dissection.

This strange episode in Newfoundland's criminal history began when Captain Arthur Morris of the HMS *Boston* obtained
permission from the governor of Newfoundland to seek volunteers from residents of St. John's to fill vacancies in his crew.
The effort was unsuccessful and the captain invoked his right
to press (conscript) men into His Majesty's service. The ship's
press gang searched every public house in the city and brought
fifteen men to the captain. Eight of these provided the captain

with good excuses as to why they couldn't serve and were released. The remaining seven were ordered to serve.

Among these were two Irishmen who asked for permission to go ashore and gather some personal belongings. Lieutenant Richard Laury, with a group of four sailors, escorted the two ashore. In the area now occupied by Steers Cove, a gang attacked the escort, killed Laury, and set the two Irishmen free.

In a matter of hours, the British had the ring leaders of the gang in custody. The two men were tried on Wednesday, October 29th, had their appeal heard on October 30th and were executed on October 31st.

The two men dressed in white turbans, which were made of two to three yards of linen, were escorted from the waterfront to the gallows at the Barrens, near Fort Townsend. The executioner wore a long black cape, face mask and a wig made of black sheep's wool. After the execution, the bodies of the men were turned over to local surgeons for dissection.

70. Russians Spied on Newfoundland during World War II

Red Star, the Russian Army magazine, displayed seven pictures of American Army bases in Newfoundland taken shortly after World War II. The photo display included two pictures of Fort Pepperrell (Pleasantville), St. John's; two of Gander, one of Argentia and two of Harmon Field. It would have been easy to get a picture of Gander, but no pictures of military bases were permitted. Canadian authorities could not explain how the Russians obtained their pictures. There was speculation that Russian agents had obtained pictures either directly or indirectly from sources on shore. The pictures showed: landing strips in Harmon, warehouses in Argentia, hospital facilities in Fort Pepperrell and the entrance gates to the bases.

Soon after North Americans became aware of the magazine's pictures, the United States tightened security at its Newfoundland bases.

71. Clever, Witty, Letters

Among Newfoundland's archival records is mention of a dispute between a private citizen and the old Newfoundland railway. The dispute itself was not unusual but the letters exchanged between the complainant and the railway were clever and witty.

In 1916, a Witless Bay farmer claimed damages against the Reid Newfoundland Company because its number nine train frightened his pig and caused it to charge and destroy a fence on his property. The pig died from injuries sustained in the mishap. His complaint to railway officials took the following form:

Dear Sir:
My razor back went on your track
One week ago today,
When Number nine came down the line
And snuffed his life away.
Now razor back through no fault of mine
Broke down my garden gate.
So please sir, pen a cheque for ten
This claim to liquidate.
Sgd. V. Tobin

C.W. Chard, claims agent for the railway responded to Mr. Tobin:

If your razor back went on our track
Sure everybody knows,
That razor backs on railway tracks
Are bound to meet their woes.
No swine kind was on our mind
The day we laid the track
The branch was built for number nine
And not for razor back.

Sgd. C. W. Chard

Case Closed.

72. Steal One-Gallon of Rum, Get Seventy-Two Lashes

On December 31, 1792, Andrew Furlong was given an un-usual punishment for stealing one-gallon of rum from Richard Tydell's Ferryland store. Furlong pleaded guilty and was sentenced to seventy-two lashes on the bare back.

The punishment involved taking the prisoner to several areas of Ferryland and partially administering the lashes in each area, so all of the population would have a chance to witness justice being served. He was first taken to the north side of Ferryland Harbour and tied to a post, where twenty-four lashes were administered. The same punishment was given at the south side of the harbour, and the final lashes were given in front of the Ferryland court house.

Part 5

73. The Phenomena on Lower Country Road

An event in Corner Brook history that took place during October, 1941, became known as "The Phenomena on the Lower Country Road," and remains among one of the unexplained stories from Newfoundland and Labrador's colourful past. The story began with a loud explosion in the area of Lower Country Road followed by lumber and glass being propelled high into the air, accompanied by a great cloud of smoke. First thoughts were that it had been caused by dynamite or a bomb.

The occurrence startled and frightened residents and the police investigation that followed left a mystery that had residents speculating for decades as to what really happened. When the investigation could find no evidence of the source of the explosion, consideration turned to the possibility that it had been caused by a meteorite. However, there was no crater of any size in the ground.

The police report on the event stated:

At 5:30 p.m., Saturday, a calm dull evening with occasional rain showers, Mrs. Snow and her daughter aged 12 years were in the kitchen of their home when they heard a terrific noise and falling glass. Rushing to the back door of the house, they found the clothesline pole almost as large and as high as an ordinary telegraph pole uprooted and resting on a part of the pile of lumber scattered over other peoples' land between her house and the river. Two windows on the second story of her house were broken in. The house received no other damage. It is a new house large and well-built, two-storey with an attic.

Police Inspector Walsh searched but could find no trace of a bomb or meteorite. He reported:

The place where the pole had been was torn up a bit and some clay and stones were thrown upon the ground leaving a space about three feet jagged and with the appearance of having been subject to a great force of eruption. Mr. Lee measured the distance from his house to Snow's as nine hundred feet. Pieces of lumber had fallen from high in the air behind Lee's house and struck the ground with such force that they went well into the surface and broke off.

A few pieces went beyond Lee's house another two hundred feet. Mrs. Snow says her neighbors living at a higher elevation to her house about two hundred yards away said they heard the noise and saw the lumber being carried into the air very high and a great cloud of smoke. This is hard to explain because there is no sign of an explosion or burnt fragment of any kind. The ground was wet and heavy and no dust should have been blowing around. There would be no dynamite around the place. None had been used there and the land is new and away from the road. It is on a low level to surrounding houses, which is also puzzling as to why it should get the 'hit' that is, if it was really a whirlwind of the end of that Florida Twister of some days previous.

The police report concluded:

There is nothing whatever to indicate an explosion and there is no crater, clear of the hole where the pole had been. Still why the board and such a lot of them had been carried so high in the air is a matter impossible to explain.

What really happened at Lower Country Road in Corner Brook remains a mystery.

74. A Peculiar John Guy Legacy

"Owning half the harbour," is an old Newfoundland saying not heard so much in modern times, but one which had its origins in John Guy's first colony in Newfoundland, Cupids. People used the saying to describe a boastful man whom they would label as, "...being so stuck-up you would think he owned half the harbour."

John Guy founded Newfoundland's first colony at Cupids and another at Bristol's Hope. He had been given a Royal Charter from the British King which granted him all the land between Cape Bonavista and Cape St. Mary's.

Guy promoted the colonization of the entire area by offering for sale "half-a-harbour" for the price of 100-pound sterling to any adventurer willing to settle the area. One of those who took Guy up on his offer was a man named Spracklin, who purchased half of Brigus Harbour from Battery Brook to the bridge. Also, the Pynn family of Harbour Grace and Bristol's Hope are descendants of an adventurer who purchased half of Bristol's Hope, from Mosquito Point to the pond.

75. An American Record

According to a Canadian Press dispatch from Washington, D.C. on December 27, 1941, a first had been recorded by

American forces in Newfoundland. The dispatch was referring to the birth of Ann Victoria Warren at St. Clare's Mercy Hospital, St. John's, Newfoundland, on September 21, 1941.

Ann Victoria Warren became the first child to be born to any American military personnel in any of the newly organized bases outside the United States. She was born to Lieutenant and Mrs. Pratt A. Warren, Newfoundland Base Command, U.S. Army.

Lieutenant Warren was a native of Kansas and came to St. John's during 1941 with the U.S. Army Forces. In St. John's, the Warren's lived at 25 Monkstown Road.

76. Aviator Sir John Alcock had Family in St. John's.

Sir John Alcock, an outstanding figure in world aviation history, had relatives in St. John's and visited with them while in Newfoundland. Sir John was pilot of the successful Vickers-Vimy airplane which crossed the Atlantic Ocean in 1919. According to *The Evening Telegram* of July 24, 1919:

> These relatives were Magistrate Mark Alcock of Griquet, his uncle, and Mrs. Crocker of the city (St. John's) his aunt, and the sons and daughters of both, his cousins. Mrs. S.H. Butler, wife of the West End Shipwright, who was formerly an Alcock, is also his aunt, and her children by a former marriage, his cousins. Mrs. Crocker and Mrs. Butler, are brother and sisters of Sir John Alcock's father.

The Butlers at the time lived at Hillcrest on LeMarchant Road and Mr. Butler worked as shipwright in premises located at 435 Water Street.

77. The Mystery Hermit of Bay Bulls

He was known simply as "the Hermit." Nobody knew his real name, and few had heard of any names associated with him. However, he called himself Henry Bond and where he came from was a mystery. Although his name will likely remain a mystery for all time, there were some things known:

Henry Bond lived in seclusion near St. John's for eight years. He resided in a dilapidated hut in Bay Bulls Big Pond. There is no indication that he ever had any visitors or that anyone saw the inside of the place. One suggestion is that most people stayed away from it because they felt the hut was haunted.

Bond earned a living by catching and selling trout and from making and selling birch brooms. Even at that time in St. John's, the 1860s, few people knew him as Henry Bond. They referred to him only as the Hermit as they watched him shuffle along Water Street in his rags and tatters, with a water pail on his arm, trying to drum up customers for his trout and birch brooms.

The Hermit was not above begging for a handout when needed. However, he showed signs that he had known more prosperous times. A contemporary report described him as, "A fine looking man, six feet tall, about thirty years of age, and notwithstanding his tattered garments, he bore the appearance of a person who had seen better days and enjoyed a high degree of society."

Bond rejected all attempts to discover his identity. To any questions along this line he would simply respond, "Well sir, I always endeavour to mind my own business." Then one day in June, 1871, he strolled into St. John's decked out in a gentleman's apparel, to announce to those who met on a daily basis that he was leaving Newfoundland. He would not tell anyone where he was going.

His response to questions of this nature was, "I dropped into town unknown and people know no more about me now than then." Bond told people who stopped to chat with him that he would drop into some other country in the same manner as he did St. John's. "Perhaps Australia," he suggested. The Hermit of Bay Bulls left St. John's on the S.S. *City of Halifax*. He was never heard from again. Many thought he was a criminal or a politician in exile. The Hermit remains as much a mystery today as he was over one hundred years ago.

78. The *Cape Clear* – Strange but True

When the sailing ship, *Cape Clear*, set sail from St. John's, Newfoundland on January 17, 1925, Jim Chancy, a member of the crew, gave no thought to danger, and in his wildest dreams would not likely imagine the ordeal he was about to face, or the ingenuity of the ship's cook which would save his life.

The *Cape Clear* was on a routine trip to deliver a cargo of fish to Naples, Italy. Near the Azores, the weather suddenly became calm and the wind decreased until there was no breeze at all. To avoid disaster, the captain dropped anchor to await the return of the wind. In the darkness of night, a wind storm suddenly struck and the captain gave orders to immediately pull anchor. First Mate Chancy was following orders when his right leg became entrapped in the windlass and, to the horror of all present, was completely severed.

Fortunately, the cook was on deck when the potentially fatal accident struck. The cook realized that if something was not done right away to stop the bleeding Chancey would certainly bleed to death. He wasted no time in soliciting the help of several crew men to bring Chancey to the forecastle. Using an axe, he broke open the top of a barrel of flour and then with the assistance of the others placed the mate's stump into the barrel.

The flour congealed with the blood and stopped the bleeding. Almost a week after the near tragedy, the *Cape Clear* arrived at Gibraltar and Jim Chancey was rushed to a hospital.

However, upon examination, the doctor discovered the wound was clean and beginning to heal.

79. St. Swithin's Day

July 15th each year was St. Swithin's Day and was always acknowledged throughout Newfoundland. The following rhyme was associated with that day:

> St. Swithin's Day, if thou dost rain
> Forty days it will remain.
> St. Swithin's Day, if thou are fair
> For forty days t'will rain
> beware!

St. Swithin's name became associated with weather long after his death. In life, he had been the bishop of Winchester, England. On his death bed, he requested that after he passed away his remains be buried in the Winchester churchyard under the dripping eaves so he would be near the working people.

In accordance with his wishes, the bishop was buried in the churchyard. A century later, church authorities decided that the Saint should be buried inside the church. The day that his body was exhumed and placed inside the church was July 15th.

As the holy bones were brought inside the church, the skies broke open and it began to pour out of the heavens. The rainstorm lasted forty days and the monks took this as a sign that the Saint's dying wish be honoured. His bones were returned to their original resting place in the churchyard.

80. Archway Across St. John's Harbour

The plans for decorating St. John's Harbour for the visit of the Duke of York, later King Edward VII, in 1860 were amazing, but were never carried out. However, because the plan was quite possible to implement it is worth recalling. A city resident, Stephen March, who contributed to decorating the town for the 1860 visit, suggested that a welcoming archway be constructed across the Narrows.

Officers of the British Navy, in port on the HMS *Styx*, carried out a survey at the Narrows to determine the scheme's feasibility and concluded it could be done.

It was to be a spectacular archway, stretching from one side of the Narrows to the other while leaving sufficient space for ships to enter and leave the St. John's port. This arch was to be festooned with flags, bunting and streamers for the daytime and multi-coloured lanterns for the night.

The idea was met with enthusiasm by Newfoundland officials but was not acted upon because of its cost.

81. A Source of Religious Friction

July 12th has always been an important day in Newfoundland history, as it marks the holiday for the traditional Orangeman's Day. On July 12, 1690, the Battle of the Boyne took place in which the Orange forces of King William defeated the Roman Catholic supporters of King James for the second time.

The famous battle was fought among the Irish with the Roman Catholics facing off against the Protestants of Ireland. In this era, Ireland was under British rule but when King James II, a Roman Catholic of the Stuart line, was deposed by the British, they then gave his throne to William of Orange. (Orange was a principality in northern France).

Irish Protestants supporting King William and Catholics supporting King James each formed an army of about 30,000 men. The two armies faced off on the banks of the river Boyne.

King William's forces were victorious. While the Catholics organized secret societies aimed at overthrowing King William, the Protestants formed the Loyal Orange Institution to support King William and maintain the connection with England.

Irish Protestants immigrating to Newfoundland brought with them the Loyal Orange Society and the tradition of honouring the Battle of the Boyne on July 12th.

82. Original Name of Church Hill, St. John's

Two of the best-known streets in the old part of St. John's are Church Hill and Cathedral Street. They are located opposite the court house on Duckworth Street and mark the eastern and western boundaries of the Anglican Cathedral property. However, according to an 1854 map of old St. John's and a *Daily News* item published July, 1914, there were different names for these streets. Church Hill was called Cathedral Hill in 1851. Court House Lane was renamed Cathedral Hill, and today is Cathedral Street. The original Cathedral Hill was renamed Church Hill.

Just west of today's Gower Street United Church was a small Wesleyan Cemetery which is long forgotten to history.

83. A 610-Year-Old Coin

The following news item comes from *The Evening Telegram*, July 23, 1898:

A correspondent writing from King's Cove tells of a very curious coin picked up there a few days ago by a resident and bearing the date 1288. He says, 'It is a copper coin and about the size of an ordinary English penny. Strange to say it is not worn much and the date is quite unmistakable. There is no other inscription on it, except two characters resembling Hebrew and Chinese letters, and these are on the same side as the date. They resemble also short-hand

111

characters. On the obverse side are two isosceles triangles interwoven, the apex of each touching the base of the other.

It was found embedded in turf, which will account for its excellent state of preservation.

84. British Naval Tradition Explained

There is a tradition in the British Navy for sailors to salute the quarter deck. This tradition is traced back to when England was Catholic, and all the men of the British Navy were of that faith. Premier Joseph R. Smallwood, while host of *The Barrelman Radio Show*, explained,

> On the poop aft, on the quarter deck, there would always be a religious statue — and as the men approached the quarter deck they would remove their caps. Long after the Reformation, after the statues were no longer there, the habit of removing the cap was continued, until eventually it developed into the present day salute.
> Now the salute is to the quarter deck in the connection being emblematic of the ship herself — and, of course, every sailor looks upon his ship, not as a mere aggregation of pieces of wood and metal, but as an actual entity, with a personality of her own.[1]

85. The Gutsy Mrs. Traverse

In 1834, with the new House of Assembly for Newfoundland in its second session, an embarrassing event took place that still stands out in history almost 200 years later.

Representative government was introduced to Newfound-

---

[1] *The Best of the Barrelman* (1938-1940) Joseph R. Smallwood, edited by William Connors p76, Creative Publishers, 1998.

land with a general election held in 1832, and the first session of the new House of Assembly taking place in 1833.

The battle for Representative government was fought over a fifteen-year period but, when granted, the country was not really prepared for it. The Colonial Building had not yet been built and the new government had no place to hold its legislative meeting.

It might be peculiar for young people today to learn that Newfoundland's first democratically elected legislature held its first meeting in the house of Mary Traverse during the winter of 1833. Traverse was located on Duckworth Street on the eastern corner of King's Road. Although hardly large enough to suit the purpose, it just had to do.

By 1834, government had found a more suitable accommodation in the court house, which was then located on the east side of today's court house and midway between Duckworth and Water streets. The legislators faced one major problem when they entered the building for their first sitting — there was not a stick of furniture!

The sergeant-at-arms entered the confused gathering, bearing upsetting news. He informed the members that Mrs. Traverse had refused to allow anyone to remove the furniture belonging to The House of Assembly until the unpaid rent for use of her premises had been paid.

This embarrassment was able to develop because the legislators had neglected to submit and approve the rent payment to Mrs. Traverse at their last session. Until payment was approved by the legislature, the bill could not be paid. While waiting for this to happen, Mrs. Traverse did not trust the government and insisted on having the money in her hands before releasing the furniture.

Government responded with a threat to their former landlord that unless she released their furniture, she would be arrested. Traverse refused two such threats, which left the legislators not knowing what to do or where to turn.

Just how the members proceeded with their first meeting in the court house is not clear, but the situation was resolved later that week when the governor intervened and persuaded her to return the furniture and assured her full-payment without delay. Traverse obliged His Excellency, and the episode came to an end.

86. Portuguese Give Fatima Shrine to St. John's

A remarkable piece of St. John's history is the Shrine of Our Lady of Fatima, located inside the Roman Catholic Basilica on Military Road. It was a gift from the people of Portugal to the people of Newfoundland.

In the tourist guide to the Basilica the following description is written:

Beyond the Sacred Heart Altar stands the Shrine of Our Lady of Fatima, comprising a group of nine statues, of polychrome and gilt plaster. A gift of the Portuguese people, whose ties with Newfoundland are well-documented, the statues were presented to the Basilica during the Centenary Celebrations in 1955. On May 27 that year, the statues were borne in procession by thousands of Portuguese fishermen from their ships on the waterfront to the Basilica. Following a special ceremony, they were transferred to their present location. This shrine is visited regularly by the Portuguese fishermen when their vessels are in port, and is held in high esteem by the Catholic population of St. John's.

87. The Mystery Man Escorted by FBI in St. John's

During August, 1941, a train set out from St. John's carrying some prominent Newfoundlanders and an American soldier whose identity was a mystery to the railway staff. The workers became more curious after learning that the mystery man had FBI officers accompanying him.

Guy McDonald was the engineer of the train that night and his son Kevin, who followed in his dad's footsteps later, revealed the mystery. He recalled, "Dad was the engineer of a special train that left St. John's for Argentia that night carrying Governor Walwyn, Sir Leonard Outerbridge and many other VIPs. The only order he had before leaving was that he was to rendezvous at Placentia Junction with a special train from Gander. He didn't know that this train would carry Lord Beaverbrook and other distinguished British dignitaries to Argentia to an event that was to be one of the most important in the history of Newfoundland and the whole world."

McDonald became suspicious when he noticed the plain-clothed men followed him at each stop when he went outside to carry out an inspection of the engine. When the trip was over he learned these men were FBI. He was then introduced to Colonel Elliott Roosevelt the son of President Franklin D. Roosevelt, president of the United States.

The meeting in Placentia Bay between the president and Prime Minister Sir Winston Churchill marked the start of a turning point in World War II. Churchill sent a telegraph message to Russian President Joseph Stalin telling him of what had been achieved at the top secret meeting. A document was drawn up to use a cover story for the real purpose of the meeting. The real details of that meeting and message to Stalin were disclosed in Churchill's writings after the war.[2]

88. Pirates and Ghosts of Quidi Vidi Lake

A pirate vessel attempting to evade capture by the British Navy during the early 1800s pulled into Quidi Vidi Harbour and carted a treasure of silver and gold to a site adjacent to Quidi

[2] *Battlefront Newfoundland,* Jack Fitzgerald, Creative Publishers, 2010

Vidi Lake and buried it, with hopes of returning during safer times to recover it.

In 1820, one of the pirates returned to claim the gold for himself. While in St. John's he stayed at the home of a Mr. O'Regan, who operated a shoe store in the city's west end. However, before he could get a chance to search for the treasure he became gravely ill and passed away. Before dying, Father Forestall was called to the home by Mr. O'Regan and the dying man's confession was heard and last rites administered. In appreciation for O'Regan's Christian kindness, the dying man confessed to his friend that he had been a pirate and he gave him a map showing where in Quidi Vidi the pirates had hidden their gold.

The map described Bennett's Grove adjacent to Quidi Vidi Lake in the vicinity of Dribbling Brook (east of the boathouse). The place to dig was thirty paces west of the brook. O'Regan employed several fishermen from Quidi Vidi Village to help him dig for the gold and silver. The men were William Quigley, Richard Mallard and William Smithwick. The trio spent three days digging without any success. O'Regan ordered the men to stop their digging, as he had discovered the buried treasure and planned to remove it himself. However, he had not anticipated that another group was already heading for Bennett's Grove to seek the treasure. A small group headed by Kenneth Connors worked at night to avoid arousing suspicion.

While working one night, an eerie cry rang out through the area. The cry startled the men and one commented, "It's the cry of the banshee." Around the same time, a misty-type figure began moving slowly towards the men and waving a sword over his head. Kenneth Connors had a heart attack and dropped dead. Another man ran from the area screaming. Days later, he was still in shock and eventually was admitted to the asylum, where he spent the rest of his days. By the time Kenneth Connors was buried, there were no non-believers of ghosts in town. However, as the treasure story became known speculation grew that

O'Regan had disguised himself as a phantom pirate with sword to scare the treasure seekers from his dig. O'Regan left a few months later to settle in the United States and the local people believed he had taken a portion, if not all, of the Quidi Vidi treasure with him.

The treasure fever, and ghost story, faded from public memory until a little over a decade later when a stranger arrived in St. John's on board the S.S. *Florizel*. A man from Boston, sought and received permission from the Honourable A.M. MacKay to dig on his property in Dribbling Brook. A Mr. Eddie who operated a coal yard on Carter's Hill befriended the stranger and sometimes helped with the digging.

Mr. Eddie learned from the stranger that a man named O'Regan had passed away in Boston and before dying had given him the treasure map. Although the American placed some trust in Mr. Eddie, he would withdraw into the woods whenever others approached him.

Then one morning at daylight, a resident of the area saw the American row a boat up from the foot of the lake to the cove, near where he was digging, and lift on board a large box from the grove. The stranger then rowed back to the end of the lake where he loaded the box onto a horse and buggy and drove away. The resident went to the grove but found only an empty hole with about eight feet of clay piled up along its side.

By this time, Dribbling Brook had changed direction and the stranger had searched for the treasure on the dried up riverbed that a 100 years before was Dribbling Brook. Meanwhile, Mr. Eddie was not ready to give up and he was convinced there was some treasure still in the area. His belief was based on information he picked up from the visitor that one man could not carry all the treasure hidden near the brook.

Mr. Eddie formed a group, which included the Honourable J. Mackay and Thomas Kent of Quidi Vidi. They agreed to share the treasure equally and to pay diggers $1 per day to do the labour for them. After seven days of unsuccessful digging, the project was called off. Rumours spread that one of the diggers had found some gold coins and kept them. Mackay and his group felt there was still a sizeable treasure in the area but because the brook had changed direction they could never locate it.

Well into the 1950s, many people of the city felt that Bennett's Grove was haunted and would avoid that area after dark.

89. Quidi Vidi Man Hanged as Cow-Killer

In 1759, William Gilmore operated a successful business in his home in Quidi Vidi Village selling liquor to soldiers from the Garrison in St. John's. During April of the same year, Gilmore was executed at Gallows Hill (corner Queen's Road and Bates Hill) by hanging for his part in stealing a cow.

Gilmore had encouraged two friends to kill one of the cows grazing in a meadow in the area now occupied by Government House. He planned the crime and arranged to hide the meat in his well.

The duo killed the cow but left the knife given to them by Gilmore at the site of the crime. Authorities found the knife, and Gilmore's wife identified it as her husband's. Justice was swift, and within days the trial and execution had been completed. Historical records are not clear on what happened to the two young men who did the bidding of William Gilmore.

In the eighteenth century there were more than 122 offences for which a person could be executed, one of which was stealing a cow.

90. Pokeham Path's Carroll's Well

Before St. John's installed 'water tanks' throughout the city, from which residents were able to access fresh water on a daily basis, people carried their water in buckets from neighbourhood wells. Included among these were Wishing Well, Penny Well, Carroll's Well and Apple Tree Well.

Carroll's Well served the Pokeham Path area, (Hamilton Avenue) and was located on the property today occupied by Riverhead Towers. A natural well formed there from water flowing from Mundy Pond. Early records show the name as 'Monday Pond'. However, there was a family in the area named Mundy and it seems that many people upon hearing the name recorded it as Monday Pond. It was from the family name Mundy that the pond got its name. This would explain the difference in spellings in earlier records.

Rocks and stones from the area were cemented together to form the well in 1859. Flagstone was used to form three outlets into Carroll Well. The water that flowed into this old well can still be heard from the basement of Riverhead Towers.

In the early 1900s, a pipe was laid from Mundy Pond to connect the old river that ran the Pleasant Street-New Gower Street route to St. John's Harbour. At the site, occupied up until the late 1960s by Mrs. Power's Candy Store and Wadden's Confectionary, was one of the town's old "Barking Kettles." Also, in that same area was the Salvation Army Citadel, which in later years moved to the lower-west side of Springdale Street where the St. Vincent de Paul Society had operated. Barking Kettles[3] were used by fishermen for barking their fishing nets.

91. St. John's Oldest Surviving Theatre Building

The old stone structure on Queen Street, today known as the Cotton Club, has quite a history. Along with being the site of the second-oldest Catholic church in St. John's, it is also the city's oldest surviving theatre. After its construction in 1861, it

[3] A Barking Kettle is described in the *Dictionary of Newfoundland English* as the process consisting of immersing a fishing net into a liquid steeped from the bark and buds of conifer trees.

119

was used as the Fisherman's Hall. Prior to that, Maurice Cullen, the father of the internationally famous artist Maurice Cullen, occupied the house that stood on that site.

The Catholic church took over the property in 1873. The Star of the Sea was founded there on February 28, 1871. The upstairs was consecrated as St. Peter's Church and the first floor became a convent school, which the Sisters of Mercy operated. St. Peter's Church was closed down when St. Patrick's Church opened in 1883. The entire St. Peter's building then became a convent school.

St. Peter's was no longer needed by 1903, when it was sold to businessman Frank McNamara who turned it into a warehouse and offices. It became a night club in the 1970s and has had a series of owners.

92. Cash's Indian on Water Street

Cash's Indian was a famous fixture in old St. John's. It got its name from Cash's Tobacco Store, located at the north side Water Street. The popular wooden Indian stood outside Cash's Store from 1885 to 1963. When Mr. Cash died, according to author Michael Harrington, the store was taken over by his heirs, the Trainor family of St. John's.

The Honourable Edward Roberts, often described by Smallwood as one of Newfoundland's most brilliant men, once told the story of when he was campaigning in the district of White Bay North and a resident told him not to worry because, "... if Mr. Smallwood sent Cash's Indian down here we'd vote for him."

Even when the store was leased to a new operator who discontinued the tobacco operation in favour of a confectionery store, Cash's Indian remained at its honoured spot outside the store. Wooden Indians were used in the nineteenth and early twentieth centuries to draw attention to buildings where tobacco stores operated. James Patrick Cash started his tobacco store on November 10, 1880.

According to Harrington, in an article published in the *Atlantic Advocate*, September, 1963, Cash was said to be the sole importer of cigars into Newfoundland, and was given the Indian by his supplier for likely making the largest sale of cigars and tobacco over a specified period.

The Indian was on display for so long that it became a landmark in the city. Any person seeking directions to a place in the eastern area of Water Street would be asked, "Do you know where Cash's Indian is located? If the person answered, "Yes," he would be told where the place he was seeking was in proximity to the wooden Indian. Others would be told to, "Keeping walking east on Water Street until you come to Cash's Indian then turn, etc."

Another city landmark was 'Connors' Horse.' Connors operated a harness-maker's shop several doors east of Cash's Store. He had on display in his shop window a life-size statue of a horse in harness and saddle. After Confederation and the closing of the store, the horse was purchased by Premier Joseph Smallwood's son-in-law, who had it mounted on a concrete setting and placed on the top of a hill overlooking Roaches Line.

The horse was the source of a humorous exchange in the Newfoundland Legislature between Joey Smallwood and Billy Browne. While criticizing Smallwood's son-in-law about moving the horse to the top of a hill approaching his Roaches Line residence, Billy pointed out, "...and the horse's rear end is facing the road." Smallwood interjected, "Mr. Speaker, perhaps the horse saw who was coming."

93. Low-Flying Plane Hits Southside Hills, St. John's

At 10:00 a.m. on Thursday, April 6, 1945, a small single-engine RCAF plane spiralled out of control and crashed into Southside Hills, St. John's. The pilot, the only occupant, died instantly in the tragedy. Some men working on the north side of St. John's Harbour watched the craft spin out of control then explode into flames upon impact.

As the RCN Firefighting Unit rushed to the scene to combat the fire, thousands of St. John's residents watched from city streets in amazement. The plane crashed on a site about 300 feet behind the Job's Wharf on the Southside. Lieutenant-Commander Charles Spinney directed the firefighting battle to extinguish the flames.

The next day, *The Evening Telegram* described what remained, only the framework of the fuselage remained partially intact with seared and shattered pieces of the aluminium body on the ground by the wreckage. The wings and the tail assembly were also riddled with holes and detached from the main body of the plane, while the motor, with twisted propeller and the cockpit lay near a boulder.

About six months later a plane crash in northern Newfoundland, with a St. John's native on board, attracted attention throughout Newfoundland and Labrador. Flying Officer J.D. Sinnott of Queen's Road, St. John's, was among the crew of a Canso plane which, after making a forced landing at sea, was pounded to pieces by heavy seas near Belle Isle. The Canso was on an errand of mercy to take the lightkeeper from Belle Isle to the hospital for emergency treatment.

Sinnott and eight others on board were rescued in a dory by the lightkeeper's assistant just minutes before the plane sank.

Part 6

94. A Peculiar Tombstone

Almost a 100 years ago, Manuel's River in Topsail, near St. John's, was called Holystone River. Its name was derived from the fact that about fifteen miles up the river from Topsail there was an eight-foot tombstone rising above the water in the middle of the river. This stone appeared to be perfectly square and carved by hand. People believed it was actually a tombstone which had been there long before the river.

In the 1930s, archaeologists discovered ancient fossils at Manuel's River, and claimed it to be one of the oldest rivers in the entire world. This unusual stone has not been seen since the 1940s; it might now be underwater or possibly moved.

95. Devil's Cove, Newfoundland

Devil's Cove was located in the district of Bay de Verde, but the name became such a burden to residents that they initiated legal action to change it to something more acceptable to their Christian beliefs. In 1812, after surviving for more than fifty years, the name was officially changed to Job's Cove.
The change was published in the *Royal Gazette* in 1812. It read:

We, the undersigned inhabitants, conceiving the utility and benefits resulting from an early conception and sense of Religion instilled into the tender minds of our children, and of the rising generation, do unanimously resolve to change and after the barbarous, execrable and impious name of *Devil's Cove*, into the ancient, venerable and celebrated name of *Job's Cove*; and that the public newspaper of St. John's will publish these our resolutions three different times, so that every person in the island may come to this knowledge, and none may plead ignorance, by saying when they pronounce *Devil's Cove*, that it is from want of knowing better how to preclude any tergiversations, or vain excuses. After the publication of this Act we do declare, that our resolution is fixed and that this Cove which underwent the appellation of *Devil's Cove* these 50 years and upwards to the scandal and detriment of God's honour and veneration, be altered and changed, and every one for the time to come, and always, will call it after the name we freely give it, to wit, *Job's Cove*, and that all persons may hereafter take notice of these our resolutions we sign our names.

Thomas English, Moses Sandy, Richard English, Richard Woodfine, James English, William Bearns, T. Edward English, John Johnson, Ned English, Wm. Johnson, Jos. Murphy, James Walsh, John Murphy, J. Murphy, Jr., George.

Another place in Newfoundland which carried the Devil's name was on the province's south coast. The Devil's Stairway was the name once given to the headland rising about 300 feet above the sea at Cape Broyle. There is a fascinating legend associated with the origins of the name. Early in the nineteenth century, an ill-tempered sea captain became very angry when his vessel was becalmed off this headland and was dragged towards shore by the tide.

The frustrated captain began shouting and cursing his crew, his ship, the sea and anything else he could think of. At his peak of anger, he exclaimed, "May the Devil take this vessel, cargo and all of us!"

Suddenly, so the legend claims, just as the ship was about to go aground a great hand seized her and she was bodily hauled up the face of the cliff to the top. The residents had no doubt that it was the work of Satan because he left his footprints embedded in the rock on top of the cliff.

While recalling this old legend, Ambrose Cahill said, "There are fourteen prints like a cloven hoof still there, in a direct line, there was also the remnants of an old wrecked vessel. How did it get there? Certainly, no human hand dragged them up an almost perpendicular high cliff."

96. Smartest Man

Theophilus Hart of Lady Cove, Newfoundland, was an amazing Newfoundlander because of his superior mathematical skills. His mind worked like a computer in calculating complicated and lengthy accounting problems. Judge Johnson, a Newfoundland Supreme Court Justice, who was a friend of Hart and aware of his abilities, described him as, "The smartest, uneducated man in the world."

Joe Smallwood, on his *The Barrelman Radio Show* during December, 1938, told his listening audience:

He [Hart] couldn't write or read his name. No pencil or pen was ever seen in his hand. And yet, Theophilus Hart of Lady Cove, Trinity Bay, was by all accounts absolutely a mathematical genius and I cannot help wondering what he might have become had he only received a good education — probably another Albert Einstein or Bertrand Russell.

Hart took only moments to calculate problems involving numbers and fractions. No accountant could match his ability. Smallwood told listeners of one of Hart's most famous feats. He solved a business calculation in a fraction of the period taken by the merchant's bookkeepers. And he did it without the aid of pen, pencil or adding machine. Smallwood explained:

Once he was aboard a Trinity Bay schooner loaded with lumber of all kinds and sizes. The lumber was consigned to no less than twenty-three different people, and after it was all delivered and the vessel was empty, the owner of the lumber, Mr. W.H. Gulliford, together with another man on the schooner, got out their paper and pencils and began to figure the thing out — how much money was coming to each of the twenty-three men.

Theophilus Hart, with no pencil or paper, began to figure the thing in his head. By two o'clock in the morning the two men with pencils and paper had arrived at their totals. Mr. Hart had got his totals quite a while before they did. And when they were all finished neither one's figure agreed with the other two, all three totals were different. So next morning, the skipper called aboard a man from ashore, a competent accountant, who figured it all out for him, and what do you suppose?

The only man who had figured it correctly was Theophilus Hart.[1]

97. The Glue Pot Fire

An overheated glue pot at Hamlyn's Cabinet Making Shop on Queen Street led to the destruction of St. John's by fire in

---

[1]*The Best of the Barrelman (1938-1940)*, edited by William Connors. Creative Publishers, 1998.

1846, which is known in history as 'The Glue Pot Fire.' This fire left 12,000 people homeless, two-thirds of the town destroyed, and property loss estimated at $3 million.

The nearby fire department was alerted to the fire at 8:00 a.m. on Tuesday, June 9, 1846, and rapidly responded. Because of the problem of getting their water pumps operating in time, the fire got out of control and flames spread quickly throughout St. John's. Things got worse in the afternoon, when the winds increased causing the spread of brands and flankers.

Leading the firefighting effort at Beck's Cove was Governor John Harvey. His strategy was to create a firebreak at this location. His first move was to have the Stabb Building on the corner of Beck's Cove blown up. Unfortunately, the explosion also killed a member of the artillery who was assisting. This action failed and the fire continued spreading.

Adding to the drama unfolding was the explosion of vats of seal oil stored on the waterfront, which spread the fire to ships in the harbour. By the time the fire was out three people were dead, one of them was an old man who was trying to save his burning bed from his home. Troops were called in to protect property and prevent looting. By 7:00 p.m. it was all over, and St. John's lay in ruins.

Many of the people whose homes were burned-out spent the night outdoors on the Government House grounds and in an area adjoining Fort Townsend. Outside help for the city began to pour in. The British government sent £5,000 and the British Parliament authorized another £25,000.

Churches throughout Britain took up collections for the victims. One of the great losses of the 1846 disaster was the destruction of many valuable historical documents. The population of St. John's at the time was 16,000, and there were 4,200 homes.

98. A Remarkable Sculpture

One of many attractions for tourists who visit the Roman Catholic Basilica annually is an outstanding sculpture called *The Dead Christ*, carved by the famous nineteenth century Irish sculptor John Hogan. Other works of Hogan include: the statue of Daniel O'Connell at the City Hall in Dublin, Ireland; a figure of Hibernia for Lord Cloncurry and the *Eve, after her Expulsion from Paradise*.

Hogan created three statues of *The Dead Christ*. All three depict Christ lying in his tomb. The first work had been ordered for a chapel in Cork but the parish was unable to raise the money to purchase it. The statue was then sold to the Roman Catholic Church on Clarendon Street, Dublin for two thousand dollars.

Hogan's work became so famous throughout Europe that Cork commissioned him to execute a duplicate of it for the city. His third statue was considered his best. Bishop Mullock of the Roman Catholic Cathedral in St. John's commissioned Hogan to his third statue of *The Dead Christ*. It cost $2,000 and was shipped to St. John's on the *Ariel*. The *Ariel* was the first Newfoundland coastal steamer. It arrived here on May 21, 1863, and was lost at Red Bay on September 12, 1875.

Hogan's masterpiece was carved from the purest Italian marble. Because the marble used in the statue was almost flawless, this third work of Hogan's was his best and most perfect. Thorvaldsen, the great Danish master of statuary, described Hogan as the best sculptor to succeed him in Rome.

Hogan was born at Tallow County, Waterford, in 1800. He gave up the study of law to become a sculptor. A wealthy Irish Lord provided the funding for him to study art in Rome. He later returned to Ireland.

There are two other Hogan pieces at the Basilica, and both were commissioned by Bishop Mullock. These are the memorials on the side-walls to Bishop Scanlan and Bishop Fleming.

99. More than One Newfoundland

In addition to our province of Newfoundland, there are four other places around the world using the same name. There is a Newfoundland in Elliott County, Kentucky; a Newfoundland in Morris County, New Jersey; another in Wayne County, Pennsylvania and we have a Newfoundland Island in Labrador.

100. Newfoundland's Peculiar Nineteenth Century Mail System

Sending trans-Atlantic messages before the Atlantic Cable was laid was handled in a peculiar way. When Joey Smallwood was host of *The Barrelman Radio Show* in 1940, he captivated his audience with the following oddity from Newfoundland's history.

He told listeners:

Up at Cape Race there was a telegraph office at the end of a land-line cable from the Cape to St. John's. Steamships coming across the Atlantic would write messages intended for Canada or America, wrap them carefully in bottles or other watertight containers, and throw them overboard in the water near Cape Race.

Boats would put out from the Cape, the messages would be picked up out of the water and then sent over the land-line cable to the western tip of Newfoundland, and then by the submarine cable across the Cabot Strait. In exactly the same way, steamships going across the Atlantic would pick up messages thrown overboard at Cape Race, and carry them over. It means, at least, that if you left New York for Europe, your last news of a personal or business character wouldn't end on the day your steamer sailed, but on the day she passed Cape Race.

The great daily newspapers of the United States paid large sums of money to have the latest news picked up at Cape Race from steamships coming across the Atlantic, and forwarded by cable from Cape Race days ahead of the steamships themselves. Even that was considered a marvellous achievement in those days, crude as it seems to us today who live in an age when a man stands before a radio microphone in London or Paris, and you can hear even his breathing on this side of the Atlantic.
– May 1940.[2]

101. The Coffins of Mockbeggar

In the 1920s, the discovery of coffins at a place called Mockbeggar in Bonavista Bay developed into one of Newfoundland history's great mysteries. While digging out a canal at Mockbeggar, workmen unearthed a shocking discovery. They had discovered a burial ground with coffins containing the bodies of men, women and children.

Their bewilderment over the discovery intensified with each coffin they opened, when they discovered that each one had been pegged and not nailed together, and were made of wood not found anywhere in Newfoundland.

Speculation that these were bodies of French settlers was quickly dispelled when it was determined that the bodies were dressed in puritan-style clothing and that the French did not bring women and children to Newfoundland while fishing.

Who were the dead of Mockbeggar?

The coffins were buried below mud, which attributed to their preservation. The bodies were moved to another site and

[2]*The Best of the Barrelman (1938-1940)* Edited by William Connors. Creative Publishers, 1998.

several homes were constructed over the Mockbeggar cemetery.

Legend has it that on a dark, stormy night one can hear the sound of singing in a foreign language coming from the cemetery site.

102. Editor's Ears Cut-Off by Bigots

The barbarous attack on the editor of a St. John's newspaper resulted in both of his ears being cut off during the vicious attack. Henry Winton who resided on Queen's Road, near Long's Hill, was the editor of the *Public Ledger*. Winton was an outspoken critic of Catholic Bishop Fleming and was behind a print campaign against the priest's influence on Newfoundland politics.

Winton, accompanied by his close friend Captain Churchward, set out from Carbonear to visit friends in Harbour Grace. Winton was riding a horse while his friend walked alongside. Nearing Saddle Hill, five men disguised with painted faces rushed from a wooded area and attacked them. Winton received a heavy blow on his head from a stone tossed by one of his attackers. Two men seized Captain Churchward and took his gun.

While they restrained the captain, the others punched and kicked Winton. They filled his ears with mud and gravel. Winton feared for his life and asked if they were going to kill him. "Hold your tongue," answered an attacker. Terrified, Winton watched as the man opened a clasped knife and ordered the others to hold Winton's hands. He then grabbed Winton's right ear and sliced it from his head. The victim's agonizing screams and the shouts of protest from Captain Churchward did not deter the attackers. They proceeded to do the same to Winton's left ear, and he passed out. After regaining consciousness, his vision was blurred by the blood pouring down his forehead. Churchward was released unharmed and he rushed to aid his friend. The attackers escaped from the scene. The captain struggled to assist Winton over a mile and a half road to the home of Dr. Stirling in Harbour Grace. The doctor succeeded in stopping the bleeding and bandaged the wounds. After a short period of rest Winton and Churchward left for St. John's.

The public was outraged when news of the attack was made public. Winton's own newspaper addressed an editorial to him stating, "Yours are the scars of honour on which every man will look with admiration." Although a reward of $4,000 was offered for information leading to the arrest of the criminals responsible, the crime was never solved.[3]

103. Newfoundland's Mildest Winter

The winter of 1899 in Newfoundland was a peculiar one. The weather was remarkable because farmers were cultivating their farmland in January. On January 11th, William Woodley, a farmer on the banks adjacent to Quidi Vidi Lake, ploughed an acre of land. Farmers all around St. John's were doing the same work. After ploughing, they top-dressed their fields and set hundreds of sheep free in the fields to graze. There was no need to tap the stored reserves of hay because the fields were so bountiful.

A month later, Bannerman Park was attracting springtime crowds. A game of Newfoundland football (soccer), played at the park, was held on February 21, 1889. Some of the players included, Fred Alderdice, later prime minister of Newfoundland, Andrew Thorburn, Joseph Peters, George Langmead and George Tessier. Football in winter was something unheard of in Newfoundland.

[3]Some years ago, author Jack Fitzgerald was approached by a person who claimed knowledge of the attackers which was handed down within her family. She said the family had always known that the men who cut off Winton's ears were named Power and Yetman. Descendants of both families are today living in St. John's.

104. Flatrock's Dog Hero

A group of seaman were stranded on the ledge of a high cliff in Seal Cove, near Flatrock, for hours. Had it not been for a dog's ability to sense danger, they all would have died.

The *Emma*, owned by Bowring Brothers of St. John's, ran ashore at Seal Cove on November 9, 1856. The vessel became a total wreck. However, before it went to the bottom, the Italian cook onboard made a valiant attempt to save his mates by diving into the rolling sea in an unsuccessful attempt to get a line ashore.

Captain W. White and his crew succeeded in getting safely to shore, but they became trapped on the ledge of a high cliff. They called for help for hours, but nobody heard them. It was a cold, windy night and they feared the worst.

About a half-mile away, a fisherman's dog was alerted and badgered the old fisherman, named Mayo, repeatedly until he awoke. He then led the fisherman to the top of the cliff where the sailors were in peril.

Mayo could hear the voices below. He went back to his house, acquired some rope and returned to the stranded men. Mayo managed to secure the rope, lowered it and succeeded in bringing the captain and his crew, one by one, to safety. The distance from the cliff to the surface where Mayo and the dog stood was seventy feet.

Mayo was quite the hero, but so was the dog. If the dog had not awakened his master and led him to the men, the outcome would certainly have been tragic.

105. Mystery on the *Terra Nova*

After arriving in a Scottish port, while giving their ship the *Terra Nova* a once-over, the crew men came across a strange object they could not identify. It was discovered on the top

133

shelf of a cupboard in the galley, and by all appearances looked and felt like a piece of wood. However, it was unlike any they had seen before. John Grant, the ship's cook, looked on with interest and, although amused by the speculation, offered no opinion.

The men wrapped the object and brought it ashore to seek the opinion of a shipbuilder nearby. This expert sawed the object in half and concluded it was some kind of hardwood, but was unable to be more definite. A few days later the *Terra Nova* began its return trip to Newfoundland. The item continued to attract the attention of the crew.

Finally, the cook came forward and holding up the item said he was ready to solve the mystery. John Grant was famous for his figgy duffs. He made these from water, flour and molasses, and then boiled them in a cotton bag. Two years earlier, after preparing figgy duff for the crew, he was left with one serving which he stored on the top shelf in the galley and then forgot about it. Over time the heat caused the duff to harden. Holding the mystery object above his head for all to see he said, "This, my friends, is that duff."

106. Truck Fell into a Vault on Water Street

On May 12, 1943, *The Evening Telegram* reported:

A truck belonging to a construction contractor hauling a heavy load of reinforcing from along Water Street about ten o'clock this morning caused a section of the paving opposite James Baird Ltd. to collapse. The left rear wheel of the truck went down to the axle and the load of iron had to be shifted to another vehicle before the truck could be taken out of the hole.

The cave-in occurred close to the curb and over the site of one of the old brick vaults which were built along

this section of the street nearly one hundred years ago
and went out of use after the fire 1892.

107. First Arrival of Air Service at Torbay Airport

Under low-lying clouds, but with the airport at Torbay brilliant in the late afternoon sunshine, the first Trans-Canada Air-
lines (TCA) flight, on a regular passenger and air mail service,
arrived at 4:15 p.m. on May 1, 1942. The plane was discerned
by onlookers for a few minutes before coming in to land from a
westerly direction. Shortly afterwards, it made a perfect landing.

Immediately on coming to a standstill in front of the TCA
office, the passengers, five in total, disembarked. They were Canadian Army nurses E. Baker and E. Buffett; Sergeant F. B. Cahill,
RCAF and Messrs' J.L. and J.P. Courtney. The first to emerge was
stewardess Dorothy Reid of Sydney, N.S., who looked smart in a
navy blue jacket and skirt, the uniform of TCA stewardess. Next
were co-pilots captains Terrice and Fowler. Harvey & Co were
local agents for TCA. The plane, a twin engine Lockheed Lode-
star, had a top speed 265 miles per hour and a cruising speed of
200 mph. It had a capacity for twelve passengers.

108. Amazing Newfoundland Fisherwomen

Newfoundland Governor Sir Erasmus Gower was impressed
by the hard-working Newfoundland women. These women
worked side-by-side with the men in the fishery during the
nineteenth century, and were not even deterred from their ex-
hausting work by pregnancy. In fact, when women joined their
husbands in the fishery, they even took along midwives.

This practice of family participation gave our first settlers
an advantage over the fishing captains, who pursued the Grand
Bank fishery and had to pay wages to hire men to cure and
prepare fish for market. Although the men did the fishing, the

women and children formed a shore gang and split, salted and cured the fish as part of their daily routine.

During the early nineteenth century, families often left their homes to go to the French Shore to fish. Governor Gower noted, "The activity of these industrious people is so great that the women, even in advanced pregnancy, rather than stay at home, take midwives with them on this expedition."

109. Sir John Crosbie Battled Unions

G'way Back, Johnny!" was a poem written by a longshoreman during an LSPU (Longshoremen's Protective Union) strike in St. John's during September, 1911. It was directed at Sir John Crosbie, owner of the Newfoundland Produce Company.

Over 500 longshoremen held an emergency meeting to discuss an ongoing strike at Crosbie's company. *The Evening Telegram*'s account of that meeting noted, "The Union men say that though they may not be able to stop the work at Crosbie's wharf, still they will prevent shipping for him at all other wharves. They will refuse to handle any freight of the Newfoundland Produce Company boats." The Union sent out circulars to all city merchants warning them that they would not handle any freight for Crosbie's.

A few days later on September 15th the poem "G'way Back, Johnny!" appeared in *The Evening Telegram* under the pseudonym 'En Quad':

"G'way Back, Johnny"

G'way back an sit down, Johnny.
You an' others had yer day!
There will be Unions in dis city
When yer cold and laid away.
Let me tell yer, Mistah Johnny,

(An I'm telling you what's true)
You struck a snag now, fer certin,
In the LSPU.

You ain't got the pull, Mistah Johnny,
To knock us under in dis fight.
You can't twist an' turn till doomsday
An' you can't prove wrong is right.
Easy 'nough fer you to holler,
An' tell folks what YOU will do,
But I'm bankin' my last dollar
On the LSPU.

So quit yer cussedness, Mistah Johnny,
'Tain't no use to shout and rage,
We are out fer fair play merely,
Askin' only a livin' wage.
We've right an' numbers wid us Johnny,
(Excuse me, please, fer tellin' you)
Western Bay pranks ain't one bit popular

- Wid de L.S.P.U.

The strike was settled shortly after, and afterwards the LSPU became a dominant force in St. John's for over half a century.

110. It's The Truth

George Summers was castigated at a city council meeting during March, 1938, and he didn't take the attack lying down. He hired one of the most brilliant lawyers in St. John's and met council head on in the Council Chambers.

The incident began during the weekly meeting of city council when Councillor Meaney accused Summers of exploiting workers by underpaying them and by failing to meet the conditions of a snow clearing contract with the city.

St. John's had been paralysed after a major snowfall early in March. Summers offered to provide snow clearing on Duckworth Street, New Gower Street and Water Street for eleven hundred dollars. City council appealed to the Commission of Government to pay the ($1,200) snow clearing contract. The Commission agreed to pay half the cost, and the city ended up with a commitment of $600 rather than $550 dollars.

When Summers offered to hire an extra forty men to shovel snow for an additional $100 the city agreed. It was during the Depression, and council, to its credit, never missed a chance to hire labourers when financial resources were available. However, when it came time to pay Mr. Summers, Councillor Meaney stood-up in council and demanded that $200 be held back because he had evidence that Summers had not fulfilled the conditions of the contract.

He then went on to castigate Summers. Meaney accused the contractor of exploiting the workers and not paying them according to commitments in the contract with the city. He said he had evidence that Summers had paid the shovelers working on Duckworth and New Gower streets twenty-five cents per hour, while those on the Water Street detail received only fourteen cents per hour. Councillor Meaney added that he had gotten many complaints that Water Street had not been properly cleared. Having maligned the character of Mr. Summers, Councillor Meaney said he would gladly apologize if it turned out he had been wrong.

George Summers was outraged. He asked, and was given permission, to appear before council with his lawyer. It was customary in those days for citizens to be allowed to appeal directly to council and to appear in person to plead their case. Summers, however, sat quietly while his lawyer presented his case.

The lawyer held a copy of the contract in his hand, and asked council to read it carefully. It was not a lengthy document. The lawyer noted that the contract mentioned that workers on the Duckworth Street and New Gower Street detail be paid twenty-five cents per hour. But it did not mention any figure for those working on Water Street. He said these workers were made aware before they started that their pay would be fourteen cents per hour. In respect to the uncompleted work on Water Street, the lawyer pointed out that there had been a snowfall after the contract was signed and George Summers was not libel for this. Council agreed and unanimously voted to release the full payment to the contractor.

The lawyer that day was later elected to city council; the House of Assembly and served as chief justice of the Supreme Court in Newfoundland. His name – Jimmy Higgins. It's the truth.

111. First Use of a Helicopter in a Rescue Mission

History's first recorded use of a helicopter rescue took place in Labrador during April, 1945. It remains among the most thrilling and spectacular rescues in the entire history of helicopters.

In that month, an R.C.M.P Canso carrying a nine-man crew left Mingan on the Gulf of St. Lawrence for Goose Bay, Labrador. While in flight, a light snowfall changed to freezing rain and began icing-up things, which forced the pilot to drop the plane to a lower altitude. The poor weather continued, and the situation worsened. The ice got into the carburetor causing one of the two engines to stall.

Adding to the crisis was the fact that nobody on board had any idea where they were. This left the pilot with only two choices: crash land into the forest below or continue, and crash head-on into a mountain coming up fast in the distance.

The pilot opted to crash land among the forest below and instructed fellow crew members to brace themselves for a rough landing. The plane struck the trees and skimmed along several hundred feet before coming to a stop. Although the plane was wrecked, the crew had survived. The captain, conscious of the danger presented by the fuel tanks of the plane, quickly organized an operation to remove survival supplies from the wreck.

They successfully gathered three cases of Bendolee kits which contained: two chocolate bars, eight small biscuits, gum, matches, fishing tackle, needles, thread, adhesive, plaster, morphine capsules, eye ointment and bandages. The men also removed blankets, parachutes, flares and a pistol.

They managed to get away from the burning plane just before it exploded, sending fifty-foot high flames into the air. Fortunately, only two men were injured and there was no loss of life. Yet, the prospects for survival seemed bleak.

When the plane failed to arrive in Goose Bay, an extensive search was undertaken by the North Atlantic Command. Meanwhile, at the crash site, the men were rationing supplies. Each person was allowed one chocolate bar and four small biscuits a day. To protect themselves from weather, they constructed a lean-to made from boughs and covered by their parachutes. After using up all their flares, they lit fires and used boughs to spell out SOS in the snow.

To increase their chances of being rescued, three men volunteered to walk to Goose Bay to seek help. They thought they were ninety miles from the base but were actually 150 miles. Captain A.C. Smith, the pilot, wrote in his diary, "Sent three men to hike to Goose Bay. They carried rations for about four days. God help them and me if they don't make it by then."

About four miles into their trek, the volunteers were spotted by two C-54s which used a heliograph mirror to locate them. The spotter crafts circled before dropping emergency food, parkas, blankets etc. and then radioed their position to Goose Bay.

The trio used tree boughs as brushes to make an arrow in the snow, pointing in the direction of the wreck where their six injured friends remained. The C-54s wasted little time in getting to the area and were able to drop emergency supplies for them. However, the terrain was not suitable to make any rescue attempt, so they notified Goose Bay Airport of the location of the crash site and returned to base.

At this point, circumstances became more complicated making the actual rescue of the men far more difficult, and creating the situation in which Labrador became the first place in the world where a helicopter was used for a rescue mission. Goose Bay sent two ski-planes into the interior to bring the victims out. Upon landing on a lake near the site, the two planes collided, injuring two men in the mishap. Repairs could only be made to one of the planes, which meant that two men had to be left behind. Since a blizzard was fast approaching the area, a C-54 rushed in to drop more emergency supplies for the stranded men.

As predicted, a terrible blizzard struck forcing the suspension of all rescue efforts. The blizzard lasted two days. When the storm ended, two ski-planes piloted by captains Avent and Herr succeeded in landing on a lake near the survivors.[4] However, once again, efforts to complete a rescue were hampered. The sun had caused snow to melt, thus creating slush on the lake making a take-off impossible. The airmen relied on ingenuity in an attempt to overcome the problem. They cut some trees and used the logs to build a rugged runway in the slush.

They managed to get their own crews out. Authorities then turned to using dogs and snowmobiles, but these were useless during the early spring when the ice covered lakes and streams were beginning to open up.

Help was now sought from a veteran Arctic explorer, Lieutenant-Colonel Norman Vaughan, who was commander of the

[4] Lakes Avent and Herr in Labrador are named after the captains in honour of their deeds.

Rescue Centre of the American based centre North Atlantic Command at New Hampshire.

Vaughan came up with a rescue plan that would involve a helicopter — never before used — under Arctic conditions. One was available in New York and it was disassembled and packed into a C-54 Skymaster and flown to Goose Bay where it was re-assembled.

Meanwhile, back at the crash site, the stranded men battled to survive. They had moved into a ten-foot deep snow cave and ate roasted spruce hen and porcupine stew. Morale zoomed when they were informed that a helicopter was coming to their rescue. Two Canadian planes placed the helicopter on an isolated radio range station 150 miles from Goose Bay. The helicopter travelled at a speed of fifty miles per hour and was christened the *Flutter Buggy* by rescuers.

The rescue team made arrangements from the radio range to complete their rescue mission. When the RCAF dropped supplies of gasoline, most of it leaked out before the rescue group were able to retrieve it. Undaunted, they dug up a cache from six feet under the snow and strained it to use in the helicopter. That evening, *Flutter Buggy* flew the thirty-five miles to Lake Herr where the survivors whistled and cheered as it set down on the lake.

The helicopter had a capacity to carry only 500 pounds and could only take out one man at a time. Each trip took one and a half hours. With nightfall upon them, they ceased operations and the next morning were frustrated by a frozen engine. Captain Avent came to their rescue and flew over the area dropping a heater which they used to unthaw the motor. By 2:00 p.m. that day, four more men had been taken out.

The pilot later described his efforts:

I had my problems. We were at 2,000 feet altitude at ground level and the helicopter was not designed for efficient take-offs at high altitudes. I had to take jump take-offs but in the end it worked out. I don't think he – commanding officer – expected me to come back and pick him up. He chose to be last out because he felt that as commanding officer he should stay until everyone was rescued.

From the radio range, the eleven rescued men were flown by ski-plane to Goose Bay and examined at the RCAF hospital. There were no serious injuries. The *Flutter Buggy* was disassembled and sent back to New York having demonstrated the usefulness of the helicopter under difficult Arctic conditions.

Part 7

112. World's Smallest Case

A mechanical genius named Peter Bennett of London earned world recognition for constructing the smallest case in the world. He was summoned before Queen Victoria to demonstrate his inventions and devices, and among the items he presented was a sail needle. There was nothing remarkable about this needle, at least not at first glance, but Queen Victoria was greatly amused when Bennett opened the needle to demonstrate that it was actually a case containing three smaller needles.

Newfoundland's connection with this man is that he left England and settled in Burin where he opened a blacksmith operation. Bennett passed away in 1910 and is buried in a Burin cemetery.

113. Heir to Fortune Drowns in the Harbour

While Newfoundlanders were preparing to become Canada's tenth province, a St. John's man disappeared. Police were informed and his friends and relatives were questioned in an effort to find out what may have happened to him. Thirty days after he was reported missing, the man was found floating face down in St. John's Harbour.

Although the death was determined an accidental drowning, circumstances of the man's life caused one to wonder if foul play was involved. The man, Frank Viquers, was one of fourteen possible heirs to the multi-million dollar Garrett Estate in Pennsylvania, United States. Eleven of the heirs were Newfoundlanders. The Garrett Estate represented the fortune left by Walter Garrett and his wife who had no children. Walter made his millions from tobacco and snuff production and distribution. During World War II, the administrator of the Garrett Estate invested $15 million in Victory Bonds at three-and-a-half percent interest. By 1946, the estate had grown to $33 million.

When news of the unclaimed wealth made international news, 20,000 people claimed to be the heirs. However, legal advisers employed by the estate reduced that number to fourteen legitimate claimants; eleven of these Newfoundlanders.

Frank Viquers had been aware of the estate for more than ten years. He quietly pieced together a family history to establish his claim to the Garrett Estate. His efforts brought him in contact with Mrs. Henry Nelson of San Diego, California who became one of the fourteen acknowledged claimants. Together they shared information.

No doubt the eleven Newfoundlanders who had a chance of sharing in the fortune were relatives of Viquers in this province. Mr. Viquers had traced his family tree back to 1607. In that year, Edward and Elizabeth Garrett, of Abbott Skerwell of Devonshire, England, were the founders of the Garrett wealth. Their daughter Anne Garrett came to Newfoundland and settled in a cottage overlooking Quidi Vidi Lake. The rest of the family moved to Philadelphia. Anne Garrett married into the Ruby family, who in turn married into the Viquers family. In 1946, these families were the Garrett heirs living in Newfoundland. Frank had been making the case on their behalf.

Walter Garrett, who belonged to the Philadelphia side of the family, passed away in 1895, leaving his fortune to his wife who was of German descent. She died at age eighty-four with no heirs. The multi-million dollar fortune then reverted back to the Garrett side of the family.

Frank Viquers had lawyers in St. John's and Philadelphia advocating on behalf of the Newfoundland claimants to the estate. In 1947, the estate was being administered by the Orphan's Court in Philadelphia. However, before the matter was concluded, Viquers drowned in St. John's Harbour. There were certainly no suggestions of foul play at the time. The family accepted the explanation that Frank, who wore very thick glasses because of vision problems, likely had fallen over the Long John Bridge in the west end of St. John's while crossing to visit a brother on the south side.

114. The Lie that Saved St. John's

A deliberate lie told by a quick thinking fisherman once saved the city of St. John's from being attacked by the French Navy. This unusual episode in Newfoundland history is recorded in the papers of Governor Sir James Wallace.

It was 1776 and the revolutionists were in control of France, and St. John's was rapidly developing into a strategically important point. During this period, a large French fleet under the command of Admiral Ritcey appeared outside the Narrows at St. John's. The town was poorly protected, and certainly not capable of repelling the French forces if they decided to attack. Its only defence were 600 soldiers, three war vessels, and a boom and chain placed across the Narrows.

One advantage St. John's had was that the French had no idea as to whether or not the town had strong defences. Rather than risk a major military confrontation, the French admiral decided to attack Bay Bulls and extract military intelligence regarding St. John's defences. This was easily achieved. One prisoner was quite willing to co-operate and was taken on board the French ship the *Jupiter* for questioning.

He gained the confidence of the French officers by providing them with an accurate description of the land route to St. John's but added details of hardships and hazards that the French found discouraging. As the interrogation continued, the man told them that there were 5,000 soldiers guarding St. John's and there were 200 cannons guarding the harbour.

The French admiral carefully considered the intelligence gathered and decided that he would not risk attacking St. John's. When Governor Wallace was informed of the story the "liar" told he was delighted and told and retold the story for years after.

115. No Molasses? Let them Drink Rum!

Molasses was cheap and a common item in the working-class homes of pre-Confederation Newfoundland. However, in 1948, when the Commission of Government announced it would be bringing rum instead of molasses from the West Indies, the public questioned how they would get their supplies of molasses. People used molasses as sugar in those days to sweeten tea and for baking. It was far more essential in working-class households than rum.

Johnny Jones never achieved the fame of Johnny Burke or Burke's sidekick, Jimmy Murphy, as poet and writer but he was well-known around old St. John's from the 1940s to the 1960s for his songs and verses about the interests of the day. He wrote about wakes, the 24th of May, Christmas, Confederation, political issues and many other categories. His verses usually had a humorous twist and were popular, particularly throughout St. John's. Johnny had them printed and neighbourhood kids sold them along Water Street, Duckworth Street, and to households door-to-door. Two of his most memorable songs were "The Molasses Problem" and "The Liquor Book Song."

"The Molasses Problem"

I'm a lover of molasses,
I have always used it free;
The shortage of that precious stuff
Means quite a lot to me.
And judging from an item
In your paper, sir, I think
If yours truly wants molasses
Then it's screech I'll have to drink.

It may, or may not, sweeten
My coffee or my tea,
As yet I haven't tested it,
I'll try it out and see.
I've tried sweetin' it with Karo
It put it on the bum,
I'm getting me a permit now
And try it out with rum

Now everybody everywhere,
North, South, East and West;
Knows that it is by trying
Men have produced the best.
Who knows perhaps a drop of stuff
Put in a cup of tea;
Will solve our lassy problem
Let's try it out and see.

"The Liquor Book Song" did not become popular throughout
Newfoundland until after his death. The song was about a practice
of the 1940s and 1950s that restricted the sale of alcohol only
to those who possessed a liquor book, which was available from

the Board of Liquor Control. Liquor sales were restricted to two
bottles per week to customers with a liquor book.

"The Liquor Book Song"
(tune "Kelligrews Soiree")

After workin' all the live long year there finally comes a day
My two weeks summer holidays and a trip around the bay
And Kickin' off my overalls I marched out in my glee
Determined to get a bottle of screech to take along with me.
There were people there from everywhere Grand Falls
and Corner Brook
From Joe Batt's Arm and Billy's farm all waitin' for their book
From Greenland's icy waters and Tex's kitty brook
All waitin' tired and thirsty to get their liquor book

There were young men with curly hair and old men
with bald heads
And pretty little maidens, old maids with wooden legs
Old men with whiskers on their chin who gave an awful look
And their whiskers they grew longer as they waited
for their book
Well along came a policeman and he lines us up in twos
He had a billy in his hand so none of us refused
How much longer must we wait said one man to the cop,
He laughed and said, I guess you'll be too old to take a drop.

An old man looked like Noah hung down his weary head
He said, my God I'll have to send my grandson here instead
I saw service in the Boar War but little did I think
I'd spend my last days tryin' to get a book to get a drink
Well after waitin' two long weeks goodness know I tried
With half a dollar in my hand I finally got inside
And walkin' to the wicket along with many more

Such names and occupations I never heard before.
There were tradesmen and mechanics, McIsaacs and McInns
A couple of men of eighty years who said that they were twins
Gravediggers and undertakers, dishwashers, stewards and cooks
Wooden legs and glass eye makers all waitin' for their books.
Too late to go around the bay my book I finally got
So I bought myself a bottle of screech and drank the whole darn lot
I passed out just like a light unto the world I seen
Boy o boy while I was out what a terrible dream I dreamed

I saw Adam eat the apple and Matthew chasin' Mark
Noah with the scrubbin' bucket scrubbin' up the Ark
King Solomon tryin' to court his wives and Abel chaisin' Cain
So is there any wonder why I'll never drink again.

"The Liquor Book Song" was published in a song book to commemorate the 1977 Canada Games entitled, *The Newfoundland Song Book*. Jones is believed to have written other songs that have found their way into Newfoundland song collections for which he was not credited. There is a file at the City of St. John's Archives that contains a collection of a dozen or more songs by Johnny Jones.

116. Strange Occurrences at Belvedere Cemetery, St. John's

Jack Adams and Jack Walsh, both employed for more than twenty years with CBC television in St. John's, often told of a strange incident they witnessed one morning at Belvedere Cemetery, St. John's. It was about 5:30 a.m. on a bright sunny June morning when the two were driving along Newtown Road on their way to work.

As they approached the Belvedere Cemetery, they were amazed to see a hearse moving in their direction take a left turn and go into the cemetery. They had seen many funerals in their lifetime but this one had an uncanny feeling. It wasn't the ordinary motor-driven hearse used in today's funerals; but a horse-drawn carriage with a driver in silks and high hat and a black whip in one hand. There was no procession following the hearse as is customary in funerals.

The duo slowly passed the open gate with their eyes glued to the hearse as it moved slowly down the cemetery path. When it stopped just past mid-way, Jack and his friend decided to pull onto the side of the road and watch what was happening. At first they thought that a theatre group in the city may be putting together some kind of film. They exited the vehicle and walked to the gate. In the few seconds it took to park and walk the few feet to the open gate the black hearse had disappeared.

The two men searched all over the cemetery, but they could not find the any sign of the hearse.

They returned to their car and continued on to work totally baffled and amazed by what they had seen.

117. Haunting Near Feildian Grounds

During the mid-nineteenth century in old St. John's, claims that the spirit of a soldier on horseback haunted the bridge at Pringledale were in abundance. Pringdale was a meadow area which is now occupied by Feildian Grounds, Pringle Place and part of Rennie's Mill Road. The claim was that at night the spirit of a man murdered at Pringdale was seen by residents returning to town at night from a day in the country. The ghostly apparition was of a man in military uniform, mounted on a black stallion with blood pouring from a wound in his chest.

Stories of this nature were common for the time. However, they usually were inspired by a true event and told and re-told until they became part of the city's colourful folklore. The ghost of Pringldale had its origins in a real life drama, which unfolded in 1826 at the location and resulted in the death of a British soldier from Fort Townshend.

On March 30, 1826, a duel to the death was fought at Pringledale between two soldiers from the Garrison at Fort Townshend. Captain Mark Rudkin, a twenty-two-year veteran of the Royal Newfoundland Veteran Company and Ensign J. Philpot, known for his mean disposition, became involved in a dispute over a card game the night before at Fort Townshend.

Ensign Philpot insulted Rudkin and kicked him in the rear end as the captain left the game in disgust over Ensign's behaviour. Humiliated by young Philpot, Captain Rudkin demanded an apology, or else satisfaction would be sought in the gentlemen's way, meaning a duel. Philpot refused to apologize and on March 30th the duel at Pringledale took place.

City historian, Paul O'Neill noted in his writings that Philpot's horse shied three times before crossing the bridge at Rennie's River on the morning of the duel. Perhaps an omen of what was to happen that day.

Captain Rudkin, an expert marksman, sought only to frighten Philpot and teach him a lesson. He got off the first shot but deliberately missed his target. Philpot also missed his target but not deliberately. His intention to fight to the death was obvious by his behaviour at the duel. Prior to the duel, Ensign removed his flannel waistcoat and shirt to reduce chances of the flannel entering any wounds he might receive. He wore only a linen shirt and trousers while Captain Rudkin was dressed in full military uniform.

Rudkin was prepared to stop the duel after the first round if the young Ensign would apologize. However, Philpot flatly refused and a second round of duelling took place. This time both guns fired simultaneously, but Philpot completely missed his target. Rudkin did not. He placed a bullet straight into the heart of Ensign Philpot, who died instantly.

Although Rudkin was tried for murder, he was acquitted. Members of the jury included Tom Brookings, one of the founders of the Royal St. John's Regatta, and Benjamin Bowring, founder of Bowring Brothers Ltd.

118. Smallwood Family Tree

Joseph R. Smallwood, who led Newfoundland into Confederation with Canada, became the province's first premier and put an end to the 'Merchant Truck System,' had an interesting family tree. It is one that traces his blood-relatives back to some very interesting people: Mrs. Wilfred Pickering, owner of Green Gables, Prince Edward Island; C.W. Smallwood, inventor of the potato digger; Jim Smallwood, inventor of a shingle machine; J.C. Stead, who invented the Stead Circulating Generator for steam boilers; D.F. Blake, mayor of High River, Alberta; Honourable Donald Farquharson, premier of Prince Edward Island 1898-1901; John Lawson, editor, *Chicago Herald* and Henry B. McLean, originator of the McLean system of writing.

119. Beothuks Knew of Christianity

As early as 1715, the Beothuks in Newfoundland exhibited a knowledge and respect for Christianity. Evidence of this is found in Mark Young's experience in Twillingate that year.

Traditionally, March was referred to by Newfoundlanders as "The hungry month of March" because by then the population was running out of their winter supplies of food, which had been stored the previous fall. Mark Young was unable to store sufficient supplies in the fall because the Beothuks destroyed nearly half of his small potato patch, and an early frost took its toll on the other vegetables. Adding to Young's hardship was the fact that wild game was scarce.

A little before dawn on Christmas Eve, Mark was tramping the woods on snowshoes setting rabbit slips. The noises caused by the wind whispering through the woods may have made a less experienced hunter nervous, but Mark was used to searching the woods alone.

The sounds he had been accustomed to hearing were suddenly interrupted by a faint moaning. It was unusual enough for Mark to come to a complete stop. His mind raced to match the sound with one more familiar to him. Perhaps it was a caribou caught in some Indian trap, he thought. He moved cautiously in the direction of the sound. An arm protruding from a bank of snow caused him to pick up his speed until he reached the distressed person. It was an injured Beothuk youth.

Fearful at first of some Indian trick, Mark prepared his gun for firing. Upon closer examination of the scene, he realized the young man was perishing in the snowbank. The race of this victim was of no consequence to Mark Young, who moved quickly to free him from the snow, and then hoisted the almost lifeless body onto his back.

He brought the boy to his cabin and covered him with deer skins to keep him warm, and then lit the fireplace. Mark prepared some hot venison soup and managed to get a few spoonfuls between the boys purple lips. The young Beothuk slipped into a peaceful sleep.

When darkness fell, Mark went outside to his wood-pile to gather wood for the evening. Suddenly, three Beothuks who had been hiding nearby jumped him and took him prisoner. They bound his arms and feet and carried him into the cabin.

As they searched for things to steal, their commotion woke the boy who started to cry. With a shout of joy, one of the Indians threw his arms around the boy, who was his son.

Mark couldn't understand a word the Beothuks were saying, but the reunion was full of much joyful excitement. On a table next to the boy was a drawing of Christ in the manger. One of the Indians pointed to it saying, "Kismas" several times. They then replaced the things they had stolen and cut Mark free.

155

Bowing low as they left the cabin, each Indian said to Mark Young, "Kismas" and "good man."

Mark Young survived that harsh winter and lived to tell and retell his story to family and friends who preserved it as part of their legacy to future generations.

120. The War-like Side of Beothuks

Sir Joseph Banks, who was a world famous botanist of the nineteenth century, described an experience he encountered in Newfoundland involving the Beothuks. During his stay, he noted in his diary that he had viewed the face and scalp of a man which had been taken off by Beothuks.

The victim's last name was Frye. While swimming to his boat, Frye was attacked and killed by the Indians who used bow and arrows as weapons. After killing the man, the Indians not only scalped him but cut off his face, as well. Banks noted they had skinned the man's face right down to his upper lip. They dropped the scalp and face while being pursued by Newfoundland settlers.

According to Banks, the Beothuk population at that time was approximately 500, and they were continually at war with the white population. Sometimes the white men plundered Indian camps and stole their belongings, which often included a mixture similar to mortar made with eggs and deer's hair.

The white settlers were not the only threat to the Beothuks. In 1809, Governor Duckworth reported that the Micmacs were coming over from Nova Scotia and the Beothuks, who dreaded them, were moving to the interior. Duckworth issued a warning to the Micmacs that the penalty for killing a Beothuk was hanging, which was the same law applied in all murder cases.

Almost sixty years after the Beothuks encounter with Mark Young, the following incident occurred: A shipmaster and crew at Exploits constructed a fort at the mouth of the Exploits River.

Beothuks living in the area became curious about the fortress and came within a few hundred yards to view it.

Scott led several unarmed volunteers to bring gifts out to the Indians as a gesture of friendship. The Indians stood their ground as Scott stepped forward and extended his hand as a sign of welcome. The response from the Beothuks was quick and deadly. One of them put his arm around Scott's neck, while another plunged a knife into his back.

This response was the signal for a bow and arrow attack upon the defenseless volunteers. Five of them were killed, and the others ran safely to the fort. They took one of the bodies with the arrows still in it to authorities in St. John's. The survivors were buried on the hill overlooking Little Harbour not far from where John Peyton, who had taken Shandithit into his house as a servant, is buried.

121. The Wood Haul More Popular than the Regatta

The greatest annual event in the city of St. John's during the mid-nineteenth century was the annual "Wood Haul," which was an event that collected firewood for the Catholic Cathedral and the Presentation Convent. These events were accompanied by great demonstrations of public spirit involving people from all denominations in the city. Prominent among the wood haulers were the great sealing skippers and their crews.

In addition to providing the needed wood supplies, this annual event, which was held just before the sealers went out to the ice, served to keep the peace during the period when men were coming to St. John's from all over to find work on a sealing vessel.

A condition for the haul was that only large spruce trees would be accepted. Most participants took their dogs and sleds, three or four men to each team, and headed for the country. After gathering enough wood to fill the great drays they began the loading. The drays were made of eight-inch square timber with three runners bolted together with cross bars, sufficient to stand the weight of 1,800 to 2,000 sticks.

Three guys of strong rope were pulled by twenty-five men on each side, who were picked because they knew how to prevent loads from toppling over. Each side was equipped with a large steering stick, which was operated by seven or eight trained men to guide the huge mass of wood along the line of road. When all was in readiness, the order to man the ropes was thundered out accompanied by the loud cheering of spectators. Then off they went led by the popular Bennett's Brass Band, which provided a variety of good old-time music and shanty songs. In describing the mood of the competitors, the popular phrase used was, "They neither knew nor cared for any other."

When all participants arrived at the Cathedral grounds, each crew unloaded and stored its cargo of wood. When this was completed, they collected the hawser's chains and ropes and returned them to their owners.

At the end of the day, the men gathered in hotels or, in some cases, the homes of famous sealing masters, for refreshments and the inevitable argument over who had the largest load.

122. Interesting Facts

Newfoundland's First Newspaper

The Royal Gazette, Newfoundland's first newspaper, was first published on August 27, 1801 by John Ryan. In its first five years of operation it was located on the west side of Rennie's River near the bridge. From there it moved to Duckworth Street, three doors east of King's Road. In 1842, its office and plant moved to the O'Dwyer property which was also on Duckworth Street.

Escaping the Press Gang

A young man named Adam Ross drowned in St. John's Harbour during an effort to escape the dreaded British press gang. He was the chief mate on the brig *Swiftsure*. Ross and eleven other members of the crew jumped into the harbour to avoid being taken by the press gang. These units often combed the city to force young men into serving in the British Navy.

Champion Seal Skinner

The all-time seal skinning champion of Newfoundland is Thomas Buckley, who, in 1844, skinned 637 pelts a day for an entire week.

Buckley could also skin a seal as easily with his left hand as he could with his right. In those days, sealers were paid six cents per pelt, from which he had to pay for his berth on the merchant-owned boat.

123. The Strongest Man in Newfoundland

Jim Chant of Elliston, Trinity Bay, ranks among the strongest men in Newfoundland history. He amazed the population in his community when, after pulling a tree stump out of the ground with his bare hands, he lifted two filled pork barrels.

His many feats of lifting outrageously heavy items caused him to develop a crook in the centre of his back, where he would nestle heavy objects. For amusement, he frequently bent six-inch nails into staples, which others would try unsuccessfully to straighten out.

His most famous demonstration of strength was when he hauled the anchor of a sealing vessel out of the water.

124. Achievement Staggered Humanity

That's just how writer Paul Druger described Guglielmo Marconi's successful experiment in St. John's on Signal Hill on December 14, 1901. *The Evening Telegram*, on December 16, 1901, described Marconi as, "The most celebrated man in the world." Why? Because:

Marconi has spoken to a man 1,900 miles away with no other medium than what existed on the morning that Noah came out of the Ark. Nature grudgingly gave out the great secrets but bit by bit, Marconi made the bold venture and subdued the hidden secrets of Dame Nature to obey his own will. The very thought of it sets one aghast. The humble genius who received *The Telegram* reporter at the Cochrane Hotel makes no vain-glorious boast about what he has achieved. He is as modest as a schoolboy, and one would not think he was the wizard who wrought this awe-inspiring wonder of science, that one realizes the tales of the Arabian Nights and the stories of Jules Verne.

It is no wonder that New York stood astounded and re-fused to believe the news when it was flashed over the wires on Saturday night. Newspapers were skeptical and before sending the report to their printers, wired for con-firmation of the news. The citizens of St. John's even doubt-ed the truth of it. They had cast an occasional glance up at Signal Hill the past few days while the experiments were going on. They had seen electrically charged kites whirling in the storm tossed air over Signal Hill now and then, but did not attract much importance to the matter. They knew that Marconi was making experiments, but up to Saturday had failed. This was not the case, for he had succeeded in getting from Lizard Point, Cornwall, the letter S (...) of the Morse code distinctly at 11:30 on Wednesday, twenty-five different times, and the same success was expected on Thursday.[1]

---

[1]*Winds of History, Notable Events of Newfoundland,* William Collins, Creative Publishers 1995.

Part 8

Spooks and Spectres of Christmas

When the window pane rattles in the night, are you sure it's just the wind? Maybe it's a long lost soul attempting to manifest its presence. While walking alone along one of the old St. John's streets late at night, have you ever had the eerie feeling of being watched? Have you heard the sound of crunching snow behind you, as though someone is following you? Was it just your imagination? Or could it be a real ghost haunting the area it once inhabited as a mortal being? Who really knows?

Christmas is a fitting time to tell tales of wandering spooks and spectres. Yuletide family gatherings, in the glow of a fireplace or Christmas tree lights, make the ideal setting for tales of the supernatural.

Christmas is no doubt a wonderful time for stories because it is one of those rare occasions when families get together to relax and celebrate. No doubt, any evening of haunting tales will always conclude with questions like, "Do you believe in ghosts?" Regardless of the answer, everyone seems to enjoy a good tale of the supernatural, especially when the setting is right. Most of this city's best stories come from the nineteenth century. Over the years, they have been used to entertain and also motivate younger children to return home at a decent hour, especially on those cold wintery nights that lend themselves so readily to storytelling and in the belief of the mystical.

Most ghost stories have a spark of truth in them. The people may be real, the life experiences may be real, as in the case of Nancy Coyle, and occasionally things happen that just cannot be explained.

125. Nancy Coyle, the "Queen of the Dead"

A hundred years ago, everyone in town knew the story of Nancy Coyle, the "Queen of The Dead." Nancy lived in a cottage at the corner of Queen's Road and Carter's Hill, and some whispered she was in league with the Devil. It's not surprising then that after her death, ghostly stories of Nancy Coyle circulated and spread fear amongst the residents of the city.

The townsfolk cringed upon hearing the name Nancy Coyle. She was an unusual woman with an unusual occupation, which earned her the title of "Queen of the Dead" and inspired bizarre stories about her; some claiming she could bring the dead back to life.

During the 1840s, Nancy lived in a cottage surrounded by a beautiful garden, located on the eastern corner of Carter's Hill and Queen's Road. During this period in St. John's history, the city did not have a morgue. The government contracted Nancy Coyle to look after the unidentified and unclaimed dead, in addition to foreign seamen, who died while in port.

A horse-drawn, spring-less cart, which served as an ambulance from the hospital at Victoria Park (then Riverhead), was also used to carry the dead. This wagon was frequently seen coming and going from Coyle's picturesque cottage. Nancy's job was to clean and dress the corpses and to place them in a coffin for burial.

On several occasions, incidents happened in the home which contributed to Nancy becoming a legendary figure in old St. John's for half a century. On at least one occasion, a man who had been prepared and was being nailed into a coffin, moved and made moaning sounds. Nancy poured him a drink of rum which revived him.

On several other occasions, people thought to be dead sat up while being prepared for burial. When these stories became known among the local population, it was claimed in whispered tones that Nancy was the "Queen of the Dead." By the turn of the century, parents would tell their children stories of the "Queen of the Dead," sometimes described as a witch who brought the dead back to life. Children were told to avoid the area of Nancy Coyle's old residence.

The original residence was destroyed by fire and replaced with a new home, which was torn down during the urban renewal of the 1960s.

126. Funeral Procession Apparition

The city abounded with tales of the supernatural. This sometimes included the spectre of a phantom scene into the life of a person or persons long departed, as in the case of the Duckworth Street funeral procession. Around the same time that stories of the "Queen of the Dead" were sending chills up the spine of townsfolk, there were stories of a funeral procession apparition travelling along Duckworth Street, near the court house, also circulating.

A couple, who were out for a quiet walk in the crisp air night during Christmas of 1898, heard the sound of crunching snow behind them. Thinking it was a horse-drawn sleigh approaching, they moved in off the street and turned to have a look. To their astonishment, there was a hearse followed by a lady with her head bowed. The vision disappeared into thin air.

When the story was told, older folks remembered hearing tales of the same phantom-like apparition. It is believed it was an apparition of the funeral of Lieutenant Richard Lawry, who was murdered in 1794 by a bunch of Irish thugs in the vicinity of

163

Steers Cove. He was laid to rest in the old cemetery adjacent to the old Established Protestant Church on Church Hill. The lady behind the hearse was said to be the spirit of a girl named Molly, who met and fell in love with the young lieutenant. She was so distressed over his death that she drowned herself in the harbour.

127. The Gambler

A house near Signal Hill was believed to be haunted by a mean old man named Earl Cahill. Earl was known around town for his gambling and disrespect of the Sabbath. He is said to have lost his soul while gambling with the Devil, and was condemned to play cards with his diabolic adversary until Judgement Day.

128. The Ghost of Catherine Snow

The family who occupied a two-storey house at the lower end of Southside Road was forced out of their home by the ghost of a woman who was hanged in St. John's in 1804. The haunting started with the sound of windows rattling in the house. Nothing unusual in that, after all, the house overlooked the harbour and winds will cause windows to rattle. However, the windows rattled on nights when the sky was clear and the wind was calm.

In the downstairs kitchen, the family was haunted by the eerie sounds of footsteps walking above them, accompanied by the opening and closing of doors. As always, they would search each room only to find it empty and the sounds unexplained. Finally, a night came when the winds swept through the Narrows and a blinding snowstorm raged, but the windows did not rattle and the house was strangely quiet.

The family had gathered around the kitchen stove, when the sound of someone walking down the stairs was heard. An unsettling feeling gripped everyone in the room as the sound came closer and closer. Then the door, creaking as it slowly opened, revealed the haunting appearance of the spirit of a woman with the hangman's rope around her neck. This marked not only the end of the haunting, but one of the fastest departures from a residence ever made by any family from a house overtaken by the supernatural.

Neighbours witnessed the screaming and heard them vow never to return to the house, not even to get their belongings. That house remained vacant until it was eventually torn down years later.

The tragic history of the woman who once occupied the house might explain the source of the supernatural activities there. That very house was once occupied by Catherine Brown who, in 1804, was publically hanged in St. John's, for murdering her husband in the upstairs bedroom.

129. Murder on Military Road

At the turn of the nineteenth century, another ghost story told often around St. John's was based on a true event, which took place just east of the Roman Catholic Basilica on Military Road. Many people claimed to have witnessed a man being beaten by another man, but when approached the two figures completely disappeared.

The story was no doubt inspired by the murder which took place on Military Road on December 27, 1848. It was on that morning, the body of Kevin Wilson was found there covered in blood. Wilson had been killed from a blow to the head by a heavy object. Police were unable to solve the crime, and it remained a mystery for almost a year. Then a strange occurrence at sea solved the mystery. During August, 1849, the brigantine

Star set sail from St. John's with a new crew member on board, Isaac O'Neill. As the ship sailed along the coast, the captain noticed O'Neill's strange behaviour. He was depressed, avoided others, and said he had lost his appetite since the murder on Military Road the previous year.

Even though comforted by the captain, the murder of Wilson continued to weigh heavily on O'Neill's mind. While on watch the following night, he couldn't take it anymore and jumped overboard. Captain Bennett immediately launched a lifeboat, but O'Neill swam away from it. He turned, waved to his would-be rescuers and disappeared beneath the deep waters.

130. The Ghost of John Hearn

The story of old John Hearn's ghost was well-known throughout the city during the mid and late nineteenth centuries. Countless numbers of people claimed to have seen the body of Hearn swinging from the gallows where the eastern entrance to the Catholic Basilica stands today.

This story was inspired by a true event which took place in 1815. In that year, St. John's Harbour pilot, John Hearn, was convicted of the murder of his wife, Mary. The two quarrelled often because of her serious drinking problem.

During his trial, Hearn insisted he had not intended to kill his wife, and several neighbours swore he had treated her well. Hearn was found guilty and sentenced to be gibbeted (hanged in chains and left for days on public display). It must have lightened Hearn's heart when Governor Keats, after considering Hearn's request for an appeal of the sentence, advised him that he would remit the gibbeting portion of the sentence. Hearn was hanged from a scaffold on Military Road on September 22, 1815.

131. The Headless Man Dressed in Black

During the 1850s, children of the city were frightened by ghostly stories of the sightings of a headless man dressed in black in the area of the old Established Protestant Cemetery, adjacent to the Anglican Cathedral. The stories were inspired by the actual discovery, on July 10, 1846, of a man named George Raynes who was found in the graveyard with his throat cut. The mystery was never solved and the story embellished over subsequent years to include the beheading of Raynes in the graveyard.

132. Bute's Fortress and the Ghost of the Dead Servant

Bute's Fortress was a notable nineteenth century structure located near Long Pond, St. John's, in an area once known as the Sand Pits. It derived its name from the owner, Captain Bute, an officer of the English Garrison in St. John's.

The home was constructed to resemble a fortress and even had its own dungeon. Known for his cruelty, Bute frequently used it to discipline soldiers and servants.

An uncanny event occurred several nights after Bute imprisoned a servant in the dungeon. During a large party at the fortress, a terrible commotion interrupted the event. The sounds came from the dungeon. The terrified Bute remembered the helpless servant he had locked up below the fortress. With weapons drawn, Bute followed by several others rushed below to the dungeon. What they found startled them and caused guests to flee the building.

The servant lay dead in a corner of the dungeon. The expression on his face showed extreme terror and shock. Although Bute examined the area, he could find no explanation for either the commotion or the death. City people believed it was retribution heaped upon Bute by the soul of the dead servant.

133. Ghastly Happenings at the Foran Hotel

One of the many ghost stories from old St. John's involves the old Foran's Hotel, officially named the Atlantic Hotel. It was located on the site now occupied by the Sir Humphrey Gilbert Building on Duckworth Street.

The ghastly happenings started one cold, winter night when guests were awakened by a loud knocking sound that echoed throughout the entire building, from top to bottom. They were so spooked that they gathered in the hallways, puzzling over what was taking place. Two men left the group to conduct a search of the hotel in an effort to try and solve the mystery. They traced the sound to an upstairs room. Upon entering, the noise came to an abrupt stop. The men searched the room high and low but could not find any explanation.

Each evening, after the guests had settled down for the night, the knocking would resume, but it would always end when someone entered the vacant room. Word of the haunting noises spread throughout the city and was reported in the newspapers. It resulted in a loss of business for the hotel, as people began avoiding it. Eventually, the haunting faded away and customers began to return.

Six months later, a stranger registered. He was escorted to the haunted room by a staff member who found humour in the fact that they finally had a guest for the room. Adding to the stranger's visit was speculation among hotel staff and guests that the stranger was a hangman from Canada.

At midnight, a sudden thunderous knocking erupted and people rushed to the hallways. The noise was much louder than ever before and brought the hotel owner and manager to the scene. He went to the room and after calling to the occupant and not receiving a reply, he unlocked and open the door. The pounding stopped, but lying on the floor was the hangman with a terrifying expression on his face.

When the undertaker went into the room to remove the body, the knocking broke out again and lasted about a minute. The stranger was buried at the General Protestant Cemetery on Waterford Bridge Road, and the knocking in the hotel stopped forever. The hotel's owner was John Foran, a prominent member of the Royal St. John's Regatta Committee, who owned the boat the Placentia crew used to win the 1877 Fishermen's Race at Quidi Vidi. He was often called upon to tell the story of the ghost at Foran's Hotel.

134. The Ghost of Lady Anne Pearl

During the latter part of the nineteenth century many people claimed to have seen the phantom-like figure of a lady riding a white horse in an area west of St. John's, now part of Mount Pearl. It was believed to be an apparition of Lady Anne Pearl, wife of Captain James Pearl, for whom Mount Pearl is named.

135. Psychic Experience

While fire swept through the Knights of Columbus (K of C) on Harvey Road on December 2, 1942, Elizabeth Ryan, more than 100 miles away, sensed something was wrong. Her two sons, Gabriel and Laurence Ryan, were at the K of C that night when fire destroyed the building and claimed ninety-nine lives.

Her sense of danger was so real, that she spent most of the night in solemn prayer asking God to protect her sons and keep them safe.

The next morning, neighbours told her of the disaster from the night before at the K of C in St. John's. On the night of the fire, she had been at home listening to the radio broadcast of the *Uncle Tim's Barn Dance Show* live from the K of C. At the time the station went off-air, Mrs. Ryan assumed it had ceased operations due to technical problems.

Unaware of what was happening, she turned her radio off and began preparing for bed. Then a strange thing happened. It was at this instance she felt her sons were in danger. Most old-timers describe it as an omen or psychic warning of pending danger. While walking through the house, she felt something brush against her leg. She assumed it was the family cat. Concern for her sons increased.

She searched the house for the cat and then realized she had let the cat out earlier. Perplexed by the incident, she was confronted with the unseen force a second time. A feeling of dread gripped her. She said, "I knelt on my knees and prayed. I prayed the whole night."

The following morning, the community was alive with reports of the previous night's destruction and loss of life. Mrs. Ryan realized then, that the omen she had experienced was a warning that her sons were in danger.

Throughout that day and part of the next, the Ryan family worried and prayed as they awaited news from or about the boys. On the evening of December 14th, their prayers were answered when Mrs. Ryan received a telegram from Gabriel and Laurence stating they were both safe, and there was no need to worry.

136. The Scrooge of Water Street

Archibald Sillars, buried at the General Protestant Cemetery in St. John's, is remembered in Newfoundland's criminal history as the "Scrooge of Water Street." A peculiar gravestone marks the burial site of Sillars, who is buried just sixty feet from the cemetery's west gate on Waterford Bridge Road. The tombstone lies horizontal on the grave and bears his name, date of death and place of birth. There are several other similar tombstones in St. John's. One marks the grave of the eccentric Professor Charles Danielle in the Church of England Cemetery on Forest Road.

Sillars was shot and beaten to death in a basement office of a Water Street establishment he had sold to William Parnell. Sillars had guaranteed part of the loan raised by Parnell to purchase the general store. However, after the sale he visited the store regularly and harassed Parnell's customers, who owed Sillars money. He also tormented Parnell, his wife and children. When Parnell found it difficult to make the required payments on his loans, Sillars threatened to toss him and his family out on the street. Christmas was approaching, and the threat placed much stress and torment on the shoulders of Parnell.

On the night of November 30th, the two argued over money and Parnell accused Sillars of sticking him with useless goods that couldn't be sold. In the heat of the argument, he pulled a revolver and fired three bullets into Sillars. Sillars crawled towards the stairway but Parnell picked up a shovel and beat him over the head until he was dead.

Parnell then went to his upstairs bedroom and took poison. However, he was revived by a doctor, and when the facts surrounding the murder surfaced he was arrested and tried for murder. He was found guilty and executed at Her Majesty's penitentiary on July 8, 1889.

This marked one of several bungled hangings in Newfoundland history. Parnell was a heavy-set man and the inexperienced executioner allowed for a rope that was too long. When Parnell fell through the gallows, the rope almost completely severed his head.

137. A Ceremonial Killing

During the 1940s and early 1950s, many people would get cold shivers late at night while passing a house near the crossroads on Water Street West where one of the most bizarre murders in Newfoundland history took place.

The house was once the home of Eng Wing Kit and two partners who operated the Regal Café, which occupied its downstairs. Kit's body was discovered on the morning of July 3, 1938, by Kilbride farmer, Gordon Stanley. The press described it as a ceremonial killing. The victim had been found with a rope around his neck and tied to an iron pipe laid across the kitchen table and stove. His throat had been cut and a circular piece of flesh cut from his chest. Acting on tips given by members of the Chinese community, police arrested Quang John Shang who hailed from the same village in China as the victim.

A sensational trial followed, which resulted in Shang being acquitted. Soon after the trial he left Newfoundland and never returned. Shang died in the 1990s in British Columbia. The murder of Eng Wing Kit has never been solved. Kit is buried in the General Protestant Cemetery on Waterford Bridge Road.

138. Death of a Barmaid

During the late 1970s, a family moved out of their New Gower Street apartment because they were convinced the house was haunted. Their concerns were reinforced after they spoke with the previous tenants, who also complained of weird, unexplained happenings.

The apartment was located above a small convenience store on the north side of New Gower Street, near the Pleasant Street intersection. However, the uncanny happenings were not occurring in the occupied house but from rooms adjacent in the building next door, which housed only a grocery store and a vacant upstairs apartment.

The lady who approached me on the story claimed that soon after moving into the house, she began to hear noises from the room adjacent to her kitchen in the adjoining building. At first she thought someone had left a radio operating. This happened intermittently, and on one occasion her babysitter complained that the people next door were arguing loudly. Over subsequent weeks, the lady turned off her own radio and television and listened. Usually after 11:00 p.m. she would hear the sounds of muffled voices, doors opening and closing, and someone walking up and down the stairs.

One day, she approached the owner of the building next door and asked about who was living in the upstairs apartment. She was astonished when he told her, "Nobody. I have never rented that as an apartment." She then told him of the nightly noises. The owner was concerned and his first thoughts were that teens in the neighbourhood were breaking in and using the place, so he searched the apartment, accompanied by the tenant from next door. They could find no indication that the place was being used or any signs of a forced entry. All the windows were appropriately locked from the inside and the front and back doors were locked each evening when the store closed.

There was one room that had a padlock on it. It was the room the lady was complaining about. The storeowner then told her a tale which sent shivers up her spine. He said he didn't know the whole story, but people in the neighbourhood had told him that decades before a young girl had been shot to death in that room. Blood stains dried into the wall were still visible. He didn't know anything more about the story, or even if it was true.

When the lady approached me, I did some research on the building and learned that in the late nineteenth century it was the tavern owned and operated by Francis Canning, who had been hanged for murder. In an upstairs room in that building, Canning had shot to death his barmaid Mary Nugent of Kelligrews. Nugent had just told him that she was leaving her job to get married. Canning was very upset by the news, and confronted the young girl in the upstairs room at 3:00 p.m. on May 12,

1899. They argued over her decision, and he pulled out a revolver then shot and killed her. She did not die right away. She was taken to the General Hospital and Canning, under police escort, was allowed to visit her. Before passing away she forgave him.

Our justice system did not. He was tried, convicted of murder and sentenced to hang. Canning told guards at Her Majesty's Penitentiary, "I will never flinch when going to the scaffold." His execution took place on July 29, 1899. The night before the execution he sat and chatted with his wife, two children and his sister-in-law in his cell. They left the prison at 10:30 p.m., and at 11:00 p.m. he had a snack of tea and toast.

One of the worst thunder and lightning storms to strike the city in nearly fifty years was raging outside as the prison bell began to toll at 7:45 a.m. Canning walked firmly to the gallows, fulfilling his promise not to flinch. His last words were, "Lord, have mercy on my soul. Into thy hands, O Lord, I commend my spirit. Lord, have mercy on my soul." Canning was cut down and after doctors confirmed death had taken place; he was buried about thirty feet from the gallows.

Canning lived in a three-storey house on Theatre Hill, now Queen's Road. The house is still there today and located east of City Hall on the north side of the street. I have talked to several families who have lived in that house over the past century and none had any unusual, strange or ghostly stories to tell.

139. The Lady in White

As late as the 1950s, there were claims that the court house in St. John's was haunted by the apparition of a lady in white. Those who claimed to have seen the apparition said it never made a sound. The lady would be seen walking down a hallway and then disappearing. It is believed it was the ghost of Catherine Snow, who was hanged near the court house in 1834 after being found guilty, along with two others, of murdering her husband. Stories of ghostly appearances of Catherine Snow span more than a hundred years. There were newspaper reports that her spirit was seen in a laneway near the court house and in the buildings that occupy the site of the old court house between Duckworth Street and Water Street. A century before these court house apparitions, there was widespread discussions of similar apparitions of Snow.

During the eighteenth and nineteenth centuries, reports of supernatural happenings and ghost sightings often made the pages of local newspapers. It wasn't unusual to hear and read of such occurrences soon after an execution. Following the hanging of Catherine Snow from the gallows outside the old court house window, located off Duckworth Street, claims spread throughout St. John's of sightings of her spirit. These reported apparitions were even discussed in the newspapers of the day.

Catherine Snow was found guilty for her part in the murder of her husband, John Snow, in Port de Grave. She was sentenced to be hanged but the execution was delayed for six months once the authorities learned she was pregnant. Soon after the birth of her child, the execution date was set. Catherine Snow was executed on Monday, July 21, 1834.

There was a great sense of injustice surrounding this case, and many people felt an innocent woman had gone to the gallows. The body of Snow had never been found. Catherine had been arrested along with two others, Tobias Mandeville and Arthur Springer, with whom Catherine was having an affair. At the conclusion of the trial, the attorney general told the court that there was no direct evidence of Catherine Snow's guilt, only a chain of circumstantial evidence.

Even more peculiar was the judge's statement, "You will observe that nothing said by any of the prisoners can be admitted to implicate her in the act. However, her affair of passion with her very much younger cousin was enough to condemn her."

Efforts by the Roman Catholic clergy requesting a commutation of sentence failed.

The night prior to her execution, she accepted a glass of wine from Bishop Fleming. When asked why she refused to eat, she answered, "Oh what is nourishment to me? God calls upon me to suffer death. That I cannot avoid. But let me add as much as possible to my sufferings so that I may try to make that death worthwhile."

Before the executioner placed the rope around her neck, she said, "I was a wretched woman but as innocent of any participation in the crime of murder as an unborn child." At that period in history, the Roman Catholic Church would not approve of an executed person being buried in consecrated ground. However, the clergy in this case felt the victim was innocent, and she was given a Christian burial and laid to rest in the Catholic cemetery. At that time, the Roman Catholic cemetery was located at the foot of Long's Hill, in the area now partly occupied by the Kirk.

Many people claimed seeing the ghost of Catherine Snow in the area of the old court house and the Roman Catholic cemetery. These stories were long forgotten by the turn of the century.

I remember telling the students of Holy Cross Junior High School the tragic story of Catherine Snow during a Book Week appearance. One student asked if the remains of Catherine Snow were still buried beneath the Kirk. I answered to the amusement of those present, "I think so. The last place almighty God is going to look for a Catholic is beneath the Kirk."

Part 9

140. The Cry of the Banshee

Stories of banshees are common in Irish folklore, but surprisingly, considering our strong Irish roots, they are practically unheard of in Newfoundland's lore. However, there is an interesting banshee story which attracted public attention in St. John's during the late eighteenth century. The story involved some strange events leading up to the death of a prominent St. John's man, and widespread claims among inhabitants that he had been called by the banshee.

Most families in the city during that period had some strange tradition or unusual token associated with their family history. The family of St. John's businessman William Welsh emigrated from Ireland, bringing with them the family curse of the banshee. Welsh himself gave little credence to the curse, but his wife and three sons did. Welsh was a healthy robust fellow, who operated a public house and banquet hall on the west side of Hill O'Chips. His wife was an accomplished cook, and their banquet hall was famous.

One night, Mrs. Welsh became terror-stricken when she heard the cry of the banshee at her window. By the time she alerted her husband, it had disappeared. Describing the banshee cry, Mrs. Welsh told her husband:

It was like a weirdly wailing and sobbing Keynee (professional Irish mourner), coming nearer and nearer each moment until it reached the window. Then with a wild shriek, it died away with unearthly sobbing. Anyone hearing it would never forget it.

The next day, the Welsh's youngest son, Felix, severed an artery while cutting fire wood and almost died. Still, William would not acknowledge belief in the banshee.

Some years passed, and on his sixtieth birthday he found himself sitting at the head table in his banquet hall. He was accompanied by the most prominent citizens of St. John's who had come to celebrate Welsh's birthday.

Suddenly, the door swung open. Standing there, his face coloured deathly pale, was William's eldest son, Michael. He was oblivious to all else except his father – at whom he stared. A sudden silence fell as he made his way towards his father. "We all heard the cry tonight," he said. "Are you all right?" William, somewhat surprised, answered, "Of course I am. Why wouldn't I be? I'm as healthy as an ox."

When Michael left the room, Colonel Skinner of the regiment in St. John's asked William what Michael meant when he referred to "the cry." William then told the attentive audience the story of the banshee. He said:

The Welsh's, since time immemorial, were from the Chiefs of a Barony in Ireland, and from the first Welsh, a great Chief and Warrior, the banshee's cry always foretold either a death or some ill-fortune of one of them.

He added it was the only tradition his wife and sons firmly believed in it. When he concluded this story many in the room agreed with the family. However, Colonel Skinner was a little doubtful. But he expressed the opinion that it was certainly a

colourful piece of folklore. When the guests left, Welsh scolded
his wife and children for allowing a silly superstition to bother
them. He said, "No one should concern himself about me; I never
felt better in my life." The family then retired for the night.

The following morning at breakfast, without any warning or indication that something was wrong, Welsh died. When Colonel
Skinner heard the news, he was shocked. "I can't believe it. He
was so healthy," he said. But then, recalling Welsh's tale of the
banshee, he added, "There was something in the banshee's cry
after all."

141. A Miracle on Signal Hill

An unexplained incident involving the noon-day gun on Signal Hill, St. John's, happened during 1890, which left city people
believing a miracle had taken place. The diphtheria epidemic
that raged throughout the city that year had spread to Portugal
Cove. Among its victims were Canon Smith, the parson there,
and his four children.

Through the efforts of Judge D.W. Prowse and a Dr. Fraser,
the Smiths were taken to the hospital on Signal Hill. Three of
the Smith children had died and nine-year-old Harold was in his
last days on earth.

Parson Smith wrote in his diary of little Harold's final day. He
noted:

A strong breeze of wind was blowing on the day that
Harold died. He was a bright lad, but his nerves were
highly strung and he was easily excited. While at 10:30
a.m. I watched him as he was lying quietly in his bed,
the wind slammed one of the doors of the hospital.
The noise so affected little Harold that his face became,
for a few moments, distorted by pain and turned quite
purple. After some considerable time, he became easier.

179

Glancing at my watch, I saw it was only four minutes to 12 noon, and then I thought of the noon-gun which was planted above the hospital, right on the hill back of it. The report from that gun, I knew, would soon thunder over the hospital shaking the whole building. I was in an agony of mind as to what would happen then to little Harold.

Canon Smith was haunted by an incident many years before in which a young girl, viewing the motionless body of her dying father, screamed so loud that he sat up in bed and lingered for nearly two hours in horrible agony before death came to relieve his suffering.

Smith continued his account of his son's last day:

I was beside myself with fear of what I believed would soon be enacted in the room where my boy and I were. Then a voice spoke to my inmost soul:'seek,' it said,'and ye shall receive.'

I can't remember exactly what I said in the agony of prayer on that occasion, but I think it was something like this, 'O Lord, who did shut the mouth of lions, of thy pity muzzle that gun.' I thought that the great God would give his angels charge to shield my little lad so that he would not be disturbed by the report of the gun.

Parson Smith watched the time until 1:00 p.m., but the gun did not fire. He said, "I knew that God had answered my prayer. At 1:30 p.m. little Henry slipped peacefully into eternity."

Mr. Scott was in charge of the noon-day gun at the time, and he couldn't explain why the gun did not fire that day. He said:

Three times I put a new primer into her and pulled the lanyard, but the old girl wouldn't speak. It was all no

180

use. I feared to prime her again least some fire might be in the vent and fire the gun while I was in the act of priming it. The next day I tried her again and she answered at once to the first pull of the lanyard.

When Parson Smith recovered, he told his congregation at Portugal Cove about God's little miracle on Signal Hill.

142. Another Eerie Incident at Belvedere Cemetery

I once interviewed a retired gravedigger, who upon hearing the story of the phantom hearse at Belvedere Cemetery told me another interesting tale that took place there. He said he was working alone digging a grave, near the site where Adams and Walsh saw the strange looking black hearse, when he found a body in the grave. In cases like this, the gravedigger was always alert so as not to disturb the buried corpse. As he cleared the clay from this grave he was shocked by what he witnessed. There before his eyes was a preserved corpse, a lady with rosary beads in her hands. Buried over fifty years earlier, her body was apparently as fresh looking as the day it was put in the ground. The gravedigger eagerly tracked down his supervisor and brought him to the site as a witness. They were both astounded. Neither man had ever witnessed anything like it.

According to the story, they brought the matter to the attention of the bishop, who listened attentively then instructed them to leave the body undisturbed and not mention the discovery again. The worker complied with the instructions. However, he has never forgotten the incident. There are multiple documented cases of the bodies of some canonized saints preserved for centuries without the use of any embalming methods. Several of these are on display in churches in Italy.

143. The Haunting of the *Reliance*

The *Reliance*, a schooner owned by a merchant from Bonavista Bay, operated out of St. John's Harbour for decades. Its crew was mostly St. John's men. Some seamen from the city refused to work on the vessel because of a popular story around town that the vessel was cursed.

The basis of the claim originated when several crew men from the *Reliance* visited a gypsy in Lunenburg, Nova Scotia, to have their fortunes told. The gypsy told each sailor about incidents which each had experienced in the past with surprising accuracy. So, when she confidently told them that their ship, the *Reliance*, was haunted by spirits and destined to be lost at sea, the Newfoundland crew abandoned the ship. Over subsequent years, the ship's reputation as a haunted vessel spread throughout Newfoundland and Nova Scotia.

However, the captain did not believe in the supernatural and, undeterred, he searched St. John's until he gathered an experienced and fearless crew. They loaded the ship with fish destined for Oporto. But the night before departure, the new crew were spooked after witnessing a misty-like figure of a man at the masthead of the ship. The entire crew quit and the captain had to delay sailing long enough to hire a new crew. Crowds of curious people visited the harbour to get a look at the cursed ship before it set sail.

A week later the *Reliance* was lost at sea a couple of hundred miles out of St. John's with all hands on board; the gypsy's prediction was fulfilled.

144. The Legend of the Devil Ship

The *Black Devil* was a ship that once frequented the port of St. John's, and was believed to be cursed by Satan himself. The haunted vessel was an all-black cargo ship with the Devil's figure carved on the front. When it landed in port, children stayed away from it, and even adults would avoid the wharves after dark. In Harbour Grace, people believed the *Black Devil* was under the control of Satan.

As with most legends, this one developed from some true happenings during the late nineteenth century. Originally, the ship was one of two left by a wealthy Englishmen to his two sons. The sons got into a heated argument over the name and finally the older one said, "You may call it the *Devil* if you wish."

"The *Devil* it shall be," the second son replied.

A full-sized figure of Satan was ordered and placed at the front of the ship. The word 'Devil' in large gilded letters was painted at several positions on the ship. It was so ominous to see the all-black ship with Satan's statue sail into port that the story of the Devil ship quickly spread.

It was chartered by John Munn and Co. of Harbour Grace in 1875, and the company could not keep a steady crew. Each captain and crew drank heavily and attacked each other with whatever weapons could be found. In 1893, Captain Patrick Spry of St. John's took command and delivered a cargo from St. John's to Halifax. Captain Spry described what he claimed was a token, which scared the entire crew and left Spry himself shaken. As the *Devil* neared Halifax water, during a moderate wind and rain storm, a man was seen in the mast standing motionless but holding tightly the rigging. At first Captain Spry thought it was one of his crew members. The man did not respond to the crew, who were shouting to attract his attention. When the captain ordered two crew members to go up and persuade the man to come down; the figure turned towards them and they could see his face clearly. Captain Spry shouted, "He's a stowaway!" Without warning the man just disappeared, leaving captain and crew totally bewildered.

The vessel discharged its cargo and began its return to St. John's, and the mystery was still being debated by the captain and crew. As the ship passed Renews, a stowaway was found in a storeroom. However, before the captain could question him, he broke clear and climbed the mast. At the top, he turned and either jumped or fell into the ocean. His body was never found. When the ship arrived in St. John's, Spry and his entire crew quit, leaving no doubt in the public mind that the ship was possessed by the Devil.

Even the elements rebelled against the satanic envoy. Once during a southwest breeze, she dragged her anchor and kept battering Godden's Wharf at St. John's Harbour. Serious damage resulted to the stern and quarterdeck. When she was repaired, the local police ordered the captain and crew to board the ship and leave port.

The Devil ship legend was enhanced when the vessel completed a trip from Labrador to England in a record eight days and eight hours. Suspicion gripped the public to the extent that the British Court of Admiralty ordered the owners to change its name. The name was changed to the *Newsboy*.

While on a trip to the Mediterranean, the cursed ship was caught in a storm and sunk. It was replaced by its sister ship, the *Sheiton*, the Chinese name for "Mother of the Devil."

145. A Flaming Apparition

Another strange and ghastly phenomenon took place in a house on Bay Bulls Road in 1910. A trouting party from St. John's became stranded in that area when a sudden wind and rainstorm struck. They found refuge in a vacant house and, although they had concerns about it, they decided to wait out the storm until morning.

At midnight, they were horrified by the sudden manifestation of a burning flame. The men watched in terror as the figure of a man emerged in the middle of the flame and then threw himself against the front of the house; passing through the walls and out the other side.

This display of flames was described as being, "...red, hot, glowing, aggressive and was accompanied by a hurricane gust of wind."When the wind died down the phantom disappeared. The men recalled that during the apparition the house shook. But no visible sign was left of the phantom.

146. A Haunting on Carter's Hill

During the 1980s, I was approached by tenants of a house on Carter's Hill who claimed their house was being haunted. The person claimed that a series of strange and blood curdling happenings had taken place there during the several months he had been renting the house with two other friends. It began with the unexplained sounds of someone walking upstairs and doors opening and closing.

To rule out the possibility of the noises being caused by wind flowing through the open windows, the man closed all the windows one night and made sure the several upstairs doors were properly closed.

Several hours later, the ritual of walking and opening and closing doors resumed. The man said this was preceded by a cold feeling, which was experienced by all three tenants. On several occasions, when the house was left vacant with the door unlocked for short periods of time, they would return to find the doors locked. A back door, which could only be locked from the inside and had been deliberately left unlocked on several occasions, was locked when the tenants returned. They sought but found no explanation for the events.

All three tenants said they had felt a cold, angry presence in the house at times when strange things were happening. The final straw for them came one Christmas, when the Christmas tree began to shake on its own. Soon after, the men moved out. However, they were not the only ones to witness these poltergeist-type happenings. Neighbours claimed that a family had moved out of the same house a year before after complaining that the house was haunted.

The former tenants believed the hauntings resulted from a triple murder that took place on the street in 1922. Today, Carter's Hill runs from Livingstone Street to LeMarchant Road, however, in 1922 the section from Cabot Street to LeMarchant Road was called Murray Street. It was in a house on this street that the triple murder took place. The crime was the coldest, bloodiest murder to happen in Newfoundland since 1872, when Patrick Geehan murdered his wife and brother-in-law.

The killings took place at the Jim Lee Laundry, which was owned and occupied by the three victims. A dispute over wages, working conditions and family hostilities, carried over from China and led to the murders. Wo Fen Game, an employee at the laundry, was angered because one of the owners, Hong Loen, was threatening to fire him and throw him out on the streets. Game could not speak English and viewed this action as a death sentence. He was convinced no one else would hire him, and other Chinese businessmen would ostracize him rather than offend the Jim Lee Laundry owners, who had paid to bring Game to Newfoundland.

While this dispute was building up, Hong Loen told Game that he would die sooner or later and that Hong Wing of the Hop Wah Laundry on Casey Street intended to kill him. Wing, according to Loen, was determined to kill Game because of a dispute between the two families, which had been on going back in China for decades.

Game sought the help of his friend, Charlie Fong, operator of a Water Street restaurant. Fong met with Hong Loen in an unsuccessful attempt to conciliate the dispute. When Game learned he had been fired, he went to the Royal Stores on Water Street, purchased a gun and that evening shot and killed the three owners of Jim Lee Laundry. He then went to the Hop Wah

Laundry on Casey Street and shot Hong Wing. Fortunately, Wing was not seriously wounded. Game then walked to the top of Barron Street, raised the gun to his own head and with his hand trembling fired, but survived. He was taken to the General Hospital. Upon recovery, he was arrested and tried for murder. During the trial, he was gagged and tied. He was held at the back of the court room because his loud moaning was interrupting the proceedings.

While at Her Majesty's Penitentiary, he got hold of a gun and made an unsuccessful attempt to escape. At 8:00 a.m., on December 16, 1922, Wo Fen Game was escorted to the gallows in the prison yard. When he saw the six-foot-tall executioner approach him, dressed in an overcoat with a woollen hat partially covering his face, his whole body began to tremble. The execution was swift and the prisoner died at 8:09 a.m.

147. Apparition at St. John's Waterfront

During the early part of the nineteenth century, people in the waterfront area claimed to have seen a ghastly, fog-like apparition of a coffin moving across the St. John's Harbour at night.

Captain Patrick O'Brien often told the story to his children to keep them away from the wharves after dark. He claimed the casket was supposed to carry the body of a seaman murdered on the waterfront in the eighteenth century. Like so many other ghost stories over the centuries, this one faded from public memory. However, it appears to have had its origins in the true tale of one of the most unusual funerals ever to take place in Newfoundland.

The ghastly funeral took place at St. John's Harbour on October 28, 1794. The silence of that morning was broken by the steady and morbid beating of military drums along the shoreline as a flotilla of dories, one of them carrying a flag draped coffin, moved slowly over the harbour waters. Three companies of Newfoundland volunteer servicemen, the entire crews of six British man-of-wars and crowds of city residents stood on wharves waiting to participate in the funeral procession.

This uncanny funeral was being held to honour the slain Lieutenant Richard Lawry, who had been murdered several days before during an ambush by a group of St. John's Irish immigrants. The lieutenant was an officer on the HMS *Boston*. He had angered the locals by impressing a group of their friends into service on the *Boston*. They waited on the shore near Waldegrave Street and, when Lawry came ashore, they ambushed and beat him to death.

The governor felt that completion of a trial and execution of the guilty was absolutely necessary to preserve order throughout the island. One of the ambushers accepted the governor's offer of immunity in return for identifying the killers. As a result of this, Richard Power and Garrett Farrell were arrested and charged with murder. The trial and execution were swift.

They were tried on Wednesday, sentenced on Thursday and executed on Friday. The hangings took place near Fort Townshend. Their bodies were turned over to local surgeons for dissection, which was part of the sentence for murder.

Before departing for England, the governor offered a £50 reward for information leading to the arrest of a third man involved in the murder, William Barrows. However, Barrows is believed to have fled Newfoundland, and he was never found.

Meanwhile, the victim, Lieutenant Lawry, was laid to rest at the old Anglican cemetery opposite the present court house on Duckworth Street. Captain O'Brien said those who claim to have seen the floating coffin on the harbour believed it was the ghost of Lawry.

148. The Ghost of Alice Janes

The diary of Aaron Thomas, preserved at the Newfoundland archives, describes the area between Flower Hill (later changed to Springdale Street) and Flower Hill Street (later changed to Flower Hill) as being the most beautiful natural flower garden in the world.[1] A large field in the area was used as a race track during the early nineteenth century and the local gentry spent many an enjoyable evening there.

It was also the site haunted for a decade by the spirit of Alice Janes, who was among the city's most ardent racing enthusiasts. With her Irish-knit shawl and jug of brew, Alice was a fixture at the race track.

During one of the races there, Alice suffered a heart attack and died instantly. The whole town turned out for the funeral and she was given a respectable send-off at the old cemetery, adjoining the Anglican Cathedral.

A year passed, and on the anniversary of Alice's death a young woman was being escorted through the Flower Hill field by a male companion. Darkness was just beginning to set in and the girl complained of a strange, cold feeling, and she asked her friend to take her home. As they neared the edge of the field, they came upon a sight that sent them screaming. They later described the apparition to friends. At first, it seemed like an old woman sitting on a rock holding a jug in her hand. When the couple neared the figure, it slowly stood up and stared straight at them. Her eyes were burning red and her white hair stood out like the whisks of a broom.

The couple swore it was the ghost of Alice Janes. When word of the apparition spread throughout town, several friends of the late Alice Janes visited the field and then the gravesite to pray. While at the graveside they noticed that the wooden

---

[1] This area was better known in the pre-Gas Lamp era as "The Darby's O'Gallivan's".

Celtic cross-marker, that they had placed in the ground to indicate the grave, had disappeared. They searched the area but failed to find it.

A later newspaper account noted that the apparition of Alice haunted the Flower Hill field for a decade after. Then one day the caretaker at the cemetery, while clearing an area of the old graveyard, found the missing cross. He placed it back on the gravesite. There were no more sightings of the apparition, and old-timers believed that her spirit had finally found peace.

149. A Haunting on Duckworth Street

In 1909, a St. John's man told the story of his brush with a real spirit. He told his friends it happened between Bet Coleman's house and John White's store on Duckworth Street (northeast side, near the Majestic).

A woman who had passed away months before suddenly appeared at his side and walked along with him. When the initial shock of the vision subsided, the man tried to question the woman, but she did not speak.

After walking about 100 yards, she turned, stared into his eyes and then disappeared as quickly as she had appeared. Around the same time, a St. John's lady had another story of the supernatural to tell. She recalled that while she walked past the door of a woman who was dying, she felt an icy hand being drawn closely across her face. Moments later, she was told the dying woman had just passed away.

150. Ghostly Guardian of the Treasure in Shoal Harbour

Shoal Harbour is only minutes south of the Goulds in the west end of St. John's. It is the site of an alleged buried treasure and hauntings. The famous Diver Dobbin of St. Mary's Bay was a man of great courage and even when he witnessed a strange apparition while digging for pirate's gold at Shoal Harbour, he was not deterred.

The story of buried treasure at Shoal Harbour was well-known even in those days, and Dobbin, the veteran of many such adventures, teamed up with eight men from St. John's on a treasure hunting expedition to retrieve the gold. When they arrived at the site where the map indicated the gold was, it was too dark to start work. While discussing plans to dig for the treasure, Dobbin recalled, they were all seized with an uncanny feeling and an unidentifiable dread. To break the spell, Dobbin grabbed a pick and started to dig. After a few minutes, Captain Martin screamed and fell to the ground. When he regained consciousness, the men asked him what had frightened him, and he refused to answer.

Dobbin led the men back to a nearby house where they were staying. Captain Martin went straight to bed, while the others remained in the kitchen making light of the Martin incident. Suddenly, a loud knock was heard at the door, which was fastened by a wooden button inside. Before anyone could open the door, it flew open and a man came into the centre of the kitchen. He stood motionless on the floor and made no sound. The move was so frightening that everyone in the room, except Dobbin and Moran, passed out. Dobbin noted that he, too, was frightened but kept calm.

Then, in front of the phantom figure, there appeared the bodies of eight men lying motionless on the floor. Dobbin described the phantom as medium height and stoutly-built. He wore a cap and underneath a mass of short black curls could be seen. He wore dark, cloth pants with a blue coat, which was cut sailor-fashion square across the hips. He disappeared as suddenly as he came.

Breen, among those who passed out, fell near the fireplace. The flames from the fireplace caught fire to his pants, which shocked him out of unconsciousness. One of the men grabbed a knife and moved towards him to cut the clothing away. Another member of the party had just come into the room and thought the man was trying to kill Breen, so he tried to wrestle the knife away. Diver Dobbin intervened and took the knife away. He then put out the fire on Breen's clothing. The figure and the eight men on the floor vanished.

The treasure hunt came to an end when Captain Martin told Dobbin and the others that the ghost in the kitchen was the same ghost he had seen at the treasure site. The men pledged to leave the area and never return. The last words Captain Martin said to Dobbin were, "The gold will have to lay there till the Day of Judgement."

151. Paranormal Incident at the Chapel

There have been many tales over the decades of organ music heard late at night coming from the chapel inside Mount Carmel Cemetery, located in the east end of St. John's. The following tale differs from those just a little, because the phantom organist in this story performed in daylight.

During the last year of World War II, a young St. John's woman suddenly dropped dead while walking up Barter's Hill, towards her home on Monroe Street. The woman had been shopping downtown for a suitable gift for her brother, who was returning home from the war in Europe that week on board a Canadian Naval ship. It was Monday, and the ship was due on Saturday.

As was the practice, she was waked for two nights in her home and the burial was scheduled for Wednesday. Her parents persuaded church authorities to allow her remains to be stored in the chapel at Mount Carmel Cemetery until Friday so her brother could pay his last respects. The deceased had been a member of the Presentation Convent Girls' Choir and loved the hymn, "Ave

Maria." Her love for the "Ave Maria" was mentioned many times by her friends during the wake.

On Saturday, her brother arrived in St. John's and was taken by family in an OK Taxi to Mount Carmel Cemetery. The taxi moved slowly up the very narrow driveway and parked alongside the chapel. As the family exited the taxi, they could hear an organist playing the "Ave Maria." The music had a very soothing effect on everyone, and it was believed by the family that the parish priest had arranged the music as part of the final funeral ceremony before the deceased was laid to rest.

However, when they arrived at the door of the chapel, it was locked. The father felt it may have been jammed and tried at first to push it open but without success. Meanwhile, the organist continued to play the "Ave Maria." Then, the caretaker and priest arrived and unlocked the door. The chapel was empty except for the casket of the deceased girl. Everyone present was bewildered by what had happened and nobody could explain it.

The girl's brother, who passed away in the 1980s, believed to the day he died that the unexplained organ music was something inspired by his dead sister to let him know she was happy and at peace.

152. The Lucifer Story

Caul's Field was a large meadow between Brazil Street and Casey Street and north of Monroe Street. The boys from the old centre of town area used it as their own recreational facility when Cauls' horses were not grazing. During the early 1950s, there was an intriguing supernatural story associated with the field. For decades, people in the neighbourhood believed the field was haunted by Lucifer himself. Several people had died instantly while walking through the field at night. While the official reasons for death were heart attacks, people in the neighbourhood had another explanation.

There were widely-told stories of people seeing a mystical dark figure, believed to be Lucifer, moving around the field at night. The story was frightening enough to keep school age children from frequenting the area after sundown. Yet, it wasn't credible enough to keep the older boys from the neighbourhood from hanging out in the field late at night.

On one such night, the boys from Flower Hill, including: Dinty Hearn, Fatso Ryall, Trapper Gillett, Dave Roache, Jack Leonard, Kip Malone, Dickey Murphy and a few others, after playing a game of baseball, stayed around until long after dark telling ghost stories. One which gave the boys goose pimples was the Lucifer story. As it neared midnight, one by one the boys began leaving the field to go home. However, Dinty passed out and the boys left him sleeping near an old shed.

Soon after midnight, Dinty awoke and was angry about being left alone by his friends. With the Lucifer story foremost in his mind, he walked towards the Brazil Street exit at a rapid pace while gripping his baseball bat tightly in his hands. The sudden sighting of a huge, menacing black figure stationed between him and the exit lane sent a cold chill down his spine. He froze. But Dinty was one of the gutsiest fellows in town and he wasn't ready to back down, not even from Lucifer himself.

Dinty raised his baseball bat in the air and when he got near enough to Lucifer, he swung it with all his might, striking the mystical figure with great force. Unexpectedly, Dinty Hearn found himself flying arse over kettle through the air and landed in the nearby bushes. When he came to, the dark figure was just a few feet away from him and he was able to see it clearly for the first time.

Lucifer turned out to be Billy Caul's black stallion. The stallion had responded to Dinty's assault with a well-placed kick of his own.

Part 10

153. The Christmas Day Riot on Water Street

On the evening of Christmas Day, 1942, the Chinese owners of the Imperial Café, located on the north side of Water Street near the Prescott Street intersection, were entertaining some friends in their restaurant. The Imperial Café, like all other city businesses, was closed to the public on that day. Three sailors from a British Naval vessel, which was tied up at St. John's Harbour, had walked the whole length of Water Street looking for an open restaurant, club or store, but without success. As they neared the Prescott Street intersection, they noticed the Imperial Café had their lights on and appeared to be doing business. However, when they tried to enter through the front door, they discovered it was locked. One of the seamen knocked on the door, but the manager, visible through the window, raised his hand and shook his head to indicate the restaurant was closed. This angered the sailors, who perhaps misunderstood the manager's hand signals.

One of the men took a step back, raised his foot and delivered a swift, hard kick to the door, which sent it swinging wide open. Several Chinese men attending the party rushed to the aid of the owner. During the ensuing struggle, which spilled over onto Water Street, the sailors took a beating from the Chinese. One of the sailors was struck on the head with a bottle, which almost knocked him unconscious. Defeated, the trio left the Imperial Café and returned to their ship. The Chinese made temporary repairs to the broken door and continued on with their celebration.

Meanwhile, the three sailors were spreading the word among their shipmates of the beating they had received from a group of Chinese.The crew members felt the beating was an insult to the British Navy as well as to their comrades, and they began to leave the ship to head towards the Imperial Café. In a matter of minutes, the ship's full company of 150 sailors were marching down Water Street to avenge their honour.

A Chinese guest at the Imperial Café couldn't believe his eyes when he looked out the window to see what all the commotion outside was, only to see the horde of English sailors approaching the front door of the café.The man shouted out in Chinese and everyone in the café began running for safety. Some ran through the back door, while others locked themselves in an upstairs room for protection.

The sailors kicked in the front door once more, and the destruction began. They beat out the restaurant's plate glass windows, broke the glass in the door, took the door off its hinges and tossed the furniture out into the middle of Water Street. Grabbing whatever food was available, and emptying the fridges, the men painted the walls and ceiling with rice, coconut cream pie, lemon pie, ketchup and sugar. They poured soup over the floor and emptied a bag of flour on top of it.

Several local policemen and a Navy patrol arrived on the scene and dispersed the crowd.When the British left, the Imperial Café was in shambles. Luckily, there had been no personal injuries. Local authorities were concerned that there might be further attacks on other Chinese establishments in the city. They immediately advised all Chinese to keep their businesses closed and stay off the streets until things settled down. The British confined all their men to their ships and put on extra police patrols.

The matter did settle down and there was no further trouble. The British sailors felt they had succeeded in getting revenge for the beating their friends had taken.

154. Old-time Christmas in St. John's

In nineteenth-century St. John's, smoked ham, black pudding and herring were popular foods during the Christmas season. Preparation for the season started during the time of the November full moon. Back-junk, better known as the yule log, was cut and placed in the fireplace, where it burned throughout the Christmas season. In those times, all houses had fireplaces, which were essential to heating the home during the cold winter months.

It was in the large open chimneys of these fireplaces where the process of smoking meat and fish took place. Ham, herring and black pudding were hung in the chimneys and cured by the wood smoke. Poultry and fresh meats were cheap. Vessels arrived almost daily from Prince Edward Island carrying cargoes of fresh meat, vegetables and fruit, which people could buy directly from the ship or at an auction. It was said that even the poorest family could easily buy the best of Christmas dinners.

During November, the wood for winter was cut, and livestock and poultry killed. While the men gathered wood, tended to the animals, and carried out other winter and Christmas preparations, the women spent their days polishing dishes and tinware until they sparkled. P.K. Devine wrote in one of his Christmas columns that, "Following a reckless expenditure of powder, the big, seven-foot 'Poole' guns were put away on racks in the kitchen ceiling or over the fireplace."

The kitchen was lit by "train-oil" or cod-oil lamps and candles were used for other rooms and the hallways. Christmas house parties were popular and people danced the eight-handed reel, cotillion and Sir Roger or country dance. In many communities, a visit by the mummers was traditional.

In St. John's, cake and poultry raffles were a very popular tradition. The most popular raffles were held at Lash's Bakery, where the Arcade Stores once operated. Devine noted that the winner of the Lash's huge Christmas cake became the hero of the hour.

Sleigh riding and ice skating were popular winter activities in old St. John's, especially during the Christmas season. There were two skating rinks on Military Road, near Bannerman Park, and these were always crowded. The merchant had his coach and a fur-coated coachman sitting in the driver's seat, which according to author Michael Harrington, drove to the nearby inns and taverns. He wrote, "Imagine the panting, steaming horses, the bright-colored sleighs, the fur-clad occupants, the jingling harness, tinkling bells, snap of the whip, and joyous shouts on the frosty air...like something on an old-fashioned drawing or a Christmas card."

A quaint aspect of an old St. John's Christmas was the many arches of green boughs and trees constructed throughout the downtown area of the city. Businesses would close for the twelve days of Christmas and celebrations would last until the twelfth night.

155. Some Newfoundland Christmas Traditions

Newfoundland's colourful past includes a variety of Christmas traditions from 'hauling' and 'clingers' to 'mummering.' Confederation brought a dramatic change in our culture and caused most of these practices to die out. However, over the past two decades, we have seen an accelerated interest in our Newfoundland heritage, and in many communities some of the old traditions are being revived.

156. Bless the House

An interesting Christmas tradition was observed in the Bonavista Bay area. On Christmas Eve, the family would gather and scatter a freshly baked Christmas loaf of bread to the four corners of the house to ensure good luck for the following year.

157. Hauling

In Port de Grace, citizens carried on a tradition known as 'hauling.' If any person in the community was caught working on Christmas Day, neighbours would force the guilty person onto a long board, usually an old gate, door or ladder, and carry him around the settlement. The offender was then required to treat his tormentors with Christmas cheer. Sometimes, the offender was auctioned off to raise the money to pay for a dram of rum for each member of the hauling gang.

158. Sleigh Rides

In St. John's, the merchants held sleighing parties. These involved sleigh rides to the countryside followed by a party and dancing. These events added a picturesque aspect to Christmas in the city, as a line of horse-drawn sleighs, bells tinkling, made their way through city streets and out over the roads to Midstream (Bowring Park) and other popular sites.

159. The Yule Log

Burning the yule log was a custom practiced on the French Shore. This practice involved cutting a log or birch junk before Christmas and at sunset on Christmas Eve placing it at the back of the hearth. A burning cinder was taken from the log on

Christmas Eve and tossed over the house to protect the house from danger of fire during the coming year.

160. Clingers

In St. John's, during the 1940s and 1950s, children went door to door similar to the practice of Halloween. They would ask to be invited into a home to see the Christmas tree. The host would offer candy, fruit or syrup and cake (clingers), and would often ask the children to sing or entertain before leaving. There were no artificial trees in those days. The children showed politeness and complimented the host on the fine tree, regardless of how badly it was decorated. To do otherwise would risk the chance of not being treated to refreshments by the host.

161. Shooting the Pudding from the Pot

In some communities, a practice developed that was a sort of Christmas Day community contest. It was known as, "shooting the pudding from the pot." After church services in the morning on Christmas Day, the ladies set about the task of preparing the Christmas dinner. This always included the hot pudding. As soon as a pudding was cooked and removed from the pot, the man of the house went outside and fired his gun in the air. The first gunfire heralded to neighbours that the first hot Christmas pudding was cooked. The winner earned the right to host the Christmas Night Time for the community. This was a house party, and people provided their own entertainment.

162. Mummering, Swabs and Eunchucks

One Newfoundland tradition that has all but disappeared from our culture is mummering, although in recent years groups in St. John's have revived the spirit, which was once looked upon a nuisance and a threat to public safety.

A mummering tradition in old St. John's, which is rarely mentioned when the tradition is discussed, is the golden opportunity it presented for enemies to exact revenge and get away with it. Judge David Prowse in his history of Newfoundland wrote, "...there were plenty of fights when the 'fools' or mummers came out from Christmas to twelfth day."

Fools wore an outfit made up of high-triangular forms of white hats decorated with ribbons. White shirts were adorned with ribbons and streamers, which were sewed on and were an essential part of the costume. Prowse said that a good outfit cost "...both time and money."

A distinguishing element of the costume was called the "swab" a sort of mop, which was made of a canvas-covered bladder with a cow's tail often attached to it. Some men dressed as women and wore long garments and masks. These were called "eunchucks." Prowse said, these fools ran at passers-by with an Indian yell, and spoke in a falsetto voice. Men were often beaten badly for old grievances by the fools."[1]

During 1860 and 1861, a series of incidents in St. John's and throughout Conception Bay finally led to mummering being banned by law. During this period, there was a lot of political unrest, with riots breaking out in the city and elsewhere. In Bay Roberts, Isaac Mercer was attacked and murdered by a group of mummers. Inflamed by religious rivalry, that tragic event was followed by riots throughout Conception Bay.

Public pressure began to mount, led by Anglican Bishop Feild, who wrote letters to local newspapers demanding the outlawing of mummering. He referred to Mercer's murder and Christmas disturbances in St. John's as evidence of the generally disorderly condition of the colony. An editorial in the

[1] *A History of Newfoundland*, D.W.Prowse, Boulder Press, St. John's, Newfoundland.

Newfoundlander argued in favour of mummering, pointing out that, "The death of the unfortunate man was but an accidental result of the sport of Christmas mummering, and not of any deadly intent."

Legislation banning mummering was passed on June 25, 1861 and one letter appearing in a St. John's newspaper noted: "Every well-disposed citizen must be gratified at the proclamation issued by the police magistrates to suppress mummering with its disgusting attendants; rioting, drunkenness and profanity."

Authorities were concerned that those with grudges would use the practice to conceal their attacks on enemies. People indebted to the merchants often used mummering to harass them. It also provided a cover for religious factions to attack each other.

Generally, mummering sparked fun and entertainment in a community. In one case, a Harbour Grace doctor led a group of mummers on an escapade in which they captured the local constable and locked him in his own handcuffs. They then dropped him off at the magistrate's house. The practice of mummering, although outlawed, continued until the 1920s and was revived again in some parts in the 1970s. The law banning mummering was never repealed. The penalty for mummering was seven days in jail or a twenty-shilling fine.

In Newfoundland, St. Stephen's Day, the day after Christmas, was officially changed to Boxing Day by the Commission of Government in 1934.

163. Candlemas Day Mummers

The people of Codroy Valley, on Newfoundland's west coast, practiced a different type of mummering during the nineteenth century, and it wasn't during the Christmas season. It was their traditional way of celebrating Candlemas Day which is February

2nd. It involved the whole community and was always an up-roariously hilarious time for all concerned.

A recorded account of the practice appeared in the December, 1948 edition of the *Newfoundlander.* It read:

'When Candlemas Day is fair and fine half the winter is left behind,' is an old saying, but sixty or seventy years ago in the Codroy Valley on the west coast, Candlemas was a very festive occasion.

It was sponsored by the men, and they were usually about three weeks preparing for it. Coasting (sliding) formed an important part in the program, and each man exerted his skill to build a fine sled. Competition was rampant. The women took very little active part in the preparation, but each had to provide a bow or ribbon, and woe betide the woman who had no ribbon – she might then just as well stay home from the feast.

When the great day arrived all the men gathered at one house, and he who had been the most popular all-round sport of the previous year was selected as the king. He walked from door to door ahead of the procession, carrying a fancy carved cane or staff. On entering each house the king sang a song which described their feast, and explained what portion or kind of food they expected to receive from that house, many parts of the song being acted.

The cane or staff would be held out toward each woman, who was supposed to adorn it with ribbon bows. Meat and molasses were the heaviest load, and as each man was to haul only one kind of food, the strongest were picked out to haul the meat and molasses.

After all the food had been gathered in this fashion, a song of thankfulness was sung and everyone joined in dancing. The festivities which generally consisted of dancing, games, taffey-pulling, tests of skill and strength, and so forth, usually lasted as long as the food held out which was two or three days and nights.

Upon arrival at the house or hall where the feast was held, the bows of ribbon would be taken from the pole by the beaus or sweethearts of the girls who had placed them there, and brandished proudly.

164. The Crime Against Santa Claus

Everyone knows that good old St. Nicholas was the first Santa Claus. However, there is another absorbing aspect of St. Nick's history that is not so well known. This intriguing story involves how the remains of St. Nicholas got from his burial place in Myra in Asia Minor to Bari, Italy.

St. Nicholas was a native of Patara in Lycia, Asia Minor. He became a monk and served in a monastery in Myra. During his lifetime, he became a legendary figure throughout Asia Minor for his virtue of charity for the poor. The good works of St. Nicholas earned him elevation to the position of Archbishop of the See of Myra. He died in the year 342 AD and was laid to rest in a cemetery in Myra. After his death, St. Nicholas became known as the patron saint of children, and our well-known name "Santa Claus" is actually a corruption of St. Nicholas.

In the year 1087, the body of St. Nicholas disappeared from its tomb in Myra. For a while afterwards there was much speculation as to what happened to the body. Some thought it was miraculous and the body had been taken up to heaven. Others held a more horrible thought, believing it had been taken by grave robbers for reasons unknown.

As with most crimes, the mystery was eventually solved, but the story has been long forgotten. Supernatural interference had nothing at all to do with the theft of the body of St. Nicholas. In Italy at the time, there was a common belief that a saint's body brought prosperity and good fortune to the town where the remains were interred. It was this belief that motivated a crew of Italian sailors visiting Myra in the year 1087 to steal the body and bring the remains to their home town of Bari, Italy.

The townsfolk of Bari credited the saint with thirty cures and miracles in the year following the reburial. The notion of Santa Claus as a secret dispenser of gifts was enhanced by the story that St. Nicholas once saved three girls from a life of prostitution by throwing purses of gold through a window in Patara. The gift permitted a poverty-stricken nobleman to give his daughters suitable dowries as custom demanded.

In addition, St. Nicholas was credited with restoring life to three boys who had been slain and dismembered by a wicked innkeeper of Myra.[2] The body of St. Nicholas remains interred in Bari, Italy to this day. St. Nicholas became San Nicolass (Santa Claus) in the dialect of the New York Dutch.

[2]The saint is sometimes depicted in stain glass windows with three boys at his side.

Part 11

165. The Newfoundland Rangers

Prior to Confederation in 1949, two police forces maintained the peace throughout Newfoundland and Labrador. The Newfoundland Constabulary under the Department of Justice policed the Avalon and Bonavista peninsulas, while the Newfoundland Rangers policed all other parts of the province. They were the responsibility of the Department of Natural Resources.

The famous Newfoundland Ranger Force came into being during Commission of Government. The force began in July, 1935, under Sir John Hope Simpson, the first commissioner for natural resources. The first commanding officer was Major Leonard Stick, who was a veteran of World War I and had served with the Royal Newfoundland Regiment at Gallipoli and Beaumont Hamel.

The Ranger Force started with an enrolment of thirty men and two officers. For $1 per day, "Newfoundland's Finest" were expected to risk their lives in all sorts of weather, arrest lunatic murderers, deliver babies and help citizens complete government forms.

The Newfoundland Government arranged with the Canadian government for RCMP Sergeant T. Anderson to come to Newfoundland and conduct a six-week training course for the Ranger recruits.

Originally, they were headquartered in Whitbourne, but later they moved their headquarters to Kilbride.

The Ranger Force wore a distinctive uniform. It consisted of a khaki tunic and breeches with a brown stripe down the side, high leather boots and a military-style peaked cap. On the hat was a badge showing a caribou's head with the one word motto of the force, 'ubique', meaning 'everywhere.'

These men really lived up to the motto. They travelled across some of Newfoundland's toughest terrain, using boats, dog teams, horses and they also travelled on foot. One did not require a driver's licence to become a ranger. However, a ranger stationed at Clarenville was issued a motorcycle. Empowered to test others for licensing, the ranger tested himself and earned his cycle licence.

The first casualty in the force occurred during the winter of 1938, when Ranger Danny Corcoran was lost while on patrol. He was found two weeks later, but died at the hospital in St. Anthony. In 1939, Ranger Mike Green and his horse fell through the ice while on a patrol near Lamaline. He struggled to land, but died of exposure. The Ranger Force was disbanded on July 31, 1950, with most of the Rangers joining the RCMP.

166. Name Origins of Bay Bulls and Kelligrews

The town of Bay Bulls, about twenty miles southwest of St. John's, got its name from the bull walrus, which were plentiful there during the early days of settlement in Newfoundland. They were sought after by hunters, and in time, they could no longer be found except in the far north of Newfoundland and Labrador. According to author Harold Horwood, Bay Bulls was the site of the last French attack on Newfoundland during the Napoleonic wars.

The community of Kelligrews, made famous in Johnny Burke's "Kelligrews Soiree," got its name from the wealthy Cornish family, the Killigrews[1], remembered in history as "the Robber Barons" of Land's End, England. Their large castle called Pen Dennis in Falmouth was used by them as a refuge place for pirates. It was the Killigrews who helped the notorious pirate, Peter Easton, build a fleet of forty armed ships. Easton fortified Harbour Grace and later set up a stronghold on Kelly's Island on the other side of Conception Bay, from Kelligrews.

167. No Other Criminal Sentence Compares!

Throughout the history of justice in Newfoundland, I doubt if any judge has ever made the same decision as did a judge in Harbour Main in the late seventeenth century. When faced with making a judgment on a dispute between a fisherman and his master, the judge made an extraordinarily unorthodox ruling.

A fishing master named Edward Fahey was a bully who abused Tim O'Rourke, a young Irishman employed by him during Tim's first season of work in Newfoundland. As was the practice at the time, employees were paid at the end of the season. When it came time to make payment, Fahey deliberately picked a fight with young Tim to avoid having to pay him for his season's work.

Tim O'Rourke took his complaint to the local judge and explained what had happened. He said he was going back to fight Mr. Fahey and to get his just pay. He said, "I ask ye'r honour's permission to defend meself."

The judge, who was outraged by what Fahey had done, gave O'Rourke permission to defend himself, and added, "Go out and give him a taste of his own medicine. Kick the stuffing out of him."

Tim took a few days to train for the fight. When ready, he marched straight down to the wharf, followed by a few curious

---

[1]The family spelled their name Killigrews. In Newfoundland this became Kelligrews.

villagers, and went unannounced aboard Fahey's boat. "I wants me pay right now. I worked for it!"Tim told Fahey.

Fahey raised his fist to strike Tim and said, "There's no pay here for troublemakers!"

This was just what Tim O'Rourke was expecting to hear. The fight was on. Fahey had never had an employee fight back before, and he proved to be no match for the angry Irishman. Tim made good on the judge's instruction and he beat Fahey from one end of the boat to the other. When Fahey couldn't take anymore, he gave up. He paid Tim his wages and said, "Let by-gones be by-gones. I'd be happy to have you work for me again."

Tim accepted the offer and the two became longtime friends.

168. Plane in Trouble over Gander

People in the Gander area were startled on January 19, 1962, to witness a Trans-Canada Airline (TCA) plane dive bomb towards the ground, then pull up and repeat the dive-bombing action. The plane didn't leave the area, but continued to circle for nearly three hours. Those watching the aircraft maneuver were not yet aware of the drama playing itself out on that TCA Flight 404.

Among the passengers on the flight was Newfoundland's Director of Tourism, Oliver L. Vardy, and St. John's businessman, Graham Mercer. The flight was carrying thirty-four passengers from Gander to St. John's. Less than ten minutes after take-off, the captain was alarmed to discover that the nose wheel would not go down. Following some discussion with ground control, he decided to remain in the Gander area and try to correct the problem. The craft was a Viscount and had a range of 1,700 miles, with sufficient fuel to remain in the air for hours. It had a cruising speed of 320 miles per hour, measured eighty-one feet long and had a ninety-three-foot wing span.

Ground control prepared for an emergency landing and quickly arranged through TCA in Halifax a direct telephone hookup between the TCA's maintenance division in Winnipeg, Manitoba and Flight 404's Captain William Gwyn. Mr. Vardy later recalled that there was no panic among passengers. He said, "When all attempts to free the wheel failed, we were informed that a crash landing would be attempted and we were given instructions on what to do."

While the crew gave passengers instructions on how to prepare for the landing, Captain Gwyn tried desperately to free the nose wheel. During these efforts, the landing gear on the wings of the plane moved into position and locked, and Gwyn took the plane to a high altitude and dive-bombed. He followed this dramatic move with bouncing the plane several times on the runway. However, all efforts failed and the front wheel remained jammed.

The captain then confided to the crew, and then the passengers, that the only choice remaining was an emergency landing. He took time to speak with every passenger on the plane to explain how the landing was going to be accomplished. Mr. Vardy said the captain's conversations and the confidence and professionalism of the crew were the factors in avoiding panic among the passengers.

On the ground, workers were preparing to handle the pending emergency landing. While the passengers were being given a briefing on crash procedures, foam was being spread over the runway to provide a smoother slide for the plane and reduce the possibility of fire on impact. Although there was no panic, tension heightened as the plane began its downward descent. Captain Gwyn lifted the nose of the plane slightly above normal to avoid a sudden nose dive and disaster as it approached the runway.

Flight 404 skidded several hundred feet over the foam-covered runway and after thirty seconds came to a halt. The passengers and crew were quickly evacuated from the aircraft. The captain had ended the near three-hour drama in the skies without any injuries or casualties. When reporters surrounded the passengers as they entered the terminal, they lavished praise upon Captain Gwyn and his crew. The crew included: Captain William Gwyn, First Officer Alex Vance and stewardesses, Solange Normanding and E.C. Gwynne all of Montreal.

Several passengers were interviewed by *The Evening Telegram* at the airport after the landing. Brenda Purchase of St. John's told the reporter that she thought, "My number was up." The most frightening part for Ms. Purchase was when the plane landed on the foam-covered runway.

Leo Tucker, who was travelling with his wife and two children, described the event as, "a harrowing experience." Frank Murphy, returning to St. John's from Nova Scotia, praised the coolness and professionalism of the captain and crew.

Gus Winter, a St. John's businessman, was accompanied by his seventeen- year-old son. He noted that he first became aware there was a problem with Flight 404 when his son pointed out that the aircraft was repeatedly circling the airport. Soon after that, Captain Gwyn announced there was a problem with the plane. Bernard Cook of Bishop's Falls was not frightened during the crisis. However, he added that he did say a prayer as the plane went in for the emergency landing.

This emergency landing marked the first time, since TCA began operations in Newfoundland, in May, 1942, that such an incident occurred.

169. Newfoundland's *Marie Celeste*

The strange fate of the brig *Resolven*, whose crew disappeared in Newfoundland's coastal waters in 1884, remains a mystery to this day. It was described in the 1920s by journalist Arthur Ainsworth of London as being in the same class as the

Marie Celeste. A dark cloud seemed to hang over the *Resolven,* and there was speculation that it was a cursed ship. From the day in August, 1884, when news of the ship's strange experience first broke, to the day it was lost in a shipwreck four years later, bad luck seemed to follow it.

The 143-ton *Resolven* was built from soft wood in Nova Scotia, and carried a crew of six men. Her captain was E. James and it hailed from Abberystwith. The *Resolven* arrived at Harbour Grace on July 14, 1884, with a cargo for John Munn & Co. Ltd. and was under charter to proceed to Labrador to take a cargo of fish to the Mediterranean. She departed Harbour Grace on August 27th and carried four passengers, who were going to Labrador to work at trimming herring for John Munn & Co. Ltd. The passengers were Doug Taylor and Bernard Colcord of Carbonear; Edward Keefe of Harbour Grace; Bill Bennett of Bell Island.

Soon after starting the voyage to Labrador, the *Resolven* experienced tragedy; the cause has remained a mystery ever since. By August 29th, just two days after departing, word was received in Harbour Grace that the ship had run into trouble on the Atlantic and was in tow to Catalina by the HMS *Mallard.* Shipwreck and tragedy were not unknown to Newfoundlanders, but when people heard the story of the *Resolven*, it sent chills up the spine of many Newfoundlanders and attracted international attention.

The vessel had been found deserted at the mouth of Trinity Bay. A rescue party could find no sign of life on board and a search of the area failed to turn up any trace of the crew, passengers, or anything that would give even the slightest hint of what the *Resolven* had encountered.

The mystery was heightened by the discovery that the sails were set, a fire was alight in the galley and no wreckage or disorder was found. The only thing out of place was the yardarm, which was broken and some ropes were left dangling.

One thing that gave them hope was the discovery that the lifeboat was missing. From all appearances, the crew and passengers had left in a hurry to escape some kind of imminent danger. No traces of the men or the missing lifeboat were ever found.

170. Bus out of Control on Long's Hill

Mike Cahill, driver of a Golden Arrow passenger bus in St. John's during the 1940s, found himself driving a bus with no brakes, full of passengers and speeding down Long's Hill. Only nerves of steel and cool-headed thinking stood between him and a major tragedy.

Cahill had just driven across LeMarchant Road where he had picked up many passengers, most of whom were heading for Bingo at the Benevolent Irish Society (BIS) on Queen's Road. At the Grace Hospital, a woman passenger got on board and took the seat near the bus driver. Old-time busses had a double seat opposite, but facing the driver and adjacent to the front window.

The ride was uneventful up until a passenger was dropped off at the top of Long's Hill, opposite Mickey Duggan's Barber Shop. When Cahill pulled away from the stop to continue downhill, he placed his foot on the brake to control the speed during the descent, and was startled to find the brakes had given out. Pumping the brakes proved to be a wasted effort. While the bus picked up speed, Cahill tried to slow it down by shifting into low gear, but this move also failed. The speed had been reduced a little but the bus continued out of control.

Only the lady in that front seat was aware of the situation and she was frozen with fear. Mr. Cahill, fearing what might happen when he reached the intersection at Long's Hill, begin flashing his lights and blowing the horn. Passengers, unaware of the loss of brakes, began shouting for the driver to slow down.

Fortunately, there was no traffic at the intersection, and the bus travelled across Queen's Road and down the slope by Gower Street Church. Cahill thought to himself that if he could turn the bus at the Gower Street intersection and then up Church Hill until she slowed down, he might be able to bring her to a slow crash and minimize injuries.

To his surprise, he was able to make the turn, and once again was able to go onto Church Hill. The bus was going fast enough to make it up Church Hill where Cahill turned right onto Queen's Road with the bus coming to a stop in front of the BIS.

While he took a deep breath and thanked God for delivering the bus from what seemed to be a certain tragedy, a woman stormed up from the back of the bus and struck him in the head with her hand. She scolded him for reckless driving and promised to contact the manager of the bus company to make sure he got fired.

At this point, the lady in the seat opposite Cahill told the angry passenger that the brakes had given out on the top of Long's Hill, and if the driver had not struggled to control the bus, they would have all likely been killed. The angry woman quickly apologized to the driver and was one of several on the bus that night who, in a letter to the bus company manager, lavished praise upon the driver's handling of the crisis.

171. Spiderman of the 'Drook'

When the *Tolsby* set sail from Galveston, Texas, on December 27, 1907, not one of the twenty-five-man crew had ever heard of the small village in Newfoundland, near Trepassey, known as the "Drook." Two weeks later, they were indebted to fishermen from that community for having saved their lives.

The *Tolsby* experienced fair sailing until January 13th, when it became engulfed in a raging blizzard. Captain C.J. Payne heard a whistle blowing at Powle's Head, but had no knowledge of any navigational aid in that area other than the one at Cape Race. He concluded the *Tolsby* was sailing a safe distance from shore and kept his course through the storm. Without warning, the ship struck something, and the captain and crew swiftly seized railings and whatever fixtures nearest to them to keep from being hurled overboard.

Unknown to the crew, the ship was heading towards land and had crashed upon the rocks at Little Seal Cove. An opening in the storm permitted them to see a towering 500-foot high cliff jutting up from the beach nearby. At first, the captain thought it would be safer to remain on the ship, rather than venture ashore. The winds increased and the waves pounded the vessel, which began to break up. The lifeboats were lowered, but were damaged in the water. One lifeboat with five men onboard made it to shore. When the *Tolsby* began to come apart, those who had not attempted to leave on lifeboats, jumped into the water and swam to ashore. It was a short distance, and all made it safely. Their joy over escaping their sinking ship was short-lived when they realized where they were. The men were now trapped on a strip of shore with a raging sea on one side and the ominous high cliffs on the other. Each time the tide rose, the men moved back towards the cliff. It seemed certain they were doomed.

Alexander Windberg and three other crew members used a marlin-spiked line to scale the cliff. By the time they reached the top, the rising seas had cut the others off from the point of ascent. An added danger to those on the beach was the falling rocks being displaced by the high winds. By dawn, the men were ready to give up when ropes suddenly appeared falling down the cliff as if coming from nowhere.

Leading the rescue effort by the fishermen from the Drook was Joe Perry. Perry knew the area well and volunteered to be lowered by rope down the cliff to rescue the stranded men.

While moving down the cliff, Perry took time to clear away large rocks to make the rescue effort easier. One by one, he sent up the *Tolsby* crewmembers until all were rescued. He was the last up the cliff. The Drook fishermen took the men to their village and gave them dry clothing, food and refreshments. When the weather cleared, the captain and crew of the *Tolsby* set out for St. John's. Before leaving, they took up a collection among themselves and presented it to Perry and his men as a token of appreciation for their courageous actions.

172. Lloyd's of London Would Not Insure this St. John's House

Lloyd's of London, the world's oldest and best-known insurers, was known to insure just about anything. A three-storey house, east of Hill O'Chips on Duckworth Street in St. John's, was one of their few exceptions. Lloyds had refused to insure the house while Smallwood lived there.

During the political battle for Confederation, there was widespread anger throughout St. John's against Joey Smallwood, who was the leading spokesman for the Confederate movement. One of the most serious incidents of the Confederation campaign erupted and was over before Smallwood knew anything about it. He was broadcasting from radio station VOCM on Parade Street when a large mob of angry anti-Confederates turned up at the door with a rope and threatened to lynch him.

Unaware of the danger lurking outside, Smallwood was delivering one of his famous speeches in support of Confederation inside. The station's owner, Joe Butler, saw the mob and called in the Newfoundland Constabulary, who quickly succeeded in dispersing them.

At the time, Smallwood was renting the bottom two flats in the Duckworth Street home. According to the former premier, "Friends of the landlord used to say that a mob would tear the house down and that he was foolish to let Smallwood live there. But the house owner merely smiled. He had, he thought, neatly provided against any such possibility for he had contacted the great Lloyd's of London insurance people and asked for a policy to fully insure against riot and civil commotion."

In fact, a crowd of 1,500 anti-Confederates who were angry at Smallwood did gather outside the house on one occasion and threatened to tear it down.

Ten years later, Joey Smallwood, then premier of Canada's newest province, recalled, "Imagine the landlord's chagrin, after it was all over. He discovered that Lloyd's had said they would not insure the house while Joe Smallwood lived there. And the local agent forgot to tell the landlord that Lloyd's would not accept the policy."

Years later, Smallwood said that all the opposition he encountered during the battle for Confederation never once made him nervous.

173. British Newspaper Recommended "Sell Newfoundland"

The prestigious London, England, newspaper, the *Times,* once advocated that England sell its oldest colony, Newfoundland, to France. Had they succeeded, Newfoundland today would be a colony of France. The famous editorial making the suggestion appeared in the *Times* on December 17, 1890. At the time, the French Shore question was a hot political issue in England, France and Newfoundland. The newspaper stated that some solution to the problem had to be found, and as France would not consider selling her claims, then England should sell all of Newfoundland to France as the easiest and quickest way to settle the matter once and for all. The matter was eventually settled with Newfoundland's colonial status remaining unchanged.

174. Law Demanded Sealers be Served Figgy Duff

A law was passed in Newfoundland in 1916 that specified exactly what meals were to be served at the annual seal hunt and on what days specified foods were to be served. This law was one of twenty-six different sections covering penalties and punishments on the owners and officers regarding the limitations of catch, load line, carrying guns, killing hood seals, bonuses to cooks, compensation for injury and conveyance home of any dead sealer. There were also eleven pages of printed reference material included.

Some of the items required to be served at meal times were: potatoes, turnip, beans, soft bread, figgy duff, and fish and brewis. The law demanded that figgy duff be served three times a week, whilst Sunday morning's breakfast was to be the popular fish and brewis.

Also, there was a law that prohibited seals to be killed on Sunday. That particular law was in effect as early as 1840. These laws were repealed in the early twentieth century.

175. Fishermen Stole Great Auk Eggs to Feed Family

One of the last homes of the Great Auk, which is now extinct, was the Funk Islands. During the late eighteenth century, taking the eggs of the Great Auk was forbidden by proclamation. In 1794, several fishermen were arrested, tried and found guilty of taking Great Auk eggs at the Funks. According to historian Judge D. Prowse, Chief Justice Reeves who tried the men was a just and impartial man, "...but in this case might have tempered justice with a little more mercy."

The fishermen were sentenced to be publicly whipped. However, the trial revealed that a man named Clarke of Greenspond, Bonavista Bay, had taken the eggs only as food for his wife and family who were in need. The chief justice weighed this factor and solemnly ordered that while the other fishermen should be publicly whipped as decreed, Mr. Clarke should only be flogged in private.

Prowse felt this was a backhanded method of showing clemency and commented, "We do not think this unfortunate victim of a cruel law appreciated the distinction."

176. Tried Renaming Newfoundland

A serious effort was made in 1829 to change the name Newfoundland to King George IV Island. At the time, there was a strong movement towards obtaining Representative Government for the colony, and some leaders of the movement felt it would help to flatter the reigning monarch of England, George the IV, by calling this country after him. Although the idea was not adopted, it took a long time to die out. Even after Representative Government was granted to Newfoundland in 1832, a bill was introduced in the legislature to rename the colony to King George IV Island. The bill was defeated and the name Newfoundland remained.

177. Pre-Confederation Dole

The reality of life for the ordinary Newfoundlander is all too often hidden by writers whose political agenda does not include telling the truth. The following is a typical one month order for food to feed a family of five in St. John's. Smaller families got less.

7 lbs. flour	Twenty cents (0.20¢)
½ lb. tea	Twenty-two cents (0.22¢)
4 tins milk	Forty-four cents (0.44¢)
7 lbs. sugar	forty-two cents (0.42¢)
2 lbs. rolled oats	ten cents (0.10¢)
2 lbs. margarine	fifty-four cents (0.44¢)
4 lbs. beef	fifty-two cents (0.52¢)

1 yeast cake	four cents (0.04¢)
2 lbs. salt	four cents (0.04¢)
3 lbs. hard bread	twenty cents (.20¢)
1 bar soap	ten cents (0.10¢)
½ gal. Kerosene oil	fifteen cents (0.15¢)
4 gal. potatoes	forty-eight cents (0.48¢)
5 lbs. salt fish	twenty-five cents (0.25¢)
5 lbs. turnip	ten cents (0.10¢)
5 pkg. matches	five cents (0.05¢)

Total $3.85

By 1948, the dole had risen to twenty-five cents per day.

Margarine was more expensive than meat. One pound of margarine cost twenty-seven cents, while one pound of beef cost thirteen cents. Margarine was protected by tariffs passed by government in the days before surrendering Newfoundland's independence in 1933. Recipients were not given money. They were issued a written order which they took to the grocery stores.

178. Catholics Paid Tax for Burial Rites

The first Catholics in Newfoundland were denied religious freedom and were treated like criminals if they were caught practicing their faith. It was a Scottish-born governor of Newfoundland who paved the way to have the law changed. He was Vice-Admiral John Campbell, who served as Newfoundland's governor and earlier as commander-in-chief of British Forces in Newfoundland from 1782 to 1786.

Alarmed over the harsh treatment of Roman Catholics by British authorities in Newfoundland, Governor Campbell issued a proclamation to allow all persons inhabiting the island to have full-liberty of conscience and the free exercise of such modes of religious worship as are not prohibited by law.

221

As a result of this action, Roman Catholic Bishop James Louis O'Donnel came to St. John's. He obtained permission to build a chapel and to perform all rites and ceremonies of the Catholic faith.

As late as 1836, Catholics in St. John's had to pay a burial fee to bury their dead. The fee amounted to twelve shillings per person. It was Bishop Fleming, his successor, who stood up to the Newfoundland government and forced the abolition of the tax.

Part 12

179. The Ice and Caterpillar Storm of 1861

The little community of Old Perlican, Trinity Bay, Newfound-land, experienced one of the most amazing storms ever to strike the province. In August, 1861, blocks of solid ice fell on Old Perlican for fifteen minutes, causing tremendous damage. Then, an amazing thing happened. When the ice melted, millions of caterpillars, which had been enclosed in the ice covered the ground, and moving onto the vegetable fields ate everything in their path.

180. Only Case Like it in the World

During the early twentieth century, a St. John's man named Moses O'Neill had the distinction of being the step-brother to a man who had died over 150 years earlier. This was believed to be the only such case in the entire world, and some kind of world record. Here's how it happened. Moses O'Neill was ninety years old at the time his story became known. O'Neill's father was married twice. His first son died, and sixty-five years later, when he was married again, at the age of over eighty, his other son, Moses O'Neill, was born. Thus, it came about that Moses O'Neill could say that his step-brother died over 150 years ago.

181. Newfoundland's Most Unusual Wedding

Perhaps the most unusual wedding ever to take place in Newfoundland and Labrador was the marriage of B.C. Bailey to a Miss Shave in Nipper's Harbour, Notre Dame Bay. Mr. Bailey was the telegraph operator in Nipper's Harbour in 1901. When Miss Shave said "yes" to his marriage proposal, the two made a visit to the local clergyman to schedule the marriage ceremony. Yet, this wedding was not to be like any other wedding.

The couple decided to wait until the end of 1899 to get married, so they could celebrate the New Year, and the new century. On New Year's Eve, December 31st, the church in Nipper's Harbour was full. Mr. Bailey and his bride-to-be came into the church just a few minutes before the stroke of the hour. While the minister pronounced the words, the groom held an open watch in his palm, to make sure that he was being married both on the last day of the nineteenth century and the first day of the twentieth century. It worked out perfectly. The Bailey's were married to each other in both centuries.

182. Moses Cutler's Friday

Moses Cutler, one of the first settlers in Fair Island, Bonavista Bay, always believed that Friday was a special day in his life. Here's why: He was born on a Friday. He joined the British Navy on a Friday. He left the Navy on a Friday. He arrived in Newfoundland on a Friday and arrived at Fair Island on a Friday. However, while Friday was a significant day in Cutler's life, his good fortune changed when, on a Friday, he got badly frost bitten and became crippled for life. Moses Cutler passed away on a Friday.

183. Vaudeville Days in Old St. John's

The first Vaudeville company to show an interest in establishing in St. John's was the Acker Vaudeville Company of Halifax. In March 1910, Mr. A. West, business representative and part owner of the company, leased the Star Hall on Henry Street to present Vaudeville shows. West and his wife were known in Vaudeville circles in Canada and the United States for their comic and acting abilities. They starred in the first Acker Vaudeville Show produced at the Star Hall on March 30, 1910. The show went on for nine nights and drew capacity crowds each night. The program included:

- The Irish Champion Dancers, Riley and Fleming.
- The comedy play, *Taming a Husband* with the Wests.
- The pretty breezy comedienne Greta Byron in *Some Class*.
- The funny jugglers, Owley and Randall in *Tumble Tom*.
- The Roberts Indoor Circus that included, "A marvelous troupe of trained bears, monkey's and dogs."

Supplying music was the famous local Star Orchestra. Two shows were held each evening at 7:15 p.m. and 9:00 p.m. Prices were ten cents for general admission and twenty-five cents for choice seating.

Mr. West told reporters, "St. John's is indeed the liveliest and prettiest little city I have visited in years." He said his company had plans to establish a full-time theatre in St. John's. These plans did not materialize, and this was the last we heard of the Acker Vaudeville's intention of permanently setting up in St. John's.

184. Vaudeville Storm the Town

Vaudeville was immensely popular in old-time St. John's and attracted full houses at performances in church halls and public theatres. Initially, the main Vaudeville theatres were the Nickel on Military Road and the Casino in the Total Abstinence Building on Duckworth Street. The British Hall later turned to Vaudeville. In 1911, the Casino Theatre brought in the Rossleys, a Scottish family famous on both sides of the Atlantic. They came to St. John's for a six-week booking, but their instant popularity with theatre goers in St. John's extended their stay at the Casino to nine months.

185. Haly Hutton at Bally Haly

The eccentric Haly Hutton amused townspeople during the 1890s. His strange behavior was explained by claims that he had been a colonial servant in British-Africa, where he suffered severe sunstroke, which affected his brain. Haly took up residence in the area now occupied by Bally Haly Country Club. He thought himself to be a grand military strategist and set up a fortification around his grounds with wooden guns and dummies.

The townsfolk encouraged Haly's military vision of himself and many would go and visit his fortifications to pass away a Sunday afternoon. Commander Haly would give an outline of his military strategies as he led them on a tour of the Haly fortification. Haly became famous around town by frequently hiring a Victorian Carriage to drive slowly up and down Water Street. He would remain standing during the ride and would raise his top hat as he gracefully bowed to all the ladies as he passed.

186. Flipper Smith and Caroline

Johnny Burke immortalized the couple Flipper Smith and Caroline in his famous Newfoundland song "The Kelligrews Soiree" as among the guests at Clara Nolan's Ball. The two were well-known in the town during Burke's time. Caroline Bowdin delighted in flowery hats and wore ribbons from head to toe. She married Flipper Smith, who got his name from selling flippers door-to-door when the sealers returned to St. John's in the spring. Flipper had a good memory for old Irish and Newfoundland ballads, and would sing them as he went about his work. Townsfolk looked forward to visits from Flipper and Caroline. There was always a "bit of sport" when the duo showed up in a neighbourhood.

Caroline's favorite saying was, "Half the world don't know how the other half lives." If Flipper was near he would interject, "With her big mouth, it's not her fault," and then he would add, "She's like an old shoe, all worn out but the tongue." The most memorable story of Caroline was after an embarrassing incident at Mount Carmel Cemetery, when she went around town with her arm in a cast, and the behind-the-back chuckles this sight attracted. In those days, women did not attend funerals. Later in the day, after a friend of Flipper and Caroline had been buried, the duo and several friends visited the grave so Caroline could pay her last respects.

When they arrived at the gravesite, they were surprised to see that the gravedigger had not yet filled it in. Caroline, known for her curiosity, stepped near the open grave to get a closer look.

When she bent over slightly to improve her view, Flipper goosed her and "the poor creature went head first into the grave." Hence the broken arm and the behind-the-back chuckles subsequently heard around town!

187. Message from Mars

Following secret experiments by Marconi in 1921, he concluded that Mars or some other planet was seeking to communicate with the world. J.C. Macbeth, the London manager of the Marconi Wireless Telegraph Co., startled people attending a luncheon in New York when he revealed the belief of Marconi and other experts. The experiments were conducted in the Mediterranean.

Mr. Macbeth told the group, which was attended by the media, that the apparatus intercepted wireless wavelengths of 150,000 metres, whereas the maximum wavelength produced in the world at that time was 14,000 metres. He added that the regularity of the wave lengths disproved the belief that it was due to electrical disturbances. The claim received media attention worldwide on October 15, 1921.

188. Ship of Dynamite Threatened St. John's

A burning ship in St. John's Harbour on November 14, 1895, carried enough explosives to wipe out the hundreds of men, women and children nearby and to cause a major destruction of property along the St. John's waterfront. It was only the incredible courage of a handful of firefighters, who, although knowing of the cargo of explosives on board, willingly risked their lives to prevent an even greater disaster.

The burning vessel was the *Aurora*, a famous whaler at the time. She was tied up at the Bowring Co. Wharf on the south side of St. John's Harbour. Dozens of ships with hundreds of workers were either tied up nearby or anchored in the harbour. Not far from the wharves was the Southside Road residential area with dozens of families; most of them were out watching the fire. The city had several fire stations. One station could be found at each of the following locations: Southside Road, the west end, centre city, and in the east end.

Fire alarm boxes were placed on poles strategically throughout the city. Each was connected to the fire hall system. In case of fire, the public used these to call in the alarm.

The steamship *Aurora* was a 356-ton vessel and carried a crew of sixty men. She participated in the whale hunt in the summer of 1895, and had battled hurricane-force winds on her return to St. John's.

It was in November that the *Auroa*, while docked in St. John's Harbour, had the potential of being the focal point of a major disaster. About 600 pounds of dynamite and 10,000 rounds of ammunition were stored below deck. The families, workers in the area and spectators who came over from the north side of the harbour did not have any knowledge of the treacherous cargo aboard the *Aurora*.

The drama on the harbour began when Second Officer Tom Walsh, standing on deck, noticed a trickling of smoke coming up the companionway. At first, he was not bothered by this, but in minutes the smoke began to billow up the companionway. When he went to investigate, he found the cabin directly below full of smoke and the captain's room on the starboard-side was engulfed in flames. Stored not far from these flames were the dynamite and ammunition.

Walsh alerted captain and crew, and a man was sent to call the alarm at Firebox 43 on South side Road. While the crew tried to control the fire with what little resources they had, firemen at the West End Station responded to the alarm. They hitched up their horses to the fire wagons, put on their suits and in just six minutes were at White's Wharf, a couple of hundred feet west of Bowring's, and ready to do battle. This was as close as the firemen could get to Bowring's Wharf that day.

Just as they were getting their hoses ready, the Southside firemen showed up. There was some confusion at first over what to do, but Captain Dunn of the West End Fire Department took control, and the firemen worked as a single unit. The two groups combined 800 feet of hosing to battle the blaze. This hosing extended from White's Wharf down over Stewart's, Tessiers' and Bowring's wharves. Captain Dunn estimated another thirty or forty feet of hose were needed. Although the central firemen were expected at any minute, Captain Dunn chose not to take a chance. He sent a man back to the West End Fire Station, near Job Street. In a short time, he was back with a sufficient length of hosing. When Captain Dunn moved onto the deck of the *Aurora* to take full control of the firefighting effort, he was joined by firemen from central, west end and the Southside.

The billowing smoke and flames from the burning vessel were attracting spectators from all around St. John's. Some came by foot while others rowed across the harbour. The firemen knew that the *Aurora* was carrying explosives and were aware of the potential for disaster. Regardless, Captain Dunn, accompanied by Sergeant Daniel Mulrooney and Fire Constable Reardon, risked their lives to go below deck and into the cabin where but a single wall separated the fire from the explosives. They remained steadfast in position until the fire was out and the threat to the public had ended.

The next day, the *Daily News* commented on the heroic deed, "They were perfectly aware that at any moment a terrible explosion might occur; that the cabin, in fact might prove their grave, but duty called and a true fireman knows no fear in such a case."

An eyewitness in a letter to the *Daily News* asked, "What would have been the result had that quantity of powder exploded. Can anyone measure the possible destruction of life and property likely to have accrued therefrom?" The writer suggested the men be recognized for their outstanding display of courage in risking their lives to bring the fire under control and to avoid certain disaster in St. John's Harbour.

The men were honoured within days by Sir Edgar Bowring, and two years later awarded medals. Sir Edgar Bowring sent a cheque for $100 to Inspector-General J.R McCowan for the men, "... as a slight recognition of the valuable services rendered by the fire brigade in so promptly suppressing the fire which broke out on the *Aurora.*

In response to this gift, Inspector General McCowan replied, "I feel proud of being in command of such men who, notwithstanding the knowledge of the extreme danger of the position in which they worked, yet performed their duty fearlessly because it was their duty." The danger was even greater than first thought because there were other vessels in the harbour carrying explosives.

Governor Murray was instrumental in having the men awarded medals in recognition for their heroism in fighting that fire. In 1897, in honour of Queen Victoria's Diamond Jubilee, the awards were presented to the following men: Inspector General McGowan, District Chief Dunn and Fire Constable John Reardon, the Silver Star; to Sergeant Daniel Mulrooney and Fire Constable James Howard, the Silver Medal for conspicuous gallantry and bravery.

189. Robbed Orphanage

One of the indications of the poor times in pre-Confederation Newfoundland was the widespread theft of food items and public begging. In October, 1921, a man named Oliver stole vegetables to feed his family from the Belvedere Orphanage in St. John's. When the police arrested him, they seized from his home a sack of turnips and cabbage.

Oliver was defended by George Ayre, who told the court he had no intention of trying to "justify larceny from an orphanage," but stressed the man's family was starving. He also noted that it was Oliver's first criminal offence. Mercy was shown by the court and the man received a suspended sentence.

The city lockup was sometimes used as an emergency shelter for homeless families. In October, 1943, a widow and five children, after being evicted from their Plank Road home, were put up in the women's cells at the courthouse. The staff at the lockup took up a collection and helped the family with money and food.

During the 1920s, large numbers of young able-bodied men, unable to find work in St. John's, moved to the forested areas around the city, including Southside Hills, in an effort to survive the hard times. They visited the city regularly and sought out food anywhere they could find it; including begging and theft.

It was a common practice for these men to go door-to-door, to the farms in the area, offering to work in return for a meal. *The Evening Telegram* reported on September 13, 1921, "This practice is so frequent as to become annoying, and farmers are fearful that, made desperate by hard times these 'out-of-works' will take to stealing. Generally, the farmers treat them well, and when considered deserving they give them a meal."

190. One Hundred Trapped Inside Train

For seventeen days during the winter of 1903, the attention of Newfoundlanders was focused on the plight of 100 passengers stranded in a train, in almost daily blizzard conditions at the Gaff Topsails. This is an area of hills in western Newfoundland described by nineteenth century surveyors as the Himalayas of Newfoundland.

The Reid Newfoundland Railway express train left St. John's on February 17th for a cross-country trip, during which passengers were dropped off and new passengers taken on at various communities along the way. The train remained on schedule until February 23rd when it neared the Gaff Topsails. Blizzard conditions had deposited fifteen to twenty-three-foot high drifts along the railway line, which forced the train to a complete stop. The telegraph operator aboard the express sent a message to St. John's that the train, which now had 100 passengers aboard, was stranded at Kitty's Brook near the Gaff Topsails, just east of Sandy Lake.

In the days that followed, newspaper reports told of the plight of those stranded on the train and the constant daily battle with snow, high winds and frost. The frost became so severe that rescue teams sent by the Railway Company could only work short shifts or they would suffer frostbite. Conditions deteriorated to the point that even when extra money was offered to workers, it was difficult to get anyone to work outside in the terrible freezing conditions.

On the train, every effort was made to make passengers as comfortable as possible. Food was provided at no cost, and passengers and the train crew joined together to cut and retrieve wood to burn, keeping the train warm for all aboard.

Snow continued to fall for fifteen days, with temperatures ranging between three and twenty-three degrees below freezing. The Railway Company sent out fifty snow-fighters and a relief train escorted by a rotary train to clear the tracks. The rotary was derailed, and the relief train became stranded in the snow. A major effort was required to get the rotary back on the tracks. The rescue train, which had been sent from Bay of Islands, exhausted its thirty tons of coal after just one day of battling conditions at the Gaff Topsails.

Some passengers decided to take the risk of walking through the storm to nearby villages. William Coombs of Brig Bay on the northern peninsula was among those who left the train. Two weeks later, he walked into his home to the amazement of friends and relatives. Coombs had walked 250 miles, stopping at Bonne Bay and Deer Lake to rest. A factor that contributed to William Coombs success was that he was an experienced outdoorsman and familiar with the area.

Eventually, with the help of snow-fighters, the train managed to move slowly, inch by inch, and on March 10th arrived at Port aux Basques. The ordeal had taken seventeen days. The train's engineer commented to a reporter, "We met the Devil and we beat him." A similar incident took place during February and March of 1905. In that instance, the train took five weeks to travel from Port aux Basques to St. John's. The train's crew was forced to resort to tearing up the railway ties behind them to use as fuel to keep the train moving. This was not the last time this practice was used to keep a train moving in desperate conditions.

In 1959, 700 passengers were stranded in two trains in Clarenville when a two-day blizzard struck. A pregnant woman among the passengers decided not to wait out the storm. She set out on foot and walked seven miles to the nearest hospital where she gave birth to a seven-pound, two-ounce baby boy.

191. St. John's First Movie Theatres

The Nickel Theatre, which became a movie theatre in 1907, was also known as The Irish. On Saturday, June 25, 1960, the Nickel showed its last movie. It was *Damn Yankees* starring Tab Hunter. The Nickel Theatre was located in the old BIS Building, opposite to the Roman Catholic Basilica on Military Road.

The Majestic Theatre opened to the public on March 3, 1919. Its original owners were Tom Coady and Tom O'Neill. It was later taken over by the famous Stan Condon of real estate fame in St. John's. The Majestic closed in early 1953 and was sold on May 15, 1953, to the firm Majestic Sales, which converted it into a retail shop and warehouse. The Majestic Theatre was located at the corner of Queens Road and Duckworth Street.

The Nickel and Majestic theatres converted to talking motion pictures in 1929, and jointly became the first theatres in Newfoundland and Labrador to feature the talkies. These first showings took place on August 26, 1929. The Nickel featured *The Desert Song*, which starred John Bola and Myrna Loy, while the Majestic featured *The Fall of Eve*, which was a narrative delivered by Patsy Ruth Miller.

The Crescent Theatre was advertising in newspapers in 1910, and may have opened before that year. It was originally owned by Patrick Laracy who drowned on the *Florizel* in 1918. J.P. Kieley, owner of the Nickel Theatre, was also a victim of the *Florizel* disaster. Edward Boulos succeeded Kieley as owner, and operated the Crescent until it closed down the late spring of 1947.

The Star Theatre was operated by Stan Condon, who leased the top floor of the Star Hall on Henry Street in 1932 after the original Star had been destroyed by fire, and was rebuilt soon after. The old Star Theatre had been showing movies since 1911 when Jack Rossley operated it, and sometimes included films with live Vaudeville shows. On its last day as a theatre on May 25, 1953, a double feature was shown: *Walking My Baby Back Home* with Donald O'Connor, Janet Leigh and Buddy Hackett followed by *Tumbleweed* staring Audi Murphy. For a short while after, it was leased by the federal government and used as a post office, while the post office on Water Street was being rebuilt.

In 1997, the old theatre was cleaned up and used for the Flower Hill reunion that year. The old theatre accommodated 500 people for a banquet and was used over the three-day reunion for live entertainment, a stage show and several dances. The opera boxes put there in 1915 by the Rossley family were still accessible in 1997.

The Regal Theatre, also known as the Little Star, was on the north side of New Gower Street, west of Casey Street. The exact date of its closure is not known, but Owen Moore of Hamilton Avenue says it was in the early 1940s. He recalled escaping from the Regal on the day it was destroyed by fire. It later became the Belmont Tavern owned by the Byrne brothers, Jack and Jim.

The Capitol Theatre, previously the Casino Theatre, opened in June, 1935. It was located on the top floor of the Total Abstinence Building on Duckworth Street, with its entrance from Henry Street. It was destroyed by fire on October 26, 1946, and was rebuilt and reopened on November 20, 1950. It changed hands several times and went out of business permanently because it couldn't compete with the new theatres at the Avalon Mall, which opened in 1967.

The Queen Theatre changed its name to the New Queen Theatre and then later the York Theatre. Talking movies came to the New Queen Theatre on May 13, 1931. The theatre had been closed for several weeks preparing for the event. The Queen's owner, Johnny Duff, had the latest RCA Photophone equipment installed in his theatre which enabled people to hear as well as see "...everything in Paramount Pictures." The first talking features shown at the opening were:

- *Paramount on Parade* – featured dance, song, comedy and drama.
- *Sweepin' the Clouds Away* – with Maurice Chavalier
- *Insurance* – with Eddie Cantor.

The admission was thirty-five cents, and there were two shows each night. The Queen was between George Street and Water Street, with its main entrance from Queen Street. Around 1939, it was connected by the construction of a long hallway to Duff's Building on Water Street, which became the main entrance to the movie theatre. It was renamed the York Theatre.

In the 1960s, the York Theatre closed and was turned into a warehouse, which was destroyed by fire around mid-May, 1988. The building was also used as The Wonderland Theatre before 1931.

The Paramount Theatre was located on Harvey Road, west of The Rooms. It was opened on September 1, 1944, and was considered the most modern and plush theatre in all of Newfoundland. It was closed down after its roof collapsed in February, 1973. The movie showing at the time was *Mary Queen of Scots*. Nobody was injured in the mishap.

The Paramount was constructed by B.D. Parsons, the same man who constructed the Old Colony, Adelaide Motors and the King's Bridge Apartments.

Newspapers described the Paramount as the showplace of Newfoundland. The theatre had a seating capacity for 1,200 people. It also had an air conditioning system, which changed the air in the theatre every five minutes.

The Paramount was financed by a group of businessmen headed by W.R. Goobie. It was turned over to the Newfoundland Amusements Ltd., a subsidiary of Famous Players Theatre, which, in turn, was owned by Paramount Pictures of Hollywood.

The Paramount was built on the same scale as the York in Montreal and the Eglington in Toronto. It was managed by Nora Hogan, who also managed the Capitol Theatre. The movie which was played at the opening of the Paramount was *Broadway Rhythm* starring George Murphy and Ginny Simms.

The Cornwall Theatre was on Lemarchant Road in a building used today as Smith Stockley Plumbing, just opposite the West End Fire Station. It opened in October, 1948, and closed in 1955. Newspapers described it as, "A well-equipped modern theatre."

The Cornwall was designed by Messrs Luke, Little and Mace of Montreal and was constructed by Concrete Products. Each seat in the theatre was accurately positioned facing the screen, thus eliminating all awkward angles.

A gold-colored stage curtain was imported from New York, and was supplied by Motion Picture Supplies Ltd. The movie equipment was made by Motiograph and was installed by C.H. Hutton & Sons of St. John's.

Alexander McKenzie of United Movies Ltd. supervised the outfitting of the theatre. Unlike other theatres in St. John's, the Cornwall hired usherettes instead of ushers. The manager of the Cornwall was Thomas Hibbs, and many movies shown there were British films.

The first movie shown was *Sun Valley Serenade* starring Sonja Heini and John Payne. Matinees were twenty cents for adults and ten cents for children. Evening admissions were forty cents for adults and twenty cents for children.

192. Explosion Tosses Baby from One Ship to Safety on Another.

In 1761, one of the most astonishing events ever to occur at sea took place on an English ship, which was taking passengers to St. John's, Newfoundland. According to the *Newfoundlander*, June 1848:

The accident sounds incredible, but its sober history, for it is recorded in the 1761 edition of the "Annual Register," an old annual publication which published all the main events in English history from year to year during a period of almost a century.

The English vessel was the *Tuscany*, hailing from Bristol in command of Captain Edward Power. She left Bristol late in April, 1761, and evidently was carrying a number of crews to engage in the Newfoundland fishery.

On the first day, they encountered the *French Duke de Biron's* privateer, which immediately opened fire on them. The *Tuscany*, in those war times was obviously carrying some explosives for the account says that when the French privateer's shots struck her, she blew up.

Out of 211 people aboard, only the captain and four or five others were saved. Among those saved was an infant. When the explosion occurred, this infant was blown completely away from the *Tuscany*, and landed on the deck of the Frenchman completely unhurt!

193. The Rooms is Built on the Site of Town's Poor House

When hundreds of families were displaced by the fire of 1846, a row of wooden sheds were constructed at Fort Townshend to temporarily house the displaced. After the city was rebuilt and people moved back to their new homes, the sheds were turned into a poor house for the paupers of the city. Forty paupers, sleeping six to a room occupied the sheds, which were then known as "The Camps." They were given weekly basic supplies which included soap, tea, molasses, hard bread, and on Sunday's a pound of beef.

194. Tuberculosis Claimed Lives of 22,000 Newfoundlanders, 1910-1945

Prior to Newfoundland becoming a province of Canada, between 1910 and 1945, 22,000 Newfoundlander's lost their lives to Tuberculosis (TB). (Over 600 lives lost per year). The TB rate in Newfoundland was the highest in North America. According to the Newfoundland Government Registrar General records the age group which suffered the most deaths were males between the ages of fifteen and nineteen and females between twenty and twenty-four.

195. Women Patients Not Accepted at Old St. John's Hospital

The military hospital on Forest Road was abandoned by the military in 1870, and used as a public hospital. Due to its size, only male patients were accepted. The hospital was a danger to health because of defects in drainage and water supply. On March 7, 1871, patients were moved to St. George's barracks, Walsh's Square, while the Forest Road hospital was being renovated. Patients were moved back by November, 1871. It had three wards and could accommodate twenty patients. It was a novelty to have indoor toilets. Patients from the Riverhead Hospital at Victoria Park in the west end of St. John's were moved there in 1871.

In 1874, two new wings were added with fifteen beds each and two small isolation wards.

In1876, a new wing was added, which allowed the admission of female patients for the first time. The hospital went without an operating room until 1885, at which time it housed sixty patients.

In 1880, expansion included an ice house and a carriage house. Trees were added in 1881, and the hospital was named the General Hospital.

196. Horse Racing Older than St. John's Regatta

In the 1830s, the area of St. John's today known as Flower Hill was a thriving race horse track. In 1833, the Turf Club met at Perkin's Hotel and organized the first horse races at the Flower Hill Race Course, which were held on September 19, 1833. Dr. William Carson's horse, Blucher, won over three others and he donated part of his winnings to the BIS Orphan Asylum on Queen's Road. The prize known as the "Queen's Plate" was for eighty dollars cash. The race was run in heavy rain.

Dr. William Carson kept his horses at Craigmiller, now known as Craigmiller Avenue. This was his country residence, and was named after Mary Stuart's castle in Scotland. Horse races were also held at Best's Farm, on Topsail Road and on Quidi Vidi Lake. Horse racing in St. John's pre-dated the annual St. John's Regatta.

197. The Start of Bowling in St. John's

In the nineteenth century, bowling was popular in St. John's. It was played in alleys on Water Street, located opposite Holloway Street. Actually, the game was the forerunner of bowling and, at that time, was known by several names including: ninepins, skittles, bowls or bowling. It was played in the open, and in 1892 had four alleys. In the 1870s, Holloway Street was called Skittles Alley.

There were other bowling alleys at Foran's (Atlantic) Hotel, Lindberg's Castle, Signal Hill and the Caribou Hut. The Holy Name Society on Harvey Road opened a bowling alley in 1927. The Duff Building, Water Street, later the York Theatre, had a bowling alley. In the 1930s, there was a bowling alley at the Radio Building near Barron and New Gower streets.

Colonial Street, originally called South West Street, had the South West Street Skating Rink. It featured summer bowling and winter skating. This was an outdoor facility. Bishop Feild College was later built on the site.

198. Best Preserved Old Water Street Buildings

The best preserved nineteenth century buildings on Water Street, St. John's, are those between Yellow Belly Corner (a.k.a. Rankin's Corner) and Mahon's Lane. These buildings were built inside the ruins of the 1846 fire. A building was torn down to make way for a firebreak between George Street and Water Street at Beck's Cove. This was owned by Jim Seaton, who

241

operated the *Newfoundland Express* newspaper, which was published three times weekly. The newspaper was on the eastern side of the firebreak and for years was called Rankin's Corner.

Mahon's Lane was originally called Blockmakers Lane because the Mahon family operated their blockmaker shop there. It was destroyed by fire in 1861. Four buildings east of William's Lane included: David Smallwood's Boot Store and Parsons Photography, owned by Simeon Parsons before and after the 1892 fire.

Nearby William's Lane was a busy street in the 1800s. It was named after Prince William, who spent a summer in Newfoundland. Three doors east of Adelaide Street was Fox's Snuff Shop. A popular attraction in its window was the bust of a man smoking a pipe, which could be activated to show him inhaling and blowing smoke from the pipe. This piece of old St. John's history was on display in the lobby at St. John's City Hall for years.

199. Hard Tack Towed 150 Miles

Hard bread, better known throughout Newfoundland history as hard tack, was used mostly for fish and brewis. Purity Factories in St. John's supplies Newfoundland's modern-day demand for the popular product, but in the nineteenth century all hard tack in the Newfoundland market was imported from Hamburg, Germany and was known as "Hamburg bread." This German-made bread was a lot harder than the modern-day article, as the following story will illustrate.

A coastal captain took a cake of Hamburg bread, bored a hole through it, inserted a line through the hole, tied a knot, and let the cake of bread down over the stern of his vessel into the water just before sailing from St. John's. He towed the hard bread for 150 miles, all the way to Seldom Come By in the Fogo district before it melted enough to break clear of the line.

200. Incredible Seal Hunt Tale

One of the most incredible true tales from the Newfoundland seal hunt took place in 1868 off Bird Island Cove, Trinity Bay, and involved the barquentine, *Eric*.[1]

The *Eric*, owned by Rorke & Sons of Carbonear, sailed from that port with sixty-four sealers under Captain Perry on March 5th. By the 25th, the vessel and crew had received such a battering and endured so many casualties that Captain Perry decided it was time to return to Carbonear.

However, one man had broken his leg and the others were on the ice hunting seals. It was March 22nd, and before Captain Perry could call the men back to the ship, the weather suddenly turned strange and a violent wind with snow struck with a vengeance. The storm hammered the area for thirty-nine hours and by the time it came to an end, two men were lost and fifteen were seriously frost bitten. Hardly a man escaped without some effect of the long exposure to the elements.

Perry organized his men and quickly got all the survivors and injured back on board. He then set out for home. On the return trip, the *Eric* encountered another snowstorm and barely avoided crashing on the breakers en route. Her anchors brought her up just in time.

There was a sea raging, and between this and the blizzard, death and destruction faced the *Eric* and her crew. The storm continued until Sunday and the men were giving up all hope of survival. Perry later recalled that every man on board was praying for a miracle. Then suddenly to the north, Captain Perry noticed a pale, low-lying narrow strip of something in the water. Using his binoculars, he took a closer look and recognized that it was a long narrow strip of ice. Strangely, it was moving toward the *Eric*.

[1] Bird Island Cove was renamed Elliston after Reverend William Ellis, and early Methodist minister in the community.

It didn't take long before the ice was brushing against the side of the sealing vessel. Gradually, it was pushed and guided between the vessel and the shore. When the captain and the men realized that this "ice out of nowhere" had formed a bridge between them and shore, they knew their prayers had been answered. All sixty-three men on the *Eric* made it safely to shore over the mysterious bridge.

Little wonder that for decades afterwards it was described as, "One of the most miraculous events to ever happen at the seal fishery."

201. Farley Mowat on Whitewashing Newfoundland History

Knowledge of the outrageous treatment of Newfoundland by British and Newfoundland merchants in the 450 years before Confederation was on its way to being whitewashed and eliminated from our history. However, recent research and writings have rescued that part of our history from eventual obliteration. This was the Newfoundland past that Canada's great writer Farley Mowat and Newfoundland's Harold Horwood often lamented, and Horwood struggled to preserve.

When Mowat passed away in May, 2014, *The Telegram* (on May 4th) published the following quote he made in 1966:

During the past seventeen years, Newfoundland has made a galvanic leap out of the morass of a feudal-primitive society into the gleaming material society of twentieth century North America. More than a century has been spanned in less than two decades.

The New Newfoundlander has now emerged; well-fed, secure in his possessions, guaranteed against oppression, healthy and hopeful. He is also, and this is very sad, rather naked, and increasingly uncertain of himself and in a condition where he is rapidly being bereft of those tenuous, but vital, links which give every man a place in the continuity of human history.

The metamorphosis which stripped him of the rags of poverty, cleansed him of the scabs of disease, and freed him from the brand of servitude – has also stripped him of his history, his story; without which he can have no culture of his own and no firm grip on certainty.[2]

Poverty among Newfoundlanders was the main battle that the Newfoundland people struggled against in the pre-Confederation days. The events of the 1930s are widely-known today but the following item describes a much earlier era.

Historian P.K Devine described the years between 1864 and 1868:

> The word 'dole', it is true was not used then, but 'poor relief,' and more than half Newfoundland was under it from 1864 to 1868. Indian meal and molasses got such a bad and bitter name that it has lasted ever since, in spite of the fact that it is an excellent food and well-off people who were not rationed, not only in Newfoundland but every other country, never thought otherwise. I am told that John D. Rockefellers' preferred diet is Indian meal, or at least it was in his younger days. In 1866-67 the able-bodied men with their five or six children could be seen going down to the Depot at Hoylestown every day to get food. In our day this job is mostly relegated to the women and girls, but the stalwart men of that day had more good sense than false pride and felt there was no disgrace involved.

---

[2] The unblemished feudal-primitive (Newfoundland) history referred to by Mowat is told in a stark naked manner in my recent books *1949: The Twilight Before the Dawn* and *Newfoundland's Era of Corruption*. Both works were published by Creative Publishers.

Thousands of Newfoundlanders fled the country and started new lives in the United States, Canada and Australia. They saw no future in Newfoundland; few ever returned.

Part 13

202. Historic Newfoundlander Encountered a Mermaid

Sir Richard Whitbourne was described by historian David Prowse as, "…our historian and Newfoundland's steadfast friend, more to us and dearer to our hearts as colonists than even the brave and most unfortunate Sir Humphrey Gilbert." He was sent to Newfoundland in 1615 to set up a formal court of justice at his own expense. Sir Richard also claimed that he came face to face with what he described in his diary as, "a mermaid." He is not the only one at that time who claimed a similar experience.

Sir Richard claimed that he came face to face with a creature in St. John's Harbour that strongly resembled a mermaid. The creature he described was also encountered by two fishermen a few miles from St. John's Narrows during 1762. The fishermen, both from Little Bay West, also said the creature was a mermaid. They claimed it came up from the ocean and attempted to climb aboard a dory near them.

Their description of the creature was similar to the one given by Sir Richard almost 150 years earlier. He wrote:

The creature came within the length of a long pike from me and was about 15 feet long. I was standing by the riverside in the harbour of St. John's when it very swiftly came swimming toward me looking carefully at my face, like a woman. The face seemed to be beautiful and well proportioned. It had about the head many blue streaks resembling hair but it certainly was not hair.

It later came to the boat and put both hands on the side. This frightened the crew and one of them struck it hard on the head causing it to fall back into the water. The men in the boats were frightened by the creature and fled to land.

What was this strange creature? Some suggested it was a seal, but others noted that a master like Sir Richard Whitbourne and an experienced Newfoundland fisherman would have known a seal if he saw one.

203. Man thought to be Dead Returned!

The entire population of Western Bay was shocked to see Captain Jim Halfyard walking through their community because they had already held a funeral service for him.

After learning that Captain Jim had fallen overboard and was lost at sea, the Western Bay community went into mourning. According to the customs of the time, window blinds in homes were lowered, and flags on land and on boats in the harbour flew at half-mast. Hardly anyone noticed the arrival, a few days later, of the brigantine *William* from Brigus. However, people became curious after the ship lowered a dory, which brought several men to shore. Everyone knew that its entire crew was from Brigus and wondered why they were in Western Bay.

Their curiosity turned into shock when the lifeboat neared shore, and residents thought they were seeing a ghost. Among those in the dory was the man they believed had already drowned at sea. Seated in the stern of the dory was the hale and hearty Captain Jim Halfyard. The captain had an amazing tale to tell.

His crew was made up entirely of his own brothers. On the night of his disappearance, a thunder and lightning storm was raging and the winds were blowing at gale force, causing high rolling seas. Captain Jim was at the helm, when a sudden lurch of his ship knocked him overboard. By the time his brothers discovered he was missing, the vessel had travelled far away from him. He fought desperately to cling onto life and prayed that the others would discover he was missing and return to search for him.

The captain's prayers seemed to be answered when his brothers became aware he had been washed overboard. They retraced their course but to no avail. They searched for hours in the storm until reaching near exhaustion. Some discussion took place among them, and after considering the storm and the time the captain had been in the water they concluded he could not have possibly survived. Totally disheartened and saddened they returned to Western Bay carrying the tragic news to family and friends.

Meanwhile, a crewman on the *William*, which was passing through the area, heard a faint cry for help and convinced Captain Whalen to go back and search. The seas were still rolling heavily and there was pelting rain. Still, despite their efforts there was no sign of anyone in the water.

Ready to give up, Captain Whalen leaned over the side and extended a boat hook into the area where the crewman had reported the cry for help. Suddenly, Whalen felt the hook catch something and he pulled it up and out of the water. It was Captain Jim Halfyard, who by then had lost consciousness. He was revived, given warm clothing and some hot tea and then taken back to Western Bay.

Commenting on his miraculous rescue, Halfyard said, "Providence sent this noble ship and her crew to rescue me. It was a miracle how they found me in the darkness and the storm. God answered my prayers after all."

204. An Unusual Reunion!

In the midst of a raging wind and rain storm off the coast of Nova Scotia, two Newfoundlanders who had not met since boyhood were suddenly reunited in a remarkable way. Captain Joe Emberley was skipper of the *Wally G.*, a sixty-eight-foot schooner. A native of English Harbour East, Fortune Bay, Captain Emberley had only one arm. His boyhood friend was Captain Lee Handrigan from nearby Rencontre East.

The two men were childhood friends who went their separate ways after leaving school to become sea captains. In the events leading up to their dramatic reunion, Captain Emberley had taken his seventeen-year-old nephew on what started out as a routine cargo trip from Halifax to the Magdalena Islands. To save time, he took a shortcut through the gut of Canso, rather than around Cape Breton Island. A sudden storm erupted. It was so violent, it wrecked the ship and sent her on the rocks at White Point.

Just before the ship went down, Emberley jumped away from it and landed in the middle of floating, dangerous wreckage. He succeeded in reaching a large piece of the deck and managed to climb onto it. From there he made a succession of attempts to rescue his nephew, who was near exhaustion and clinging to the stern of the ship.

Each time he neared the boy, he shouted for him to let go and swim to the wreckage, but the frightened boy was too weak to make the effort. Emberley said, "It was a terrible feeling to see a shipmate and a blood relative drown before your eyes."

The piece of wreckage carrying Emberley began drifting out to sea. In desperation the captain tried to attract the attention of two passing schooners, but had no success. By 5:00 a.m. the next morning, he was near exhaustion. He couldn't summon the strength to call for help to a ship passing nearby.

The captain of the passing ship was standing on deck and noticed something bobbing around in the water. He quickly ordered a lifeboat over the side and went to investigate. Captain James Emberley was astounded when he recognized the man coming to his rescue was Lee Handrigan, the childhood friend he had not seen in years. It was a reunion both men never forgot and a story still remembered in Newfoundland.

205. Phenomenon in Skies Above St. John's

There is nothing unusual about witnessing a rainbow, but the one that appeared in the skies over St. John's on March 25, 1842, brought people to the streets to witness it in awe. This event was described in Lord Bonnycastle's *History of Newfoundland*. The phenomenon was a bow, but not a rainbow, and it did not display the ordinary colours of a rainbow. Lord Bonnycastle wrote:

> On the evening of Good Friday, March 25th, 1842, with the thermometer at 30 degrees Fahrenheit and a northeast wind, a most unusual appearance was exhibited at sunset around 6:30 p.m. The western sky over St. John's was in a blaze of rosette and fire coloured angry light after the sun dipped a blaze which reflected on the eastern or sea sky to a great extent; and just as the sun had disappeared behind the hill, a perfect bow appeared in the east. This bow did not have the usual rainbow colours. It was made up of a variation of the colour red, from fiery red to the rosette. It was a perfect arch of the usual size and height of a rainbow at sunset.

According to Bonnycastle, on the previous evening the eastern sky at sunset was beautifully coloured with purple and red down to the horizon, while the western sky was not. The thermometer varied only two or three degrees above or below freezing all the time; yet both these appearances were succeeded only by light thaws.

The historian noted that while snow covered the land and ice lay offshore, there was neither snow nor rain during the two days of the unusual phenomenon. It seemed so spectacular that some thought it was the end of the world.

206. Dream led to Arctic Rescue

Captain Frank Ash of Trinity, Newfoundland, never claimed to have any psychic powers, yet he did have a disturbing dream that led a rescue expedition to rescuing seven survivors of an ill-fated Arctic expedition.

That expedition was sent to the Arctic in 1881 by the United States government. Lieutenant Adolphus Greeley, a U.S. cavalry officer was in command of the twenty-five men assigned to carry out the assignment. They took with them 140 tons of coal and provisions to last three years.

The *Proteus*, under the command of Captain Richard Pike, a Newfoundlander, took the expedition to the Arctic and waited with them until they completed building a wooden house.

The party ran into problems a year later when the Newfoundland sealing vessel the *Neptune*, carrying supplies to them, was forced to turn back after encountering severe ice conditions.

On June 29, 1883, Captain Pike took his ship to a place called Payer Harbour, which was closer to Greeley's Party than the *Neptune* had gotten. This was also an unsuccessful effort.

Ice crushed the *Proteus* causing it to break up and sink. Captain Pike managed to get three lifeboats off before the ship went down. Pike and his seven-man crew hauled and rowed their lifeboats 800 miles to Disko, Greenland.

Meanwhile, back in the U.S., Arctic experts were gravely concerned about the chances of their men ever being found. Three ships, the Bear from Scotland and the *Thetis* and *Alert,* both Newfoundland sealing vessels, were chartered by the U.S. to conduct the search. As an incentive, they offered a $25,000 reward to anyone who could locate the missing men. The three-ship fleet was manned by 102 hand-picked American sailors who were placed under the command of William Sachley. Two Newfoundland sea captains, Frank Ash of Trinity and a Captain Norman, were hired as ice pilots.

Nobody expected that Captain Ash would hold the key to finding the survivors. His insight came through a vision while sleeping. Ash had a dream that he came upon a house erected by the Greeley party. He said that the next morning, when he boarded the *Bear* he had the location etched clearly in his mind. Acting upon the information from his dream, Captain Ash directed the search.

When they located Greeley's records their expectations soared. Although it was not easy going, the searchers pushed on following Captain Ash and succeeded in finding Captain Greeley and six survivors. One man had lost both hands and feet to frostbite. A spoon was applied with a bandage around his stump in hopes of preventing infection. The bodies of those who died were exhumed from their frozen graves and returned to the United States for burial. The survivors spent two weeks in St. John's before returning home.

Captain Ash passed away in 1938, at the age of ninety-one. The reward was distributed among the successful search party members.

207. A Novena Answered

In October, 1926, Ferryland was in desperate need of food. Times were hard and the nuns at the community's Roman Catholic school organized the children to make a Novena, asking for something good to happen that would relieve their distress.

On the final day of the nine-day Novena, one child disappointingly asked the good sister why nothing had happened. She replied, "The day isn't over yet." It turned out to be a memorable day, and one which the good sister was not allowed to forget for a long, long time. Just before the end of the school day something seemingly bad happened, which turned out to be a Godsend for the community. It was interpreted as an answer to their prayers.

The event began with the wreck of the *Torhamvan* on the north side of Ferryland. The vessel was en route to Montreal, when it ran aground in a dense fog. For some time the people could hear the ship's horn blowing, but were unable to see the doomed ship as she manoeuvred between Goose Island and the reefs, which threatened to trap her.

At 5:00 p.m., the sound of wrenching metal was heard through the fog. At one point, an empty lifeboat drifted to the beach, which caused fear among bystanders who felt sure the crew had drowned. It turned out to be an empty lifeboat that had broken away from the ship.

Ferryland residents: Mike Kinsella, Billy Williams and John Will Costello went out in a small boat and successfully rescued everyone from the vessel. In the end, there was no loss of life and tragedy was avoided. However, the government impounded the cargo, but not before a good supply of paint, ham, lard and macaroni found its way into many homes. The beaches of Ferryland were literally white with macaroni for weeks afterwards.

The arrival of so much food, and the manner in which it arrived, satisfied people that the Novena had been answered. A holy display of bronze statues was removed from the ship and given to the Ferryland Catholic Church, where they have been on display ever since.

208. Child Prisoners

A newspaper reporter walking along Water Street on June 2, 1908, was appalled by the sight of three children, ranging in age from eleven to thirteen years, being carted off by the local Constabulary to Her Majesty's Penitentiary in St. John's.

The children were confined in the back of a horse-drawn police cart with three adult convicts, one of whom was a man convicted of attempted murder. The sight of the little children crying and pleading to be released attracted the attention of many people that day. But the citizens, police and prison guards could do little to help. They were victims of a justice system that treated children as adults.

The reporter stated, "To see boys being dragged along with such characters was a disgrace to the community, and only once again demonstrates the need for a reformatory." Demands for a children's reformatory were frequently made by people outraged by this form of justice. Several days after these children were jailed; a ten- year-old-boy named Woodley was arrested by police and sent to prison. He had stolen cigarettes from Annie George's Store on Water Street. He was caught by police as he puffed on a cigarette in a Water Street laneway.

Unlike the other three children, he was not given the luxury of a ride to prison. The boy was thrown together with five adult prisoners and forced to march along Water Street to the prison. The lad was wearing ragged clothes and had no shoes. The *Daily News* reported, "Such a scene is a disgrace in the chief town of Britain's oldest colony and the need for a reformatory was once more strongly demonstrated."

A thirteen-year-old boy was sent to jail for leaving his job on a fishing vessel. He had been charged and convicted of desertion. Another boy named McGrath was serving time for vagrancy, while the remaining two were jailed for theft.

William Kendall, a volunteer worker at the prison, was re-
pulsed by the scene of youngsters crying and being forced into
cells with adult prisoners. He wrote a letter to the local papers.
It read:

> Among the lads there was one poor little fellow only
> eleven years old. His little baby face was the very pic-
> ture of guilessness and innocence, his cries were heart
> rending. he pleaded that if they would let him out he
> would never do it again, but of course, the officials had
> no power to release him and there he was, little older
> than a baby, behind bars.
>
> The child shared a cell with an adult convict. Kendall
> continued, 'While making enquiries about him his eyes
> filled with tears, and his whole face was the picture of
> anguish and trouble. Your readers can form their own
> opinions of a system which consigns such as these to a
> common jail.'

Others in St. John's favoured severe punishment for children who commit crimes. The following comments appeared
in the *Daily News* in a letter signed, "Pro Bono." It read:

> If some of these unfortunate youngsters got a good
> birching the first time they come up for petty larceny,
> or kindred offences, their names would never again ap-
> pear on the police records. There are some natures and
> the only way to appeal to them is by causing physical
> suffering. They will cease their savagery for fear, when
> all other means fail. Many well-meaning but unthinking
> people will raise their hands in horror at this suggestion,
> but it is to people who know and who have had bitter
> experiences of the futility of ordinary methods, that the
> decision ought to be left.
>
> If a dozen strokes of a birch rod, humanely administered,

taught a youngster who was disposed to evil ways either from heredity or environment, then the greatest kindness that the protection of public life and property could do to such, would be to stop depravity with corporal punishment.

The reformatory issue, coupled with the spectacle of children being jailed, touched the heart of a young boy who donated three dollars from his pocket money to start a fund for a reformatory. The *Daily News* stated, "The reformatory must come, and when it does it will be largely due to the fact that public opinion was effactually aroused by his gift. To thrust children into jail is to dedicate them to crime, ever after they are known as the companions of thieves and murderers."

209. Peter from Heaven and 'Tomcat' Neil

Peter from Heaven," was a character who frequented the LeMarchant Road area of St. John's and was fond of wearing several fashionable boulder hats, all at once. He was familiar with the Bible, and would stand near the corner of Cookstown Road and LeMarchant Road, where he would preach to anyone who would listen.

Often, he would attract a crowd, mostly of people looking for a "bit of sport." Peter was able to read and quote extensively from the Bible, and would speak as passionately as any preacher. To those who tormented him he would, while staring directly at them and pointing a finger, exclaim, "Take heed, you are in danger of losing your immortal soul!"

However, "Tomcat" Neil was not as restrained. On one occasion when a bully was giving Peter a hard time, Tomcat flattened him with a single punch. With Peter still preaching in the background, Tomcat looked down on the bully and in the religious spirit set by Peter said, "We are all blessed with God-given talents; mine just happens to be beatin' up people." That bully never again bothered poor Peter.

Peter lived in a boarding house on Murphy's Range. He was described by townsfolk as being "touched." They used the same term to describe most of the characters of the era.

Mickey Neil was one of Justice Jimmy Higgins favorite old-time characters. He delighted in recalling how Neil became known, as "Tomcat. "Mickey Neil," said Higgins, "was a tall raw-boned Irishman who lived with his mother and a large yellow tomcat in a little house near the Star Hall. He was considered to be simple, hard as rocks, but not as foolish as people thought." Higgins said:

> One bitter, winter's night Tomcat was seated on the hob placidly sucking his clay pipe while his mother was ensconced in the Flour Barrel chair knitting a pair of cuffs (gloves) for him.
>
> Between them the tomcat was stretched out on the floor in front of the fire. After glancing from his mother to the cat Mickey slowly removed his pipe, spat into the fire, and said solemnly: 'Mother, there's just three of us here, you and me and the cat. One of us must go out and get some wood. It's no use sending the cat, cause he won't come back and I'M NOT GOING!'

His poor mother got the best of him at least on one occasion. Tomcat was resting on his bed when his mother came in and said, "There's a black cat in the kitchen."

"What odds, Mom," said Tomcat, "a black cat is lucky."

As his mother left the room she answered, "This one is; he's eating your dinner!"

210. Newfoundland-Owned Flag over Tokyo

A little-known piece of World War II history involves the flying of a flag over Tokyo, Japan, which had been given to the British Navy by the wife of the governor of Newfoundland. In May, 1944, the HMS *Newfoundland* visited St. John's. While in port, Governor Walwyn and his wife were guests on the ship. Before leaving the vessel, Lady Walwyn, on behalf of the Women's Patriotic Association of Newfoundland, presented the ship's captain with a silk white ensign.

In September, 1945, after the atomic bomb had been dropped on Japan, the HMS *Newfoundland* entered Tokyo Bay. A telegram message from the ship was sent that day to Lady Walwyn, Government House, St. John's, Nfld. which read: "Your ensign flying in Tokyo Bay today, September 2nd. Warmest greetings to all who presented it." Sgd. Ravenhill, HMS *Newfoundland*.
The reply sent to Captain Ravenhill from Government House read, "Thrilled and proud to receive your message."

211. No Established Currency in Newfoundland

During World War II, Newfoundland did not have an established currency. In 1939, the Commission of Government discontinued issuing Newfoundland banknotes, and made the Canadian dollar legal tender throughout Newfoundland and Labrador. However, Newfoundland currency continued to be accepted.

Around 1941, the Commission of Government began removing Newfoundland banknotes from circulation. At that time, about a quarter of a million dollars in Newfoundland $1 and $2 banknotes were removed from circulation and burned by the Finance Department. The move to make the Canadian dollar legal tender, and the destroying of Newfoundland bills, was done as an economic measure to save Newfoundland the annual redemption cost of replacing its bills.

A commentary in *The Evening Telegram*, February 20, 1946, on the practice stated:

> The Newfoundland $1 and $2 banknotes are as rare today as the Great Auk or the first issues of local postage stamps which cannot be obtained from the Newfoundland Savings Bank. Apart from the government redeeming the notes, visiting servicemen went to great trouble to obtain local banknotes for souvenirs.

212. The Origins of the Name Quidi Vidi

No book on the history of old-time Newfoundland would be complete without some discussion of the name Quidi Vidi and its origin. Dr. E.R. Seary, in his scholarly work on place names of the Avalon Peninsula, examined the many variations of the name as recorded in old documents and concluded that the most likely source was a French family name with several variations: Quidville, Quedville, Quiedville and Quetteville.

The late A.B. Perlin, respected historian and newspaper editor, disputed Seary's claim in his Wayfarer's Column (August, 1966). He argued, "I doubt that any Frenchman or Jerseyman was identified with the settlements in and around St. John's in the seventeenth century."

Dr. Seary identified many variants of the name. They include: Quilliwiddi (1671), Kitte Vitte (1675) and Quide Vide (1677).

The *English Pilot*, published in 1689, referred to two variations of the name: Quidi Vidy or Kitty Vitty. H.W. LeMessurier, who researched and collected Newfoundland history during the early part of this century, came to a different conclusion as to the origins of the name. He argued that the name might be a corruption of Guy's divide, or a line separating John Guy's plantation from that which had been subsequently formed in St. John's.

Archbishop Howley, who carried out extensive research into Newfoundland nomenclature, suggested the most likely name had been Qui dividie which he translated as "here divide."

Howley's claim was considered credible by Perlin, who observed:

> I have always felt that Quidi Vidi got its name because it was the first opening in the wall of rock immediately north of St. John's. I am not a linguist and I don't know what the Portuguese word would be for the place that divides but it may have been something like Qui or Qua Divida. And almost all the early variations tend to suggest something of the sort. It follows that, as in the case of so many other place names in Newfoundland which have been distorted by the untutored English, Qui Divida or Qua Divida could have become either Kwidi Vida-Kiddy Viddy and from Kiddy Viddy it is but a short move to Kitty Vitty.

Another respected historian of the nineteenth century, Rev. Dr. Moses Harvey suggested a widow named Kitty Vitty had operated a public house in the village and the place got its name from her. Little credibility was attached to Harvey's explanation. However, a few years ago I researched birth records at the Provincial Archives and came across the name of a resident of Quidi Vidi named "Kitty Fitty." She did operate a public house there and it does not take much imagination to connect "Going to Kitty Fitty's" to "Going down to Kitty Vitty's." That record was in the late eighteenth century.

The earliest reference to the name can be found in the journal of James Yonge, who served as surgeon to the fishing fleet in the 1660s. Yonge, who first visited Newfoundland at the age of fifteen, kept a journal of his stay. In 1669, while operating out of St. John's he wrote, "... during our being here I went once to Petty Harbour and twice to Kitty Vitty of which place I forebear a description, intending to leave that to the figures (maps) by and by, to be made of all the harbours I have been in this land."

Originally, Quidi Vidi was a plantation owned by John Downing. A census of 1682 spelled the name as Quitevide. In 1679, a statement written on behalf of the people of St. John's relating to its defence spelled the name as Que de Vide. It stated that, "... to fortify St. John's, naturally very strong, with twenty-five guns and two-hundred small arms and some small arms to defend the creek Que de Vide to prevent surprises."

In the French report on D'ibberville's capture of St. John's the name was spelled Kerividi.

Dr. Seary refers to the usage of Kitty Velle by Captain Cook in 1763. However, in Cook's chart of 1775 it is spelled Quidy Videy.

No doubt the debate over the correct pronunciation and the origins of the name Quidi Vidi will continue which in itself is another colourful aspect of the historical Regatta at Quidi Vidi.

213. How Dog of Hollywood Producer survived the *Viking* Disaster

A little-known story related to the *Viking* disaster of 1931 involved the disappearance of Varrick Frissell's dog, Cabot. A few weeks after the disaster, the lighthouse keeper on Peckford's Island, Ernest Abbott, and assistant-keeper, Allan Mouland, spotted an animal that looked like a dog, drift ashore on a pan of ice. From a distance they could not tell what kind of animal was on the ice pan, so they grabbed their guns and went to investigate. Once near the ice pan, they could see that it was a dog in an obvious weakened condition.

When approached by Abbott and Mouland, the dog attempted to escape by running from ice pan to ice pan but the two men managed to capture it, and brought it back to the lighthouse where the dog was given food, water and a warm place to rest. The dog responded well to the kindness shown and in a short time became a loyal family pet. When the men went bird hunting the dog would go along with them. The appearance of the dog on the island, however, remained a mystery for weeks afterwards.

Meanwhile, Dr. Frissell, Varrick Frissell's father, offered a reward to the public to find his son's body, and he also offered a reward for the finding the dog. At the time, it was generally believed that the dog, along with its master, had been killed in the *Viking* explosion. In the spring, when the mailboat arrived at Peckford Island, it brought with it news of the reward Frissell was offering. Dr. Frissell had sent out a picture and description of his son's dog, Cabot. He was described as having a white patch on his forehead.

When this information reached Peckford Island, the mystery of where the dog came from was solved. The rescued dog fit the description given by Frissell, and readily responded to the name, Cabot. The news of the dog's survival reached outside Newfoundland, and there was an overwhelming response. Various S.P.C.A organizations sent messages to Mr. Abbott, and one from Scotland included the annual report of the S.P.C.A and a photograph of Cabot and the Peckford Island Lighthouse. Letters also arrived from all over the United States and packages containing dog biscuits and medical supplies arrived from as far away as New Zealand and Australia.

Dr. Frissell sent Ernest Abbott a battery radio to keep him in touch with the outside world. Peckford Island was isolated, and its only contact with the outside was through the mailboat and courier. Cabot remained at Peckford Island as a family pet for the remainder of his life, which was about ten years.

This remarkable story of Cabot's survival of the *Viking* Disaster was brought to public attention by Roland Abbott in an article published in the Gander *Beacon* on March 13, 1991.

Part 14

Pre-1949 St. John's in Photos

In the first twenty years following Confederation, Newfoundland experienced what Farley Mowat described as, "A 100 years advancement compressed into just twenty years." The following are a variety of pre-1949 photographs of St. John's.

1. Two historic items in one. The noon-day gun and Cabot Tower on top of Signal Hill. Townspeople set their clocks by the daily sounding of the noon-day gun. Many stories are told of people napping during church services, but being suddenly jolted out of their sleep by the noon-day gun. One lady at the Basilica jumped to her feet shouting "Bingo!" The two ladies next to her awakened the same time and shouted "f***k!" *PANL*

2. American tanks on parade on Military Road during World War II passing Government House. *City of St. John's Archives*

3. The main post office in St. John's. The museum was also part of this building prior to 1933. It was located on Water Street, east of Queen Street. *City of St. John's Archives*

4. The Customs House at the east end of Water Street in vicinity of the War Memorial. *PANL*

5. When the banks crashed in 1894, people rushed to take their money out. The building shown here was a bank, but today houses the Supreme Court of Appeal. *PANL*

6. Ayre & Sons Department Store was a dominant part of Water Street and St. John's in the pre-1949 era. The Atlantic Building stands on that site today. *PANL*

7. The Broadway House of Fashion was located on the corner of Water Street and Bishop's Cove, opposite Adelaide Street. The Great Eastern Oil once occupied this site. *Frank "Spotty" Baird Collection*

8. This section of the Broadway House of Fashion contained a boot and shoe department and a bargain basement section. *Frank "Spotty" Baird Collection*

9. A cow and calf leisurely walking along Quidi Vidi Road in 1930s. Animals often wandered the streets of old St. John's. The city employed an official "goat catcher" to gather goats roaming streets and destroying property. *City of St. John's Archives*

10. The Crosbie Hotel on Duckworth Street (in later years re-named the Welcome Hotel) was rebuilt after the 1892 fire. *City of St. John's Archives*

11. The Springdale Street School was located at the corner of Gilbert Street and Springdale Street. Its main entrance was on Gilbert Street. *Jack Fitzgerald*

12. The old General Hospital on Forest Road. *PANL*

13. The Newfoundland Hotel opened for business on June 30, 1926. There was a public effort at the time to open the old military underground tunnel, which ran from the harbour to the hotel site, so tourists arriving by passenger ship could go directly by tunnel up to the hotel. *PANL*

14. This photo of the Newfoundland Hotel shows the area much improved by the early 1930s. *PANL*

15. During this Jubilee ceremony in 1936 trees were planted on Bannerman Road. *PANL*

16. A view of St. John's from the shores of the Battery. *PANL*

273

17. View of St. John's and harbour from Southside Hills. *City of St. John's Archives*

18. A view of the community of Riverhead in St. John's West shows the harbour waters reaching west to Leslie Street. *City of St. John's Archives*

19. The War Memorial in St. John's just before its official opening. *City of St. John's Archives*

20. A view of St. John's Narrows from Bonaventure Avenue with the old BIS Building in the forefront. *PANL*

21. Cavendish Square before the building of the Newfoundland Hotel in 1926. *City of St. John's Archives*

22. The Royal Stores located at Water Street East. An underground tunnel that ran through this area was incorporated as part of the building's basement. The tunnel was uncovered in the 1960s and efforts by *The Evening Telegram* **to save it failed.** *Frank "Spotty" Baird Collection*

23. The railway terminal ended at this site when it was located at Cavendish Square. *PANL*

24. The old Central Fire Hall on Bonaventure Avenue.
Frank "Spotty" Baird Collection

25. The St. Andrew's Presbyterian Kirk on Queen's Road was given access through the old Roman Catholic Cemetery on Queen's Road for the token sum of $1 annually. The only condition was that the access road should not interfere with the grave sites. After the 1892 fire, the graves were removed and St. Andrew's obtained rights to access the property. Catherine Snow was buried near this site after being hanged for her part in the murder of her husband. *PANL*

26. The Newfoundland Railway train better remembered as "The Newfie Bullet." *PANL*

27. This photo was taken the day after the Chinese triple-murder in St. John's. It shows the Casey Street and Baron Street intersection. The Hop Wah Laundry is to the left. One man was wounded there and the shooter stood at the intersection and made an unsuccessful effort to kill himself. *Jack Fitzgerald Collection*

28. The St. Andrew's Presbyterian Kirk at the corner of Cathedral Street and New Gower Street after being destroyed in a fire in 1848. *PANL*

29. Water Street, between Waldegrave and Queen Street, before that end of Water Street was straightened out, circa 1889. *City of St. John's Archives*

30. Water Street, circa 1880s. *City of St. John's Archives*

31. Parade moving east along Duckworth Street near Caine's Store, circa 1900. *City of St. John's Archives*

32. Water Street, east of Adelaide Street, circa 1890s. *PANL*

33. Water Street, west of Waldegrave Street, circa 1890s. *PANL*

34. Water Street 1930s, east of McBride's Hill. Atlantic Place has replaced most of the buildings on the right, which included Ayre's and The Sweet Shop. *City of St. John's Archives*

35. Bowring Brothers on Water Street, east of Beck's Cove, circa early 1900s. *PANL*

36. A Water Street shoe store, Parker and Monroe's pre-1949. Notice goods stored on shelves in boxes and five formally dressed salesmen stand by to service the customers. The chairs shown are similar to the chairs used in the very popular Power's Candy Store on New Gower Street, makers of Perfection Ice Cream and homemade candy. *PANL*

283

37. St. John's grocery store prior to 1949, and before the introduction of supermarkets to Newfoundland. Six salesmen appropriately dressed in white shirts, ties and white coats stand buy to serve customers. *PANL*

38. The corner of McBride's Hill and Water Street. Delivery horses and wagons stand by for the businesses shown in photo. *City of St. John's Archives*

39. Crotty's Taxi Service on Queen's Road, a few doors west of Carter's Hill. Street car tracks are visible in front of picture. *City of St. John's Archives*

40. A parade following the return of troops at the end of World War I as it proceeds down Job Street into Water Street. *PANL*

42. A man and young boy bringing their horse to a water trough for a drink. This trough was located on Prescott Street, Queen's Road intersection. *PANL*

44. Winter scene on Queen's Road looking west. *PANL*

45. A Sunday ride into the country by horse and sled. Near Corpus Christie Church. *PANL*

46. The Monkey's Puzzle was the name given to the row of houses that ran from Temperance Street up to Battery Road. *PANL*

47. Winter scene showing road clearing on Water Street, east of Waldegrave Street. *City of St. John's Archives*

48. Winter scene on Water Street, likely in 1930s when the city paid men twenty-five cents a day to clear the street.
City of St. John's Archives

49. Winter scene on Water Street, west of Princess Street. Snow was tossed onto the street with enough clearing left for the electric street cars. *City of St. John's Archives*

50. Water Street after a winter storm. Electric street car rails cleared. *City of St. John's Archives*

52. A ship just as it was arriving in St. John's Harbour in winter. *PANL*

53. Winter scene on Water Street pre-1949. *PANL*

51. Horse trough at foot of Hill O'Chips, which was later moved to Bowring Park. *PANL*

54. Large iceberg at Fort Amherst around 1900. Notice its size in comparison to the nearby ships. *PANL*

Bibliography

Newspaper and Journal Sources:
The Evening Telegram, St. John's, Newfoundland
The Daily News, St. John's, Newfoundland
Grand Falls Advertiser (1959, 1969, 1971)
Western Star, Corner Brook, Newfoundland, 1959, 1960
The Royal Gazette, St. John's, Newfoundland
The Newfoundlander, St. John's, Newfoundland
The Patriot, St. John's, Newfoundland
Harbour Grace Standard, Hansard, Province of Newfoundland, 1959-1960
Toronto Daily Star, February-March 1960
Montreal Star, March 1960
Montreal Gazette, March 1960
Calgary Herald, March 1960
Regina Post, March 1960.
Toronto Globe and Mail, 1971-1976
Public Ledger, the Herald the Courier (which was taken over by the *Evening Telegram*)
The Mercantile Journal
All Shipping Intelligence Columns and Obituaries

Books
Brown, Alexander Crosby. *Women and Children Last*, G. P. Putnams Sons, New York, 1961.
Cardoulis, John N., *A Friendly Invasion, The American Military in Newfoundland 1940-1990*, Breakwater Books, St.

John's, Newfoundland and Labrador, 1990.

Dollar, Robert, *One Hundred Thirty Years of Steam Navigation, a history of the merchant ship*, Privately printed for the author by Schwabacher-Frey Company, San Francisco, 1931.

Fitzgerald, Jack: *Strange But True Newfoundland Stories, Amazing Stories of Newfoundland and Labrador, Untold Newfoundland Stories, Beyond the Grave, Remarkable Stories of Newfoundland Beyond Belief, Incredible Stories of Old St. John's, Newfoundland Fireside Stories*, Creative Publishers, St. John's, Newfoundland. *Ghosts, Heroes and Oddities* (Jesperson Press Ltd., 1991)

McCarthy, Michael, *The Irish in Newfoundland*.

Prowse, D.W. *A History of Newfoundland*, Boulder Publications, St. John's, NL. 2002.

Reeves, John, Esq. *The History of the Government of Newfoundland*. J. Sewill, Cornhill, London.

Mosdell, H. M. *When Was That: a Chronological Dictionary of Important Events in Newfoundland Down to and Including the Year 1922*. 1974.

Nicholson, W.W.L. *More Fighting Newfoundlanders*. St. John's: Government of Newfoundland and Labrador, 1969.

Magazines
Atlantic Quarterly
Catholic Cadet Corps Magazine, 1920s collection
Registers, Documents
Lloyds of London Records at Marine History Archives, Memorial

University, St. John's, Newfoundland: Lloyds Lists, Lloyds Registry, Lloyds Index.
Listing of Newfoundland Sea Captains, Marine History Archives, MUN, St. John's, Nfld.
Newfoundland Board of Trade Mercantile Registry, Marine History Archives, MUN, St. John's, Nfld..
Newfoundland Directories, 1865-1930, Hunter Library, Newfoundland Collection, St. John's, Nfld.
Newfoundland Census Records
Letter books of the Colonial Secretary's Office, Vol S1. PANL
Colonial Records 1790-1792. PANL
Court of Assize Records, GN5/2A/1; Box 2A, 1804. PANL
Howley, M. F. Ecclesiastical History of Newfoundland. Boston: Doyle and Whittle, 1888.
Thomas, Aaron. The Newfoundland Journal of Aaron Thomas. Ed. Jean Murray. London: Longmans Green and Col Ltd., 1968
Gert Crosbie's collection of deaths, births and marriages, 1810-1890
Marine History Archives, MUN, St. John's, NL
City of St. John's Archives; Directories, pictures and files
Wills, Last Testaments, Justice Records, Provincial Archives of Newfoundland and Labrador Church Records, Baptismal, Burials and Marriages-1790-1930. St. John's, Harbour Grace, Bay Bulls, Bonavista, Cod Roy, Channel and Port Aux Basques(PANL) Roman Catholic Cemetery, North Sydney.

Places Visited
Graveyards Visited: Mount Carmel Cemetery, Belvedere Cemetery, General Protestant Cemetery, and Anglican Cemetery, St. John's, NL
Bay Bulls Cemetery and the cemetery at the Gunnerage, Bay Bulls, NL
Roman Catholic Cemetery, Harbour Grace, NL
Harbour Grace Museum

Newfoundland Museum, St. John's, NL
Captain Bob Bartlett Heritage Home and Museum, Brigus, NL
Cupid's Museum, Cupids, NL

Colonial Records:
PANL. MG 562 Box 1. Logbooks of Legion of Frontiersmen at Fort Waldegrave.
PANL. MG 632 Box 1. Minutes of Newfoundland Patriotic Association's monthly meetings.
PANL MG 429
PANL. GN 2/14
PANL. GN 1/10. Royal Naval Reserve, Royal Newfoundland Regiment War correspondence.

Acknowledgements

I acknowledge with sincere appreciation the help and encouragement of the following people during the writing and publishing preparation for this book. In particular I would like to thank, Bob Rumsey for reviewing the manuscript, Maurice Fitzgerald for the cover design and photograph-editing, Don Morgan for the final manuscript editing and invaluable advice. I am also grateful for the professional work and advice provided by Pam Dooley of Creative Publishers in guiding *Jack Fitzgerald's Treasury of Newfoundland Stories Volume II* along the road to its final publication. Special thanks to Donna Francis of Creative for her encouragement, support and accessibility when needed. Also the staffs at the Provincial Archives of Newfoundland and Labrador, the A.C Hunter Library (Newfoundland Collection), the Queen Elizabeth II Library, MUN, Centre of Newfoundland Studies, MUN and the City of St. John's Archives. I must also acknowledge the late Dr. Bobbi Robertson, who decades ago guided me through the entire collection of records kept by the Newfoundland Historical Society in the old Colonial Building and the help provided at that time by my friend Richard "Dick" Hartery.

Other Jack Fitzgerald Books

Jack Fitzgerald's Treasury of Newfoundland Stories,
    Volume I: True Crime and Adventure
Peculiar Facts and Tales of Newfoundland
Newfoundland's Era of Corruption: Responsible Government, 1855-1934
1949: The Twilight Before the Dawn
The Spring Rice Document
Battlefront Newfoundland
Crimes that Shocked Newfoundland
The Jack Ford Story: Newfoundland POW in Nagasaki
Legacy of Laughter
Remarkable Stories of Newfoundland
Treasure Island Revisited: A True Newfoundland Adventure Story
Ten Steps to the Gallows: True Stories of Newfoundland and Labrador
Newfoundland Adventures: In Air, On Land, At Sea
Where Angels Fear to Tread
Another Time, Another Place
Amazing Newfoundland Stories
The Hangman is Never Late
Untold Stories of Newfoundland
Beyond the Grave
Beyond Belief
Strange but True Newfoundland Stories
Jack Fitzgerald's Notebook
Ghosts and Oddities
Stroke of Champions
Up the Pond
A Day at the Races: The Story of the St. John's Regatta
Newfoundland Disasters
Rogues and Branding Irons
Convicted
Too Many Parties, Too Many Pals
Incredible Stories of Newfoundland
Newfoundland Fireside Stories

Ask your favourite bookstore or order directly from the publisher.
Creative Book Publishing
36 Austin Street
St. John's, Newfoundland
A1B 3T7

Tel: (709)-748-0813 - Fax: (709) 579-6511
E-mail: nl.books@transcontinental.ca - www.creativebookpublishing.ca

JACK FITZGERALD was born in St. John's, Newfoundland and educated at Holy Cross School, Bishop Eustace Community College, (Camden, New Jersey), the College of Trades and Technology and Memorial University. During his career he has been a journalist, a feature writer and political columnist with the St. John's *Daily News*; a reporter and public affairs writer with CJON and VOCM news services; and editor of *The Newfoundland Herald* and *The Newfoundland Chronicle*. During the Smallwood administration, he was Assistant Director of Public Relations with the Government of Newfoundland and Labrador.